"Brian Tabb takes us back to the sources Jesus's ministry. What stands out is the Often these two themes are studied separately, twined. This deft and insightful study shines a fresh light on what God accomplished through his Spirit in Christ, and it inspires us today when we recognize that God's great promises are still being fulfilled."

Thomas R. Schreiner, James Buchanan Harrison Professor of New Testament Interpretation, The Southern Baptist Theological Seminary

"In *After Emmaus*, Brian Tabb clarifies what Jesus was getting at when he said that it was necessary for the Christ to suffer before entering his glory and what that will mean for all who seek to follow him. With careful scholarship as well as scriptural insight, Tabb helpfully connects the mission of God through the person and work of Christ to the mission we've been commissioned to carry out."

Nancy Guthrie, Bible teacher; author, *Even Better than Eden*

"The last few decades have witnessed an abundance of studies on the rich ways in which the two Testaments are properly tied together. According to Luke, the resurrected Jesus held and taught strong views along these lines. Starting with a focus on Luke 24:46–47, and concentrating especially on the depiction of Jesus in Luke and the depiction of the church in Acts, Brian Tabb demonstrates how deep the links are: the Old Testament does not simply sidle up to the line and point to Jesus, but unpacks the narrative of redemption so powerfully and coherently that thoughtful readers cannot help but see how the narrative is truly fulfilled in the mission of Jesus and the mission of the church—a connection that Acts 1:1 makes explicit. This book will enrich your grasp of biblical theology while calling your heart to worship."

D. A. Carson, Cofounder and Theologian-at-Large, The Gospel Coalition

"In this beautiful blend of hermeneutics, Christology, and missiology, Brian Tabb sets forth his thesis that Jesus did not merely come to save us from our sins, but also to summon us to mission. Warmly recommended!"

Andreas J. Köstenberger, Director, Center for Biblical Studies and Research; Research Professor of New Testament and Biblical Theology, Midwestern Baptist Theological Seminary; Founder, Biblical Foundations

"Brian Tabb has proven himself to be a trusted guide and teacher. There has been a renaissance in biblical theology, but what distinguishes this book from others is the emphasis not just on Christ's fulfillment of Old Testament promises, but on his universal mission that we are invited to participate in, which then helps to address recent proposals that redefine the gospel and the church's mission. This is a learned book, wonderfully organized and skillfully presented. The thoroughness of argument will force you to grapple again with Jesus's parting words in Luke's Gospel and their implication for how we read our Bibles."

Darren Carlson, Founder and President, Training Leaders International

"*After Emmaus* beautifully blends the best features of evangelical biblical theology, exemplifying the hermeneutical benefit to be gained from following the New Testament's redemptive-historical reading of the Old Testament. Tabb surveys major motifs in the theology of Luke-Acts, displaying how its Christology, ecclesiology, and missiology are enriched by Luke's Spirit-enlightened saturation of heart and mind in God's ancient Scriptures. Moreover, *After Emmaus* applies the Spirit's instruction through Luke to the faith and life of Christians today. I enthusiastically recommend this study."

Dennis E. Johnson, Professor Emeritus of Practical Theology, Westminster Seminary California; author, *Him We Proclaim* and *Walking with Jesus through His Word*

"As the debate continues over the nature of the church's mission, Brian Tabb points us to Jesus's own words. Tabb argues that, in Luke 24:44–47, Jesus provides the hermeneutical lens by which we may clearly see how he fulfills Old Testament messianic prophecies so that we may courageously proclaim the saving message of the Scriptures. This is how the risen Christ accomplishes his mission—through Spirit-empowered witnesses who spread his message to the ends of the earth. If you long to see Jesus exalted as the promised Messiah and worshiped among all peoples, read *After Emmaus*. It will not only encourage you to be a faithful witness, but will also lead you to greater confidence in God's progressive, unified revelation about Jesus, the suffering and vindicated servant who is the hope of the nations."

Juan R. Sanchez, Senior Pastor, High Pointe Baptist Church, Austin, Texas; author, *The Leadership Formula*

"By divine design, the mission of Christ has become *our* mission. Embedded in the purpose and power of Christ's death and resurrection is his own mission through us. In *After Emmaus,* Brian Tabb pens a much-needed, rich, and rewarding missional reading of Luke-Acts (along with Matthew, John, Romans, and Peter)—not as an interpretive interest imposed on the Old and New Testaments, but as a hermeneutical mandate rooted in Scripture's own self-interpretive authority. Navigating exegesis with the dexterity of a master surgeon and the delight of a disciple of Christ, Tabb makes an illumining exegetical and biblical-theological case that Christ's 'witnesses are . . . an extension of the risen Lord's own activity.' *After Emmaus* will inform your mind, rejoice your heart, and (re)ignite your resolve unto that divinely appointed privilege: to proclaim Christ with courage and clarity."

David B. Garner, Academic Dean, Vice President of Global Ministries, and Professor of Systematic Theology, Westminster Theological Seminary

After Emmaus

After Emmaus

How the Church Fulfills the Mission of Christ

Brian J. Tabb

WHEATON, ILLINOIS

Library of Congress Cataloging-in-Publication Data

Names: Tabb, Brian J., author.
Title: After Emmaus : how the church fulfills the mission of Christ / Brian J. Tabb.
Description: Wheaton, Illinois : Crossway, [2021] | Includes bibliographical references and index.
Identifiers: LCCN 2021003022 (print) | LCCN 2021003023 (ebook) | ISBN 9781433573842 (trade paperback) | ISBN 9781433573859 (pdf) | ISBN 9781433573866 (mobi) | ISBN 9781433573873 (epub)
Subjects: LCSH: Jesus Christ—Person and offices. | Jesus Christ—Messiahship. | Bible. Luke—Criticism, interpretation, etc. | Bible. Acts—Criticism, interpretation, etc. | Bible. New Testament—Relation to the Old Testament. | Redemption—Biblical teaching. | Mission of the church.
Classification: LCC BT203 .T33 2021 (print) | LCC BT203 (ebook) | DDC 232—dc23
LC record available at https://lccn.loc.gov/2021003022
LC ebook record available at https://lccn.loc.gov/2021003023

Crossway is a publishing ministry of Good News Publishers.

VP			30	29	28	27	26	25	24	23	22	21
14	13	12	11	10	9	8	7	6	5	4	3	2	1

For my father,
William Murray Tabb
Proverbs 4:1

Contents

Preface

THIS IS A BOOK ABOUT reading the Bible with a focus on Christ and the church's mission in his name. The title *After Emmaus* draws attention to the famous narrative in Luke 24, where Jesus reveals himself to the travelers on the Emmaus road and then to his gathered disciples. The book's cover features vignettes from Diego Velázquez's painting *The Supper at Emmaus*,[1] which captures something of the mystery of the travelers' revelatory encounter with the risen Lord as "their eyes were opened, and they recognized him" (Luke 24:31). After that encounter, Jesus appears to his distressed disciples and demonstrates that he is truly alive by showing them his hands and feet and by eating fish before them (24:36–43). He then opens their minds and expounds the Scriptures:

> Then he said to them, "These are my words that I spoke to you while I was still with you, that everything written about me in the Law of Moses and the Prophets and the Psalms must be fulfilled." Then he opened their minds to understand the Scriptures, and said to them, "Thus it is written, that the Christ should suffer and on the third day rise from the dead, and that repentance for the forgiveness of sins should be proclaimed in his name to all nations, beginning from Jerusalem. You are witnesses of these things. And behold, I am sending the promise of my Father upon you. But stay in the city until you are clothed with power from on high." (24:44–49)

Our Lord explains that everything written *about him* must be fulfilled, and he focuses on his necessary suffering and resurrection according to the

---

1 Diego Velázquez, *The Supper at Emmaus*, 1622–1623, oil on canvas, The Metropolitan Museum of Art, New York, https://www.metmuseum.org/.

Scriptures. Christ's biblical-theological summary does not stop with 24:46, however. Rather, Jesus explains in verse 47 that the disciples' mission to all nations also fulfills the Scriptures. He then identifies them as "witnesses" and instructs them to wait for divine empowerment (24:48–49), recalling Old Testament prophecy (Isa. 32:15; 44:8) and preparing readers for the outpouring of the Spirit at Pentecost (Acts 2).

These are the last recorded words of the risen Lord in Luke's Gospel, and I argue that in them Jesus offers his followers a framework or lens for interpreting the Bible Christologically and missiologically. I seek to show that Jesus's teaching about his suffering, resurrection, and mission in Luke's Gospel anticipates his paradigmatic summary of the Scriptures in Luke 24:46–47. I also explain that the apostles and their associates follow the risen Lord's model for reading the Law, Prophets, and Writings with concerted focus on the Messiah and his mission. Finally, I contend that the church today should adopt the same hermeneutical lens in our Bible reading, for it grounds our gospel message and galvanizes us to participate in Christ's global work.

Abbreviations

AB	Anchor Bible
AJPS	*Asian Journal of Pentecostal Studies*
ANF	Alexander Roberts, James Donaldson, and A. Cleveland Coxe, eds., *Ante-Nicene Fathers*, 10 vols. (Buffalo, NY: Christian Literature, 1885).
BBR	*Bulletin for Biblical Research*
BBRSup	Bulletin for Biblical Research Supplement
BDAG	Walter Bauer, Frederick W. Danker, William F. Arndt, and F. Wilbur Gingrich, *A Greek-English Lexicon of the New Testament and Other Early Christian Literature*, 3rd ed. (Chicago: University of Chicago Press, 2000).
BECNT	Baker Exegetical Commentary on the New Testament
BETL	Bibliotheca Ephemeridum Theologicarum Lovaniensium
Bib	*Biblica*
BNTC	Black's New Testament Commentaries
BSac	*Bibliotheca Sacra*
BSL	Biblical Studies Library
BTB	*Biblical Theology Bulletin*
BZ	*Biblische Zeitschrift*

BZNW	Beihefte zur Zeitschrift für die neutestamentliche Wissenschaft
CBQ	*Catholic Biblical Quarterly*
CNT	Commentaire du Nouveau Testament
CurTM	*Currents in Theology and Mission*
EBC	Expositor's Bible Commentary
ECC	Eerdmans Critical Commentary
EGGNT	Exegetical Guide to the Greek New Testament
ESBT	Essential Studies in Biblical Theology
ESVEC	ESV Expository Commentary
EvQ	*Evangelical Quarterly*
ExpTim	*Expository Times*
HTA	Historisch Theologische Auslegung
ICC	International Critical Commentary
JBL	*Journal of Biblical Literature*
JCTCRS	Jewish and Christian Texts in Contexts and Related Studies
JETS	*Journal of the Evangelical Theological Society*
JPTSup	Journal of Pentecostal Theology Supplement
JSNT	*Journal for the Study of the New Testament*
JSNTSup	Journal for the Study of the New Testament Supplement Series
JSOTSup	Journal for the Study of the Old Testament Supplement Series
KEK	Kritisch-exegetischer Kommentar über das Neue Testament
LCL	Loeb Classical Library

LNTS	Library of New Testament Studies
LSJ	Henry George Liddell, Robert Scott, Henry Stuart Jones, and Roderick McKenzie, eds., *A Greek-English Lexicon*, 9th ed. (Oxford: Clarendon, 1996).
LXX	Septuagint
MT	Masoretic Text
NAC	New American Commentary
NCB	New Century Bible
NCBC	New Cambridge Bible Commentary
Neot	*Neotestamentica*
NICNT	New International Commentary on the New Testament
NICOT	New International Commentary on the Old Testament
NIDNTTE	Moisés Silva, ed., *New International Dictionary of New Testament Theology and Exegesis*, 2nd ed., 5 vols. (Grand Rapids, MI: Zondervan, 2014).
NIGTC	New International Greek Testament Commentary
NovT	*Novum Testamentum*
NovTSup	Supplements to Novum Testamentum
NSBT	New Studies in Biblical Theology
NTL	New Testament Library
NTS	*New Testament Studies*
OTL	Old Testament Library
OWC	Oxford World Classics
PNTC	Pillar New Testament Commentary
RTR	*Reformed Theological Review*

SBJT	*Southern Baptist Journal of Theology*
SCS	Septuagint Commentary Series
SNTSMS	Society for New Testament Studies Monograph Series
SSBT	Short Studies in Biblical Theology
TBei	*Theologische Beiträge*
TOTC	Tyndale Old Testament Commentary
TrinJ	*Trinity Journal*
TynBul	*Tyndale Bulletin*
VT	*Vetus Testamentum*
VTSup	Supplements to Vetus Testamentum
WBC	Word Biblical Commentary
WTJ	*Westminster Theological Journal*
WUNT	Wissenschaftliche Untersuchungen zum Neuen Testament
ZECNT	Zondervan Exegetical Commentary on the New Testament

1

Christ's Exposition after Emmaus

"These are my words that I spoke to you while I was still with you,
that everything written about me in the Law of Moses and the
Prophets and the Psalms must be fulfilled." Then he opened their
minds to understand the Scriptures, and said to them, "Thus
it is written, that the Christ should suffer and on the third day
rise from the dead, and that repentance for the forgiveness of
sins should be proclaimed in his name to all nations, beginning
from Jerusalem. You are witnesses of these things. And behold,
I am sending the promise of my Father upon you. But stay in
the city until you are clothed with power from on high."

LUKE 24:44–49

WHEN I WAS TEN YEARS OLD, I began wearing glasses. What a thrill it was to see the baseball clearly from across the diamond and to read the words on the blackboard from the back of the classroom! At each eye exam since that time, the optometrist has tested my vision and corrected my prescription to ensure that I can decipher the small letters on the eye chart. To see clearly, I've known for many years that I need the proper lenses. Without my glasses, it's easy to miss things. Once I woke up and thought the clock said 6, so I took a shower and got ready for the day. But when I put my glasses on, I realized that it was only 3 a.m.!

Just as many of us wear corrective lenses to see things clearly, so we all need the proper "lenses" when we read God's word so that we do not fail to see what is really there. Jesus's healing miracle in Mark 8:22–26 illustrates this point well. When Jesus came to Bethsaida, some people begged him to heal a blind man. Jesus spat on the man's eyes, laid hands on him, and then asked, "Do you see anything?" The man replied, "I see people, but they look like trees, walking." Jesus laid hands on the man's eyes a second time, and then he saw everything clearly.

At first reading, this is a puzzling passage. It's the only time in the Gospels when Jesus heals someone in stages. Elsewhere we read about Jesus healing people who are crippled, deaf, mute, blind, demonized, and afflicted with various incurable conditions. Several times he even raises the dead! He does not say to the lame man, "Rise and walk," then hand him crutches. These examples illustrate that Jesus does not lack the power or authority to heal instantly and fully when he so desires. So, why does Jesus only partially restore this blind man's sight at first? I think the key is to read this scene together with the next passage. Jesus asks the disciples, "But who do you say that I am?" Peter answers, "You are the Christ" (Mark 8:29). The Lord then instructs his followers that he must suffer many things, be rejected and killed, and rise again (8:31). Shockingly, Peter begins to rebuke Jesus in response to this teaching.[1] Jesus then rebukes Peter and explains to his followers the true cost of discipleship. In this passage, the apostle Peter is like the half-healed blind man. He recognizes that Jesus is the Messiah, but he does not grasp what sort of Messiah Jesus really is. The details are fuzzy for Peter and the other disciples, and they see clearly only when the risen Lord opens their minds to understand. Jesus is the master ophthalmologist, who removes the disciples' cataracts and fits them with the spectacles needed to see him and his purposes according to the Scriptures.[2]

This book proposes that Jesus gives his followers a hermeneutical *lens* with which to understand the Scriptures. In his last recorded words in the Gospel of Luke, the risen Lord summarizes the Bible's essential *message* and offers us a *model* to faithfully read the Scriptures with the proper focus on the Messiah and his mission.

---

1   Matt. 16:22 specifies that Peter objects strongly to Jesus's imminent suffering, as he says, "Far be it from you, Lord! This shall never happen to you."

2   This metaphor is inspired by Kevin J. Vanhoozer's description of pastors as eye doctors of their congregations, in *Hearers and Doers: A Pastor's Guide to Making Disciples through Scripture and Doctrine* (Bellingham, WA: Lexham, 2019), 92–93.

A number of fine studies consider how Christ fulfills the prophecies and patterns of the Old Testament.[3] For example, Dennis Johnson explains that the Old Testament predicts and prefigures various aspects of Christ's saving work as the sovereign protector of his people, the suffering servant, the final prophet, the great high priest, and the true King.[4] Similarly, Jason DeRouchie argues that "the light of Christ supplies us the needed spiritual sight for understanding the things of God," while "the lens of Christ's life, death, and resurrection provides the needed perspective for reading the Old Testament meaning to its fullness."[5]

Additionally, several scholars have offered whole-Bible treatments of mission. For example, Christopher Wright contends that the mission of God and his people is "a major key that unlocks the whole grand narrative of the canon of Scripture."[6] Wright expansively establishes the Old Testament basis for mission and insists on a holistic understanding of mission that holds together gospel proclamation and robust social engagement. More recently, Andreas Köstenberger offers an inductive biblical-theological study showing that Christ's saving mission is foundational for the mission of his people.[7]

This book is not just another study of Christ in all of Scripture. While Jesus does explain "the things concerning himself" in all the Scriptures (Luke 24:27), he asserts that his messianic suffering and resurrection *and* the mission in his name among the nations fulfill what is "written" in the Old Testament (24:46–47). The church needs to grasp the vital relationship between Christology *and* missiology so that we can rightly express the message about Christ and faithfully carry out his mission in the world. The church's mission does not begin with the Great Commission, but is integrally related to the grand storyline of Scripture and specifically to

---

3 For an introduction to the range of interpretive perspectives, see Brian J. Tabb and Andrew M. King, eds., *Five Views on Christ in the Old Testament: Genre, Authorial Intent, and the Nature of Scripture*, Counterpoints (Grand Rapids, MI: Zondervan, forthcoming).

4 Dennis E. Johnson, *Walking with Jesus through His Word: Discovering Christ in All the Scriptures* (Phillipsburg, NJ: P&R, 2015), 13.

5 Jason S. DeRouchie, "The Mystery Revealed: A Biblical Case for Christ-Centered Old Testament Interpretation," *Themelios* 44 (2019): 248.

6 Christopher J. H. Wright, *The Mission of God: Unlocking the Bible's Grand Narrative* (Downers Grove, IL: IVP Academic, 2006), 17.

7 Andreas J. Köstenberger with T. Desmond Alexander, *Salvation to the Ends of the Earth: A Biblical Theology of Mission*, 2nd ed., NSBT 53 (Downers Grove, IL: IVP Academic, 2020), 1.

the hope of the Messiah. Jesus himself expresses the scriptural expectation for his messianic work and for the universal mission that his witnesses will carry out among the nations. The risen Lord's last words offer a *lens* with which his people can see how his suffering, resurrection, and mission climactically accomplish God's ancient plan. In Acts, Jesus's witnesses follow the Lord's example of biblical exposition as they carry out his mission to "the end of the earth" (Acts 1:8). So Christ's summary of the Scriptures in Luke 24:46–47 offers a coherent *message*, a compelling *mission* among the nations, and an enduring *motivation* for us to bear witness to our risen Lord.

Let's look more closely now at Jesus's last words after Emmaus.

Famous Last Words

For thousands of years, people have understood the last words of notable individuals to have particular importance. For example, the Old Testament records Jacob's deathbed blessing to his sons, in which he prophesies that his fourth son, Judah, will bear the royal scepter (Gen. 49:8–10). Joseph promises that God will visit his people in Egypt and insists that his bones be carried to the promised land (50:24–25; cf. Ex. 13:19; Josh. 24:32). Moses's blessing recalls the exodus and previews the future for Israel's tribes preparing to enter the land (Deut. 33). The last words of King David rehearse the covenant God made with his house and stress the need for rulers after him to fear the Lord (2 Sam. 23:1–7). The Old Testament Apocrypha records the last words of the priest Mattathias, in which he charges his sons to show zeal for the law and remember the deeds of their forefathers (1 Macc. 2:49–69). To these could be added many other ancient examples, such as Socrates's enigmatic instructions to make an offering to the god of healing before he calmly drinks the hemlock[8] or Julius Caesar's stunned question to his assassin, Brutus.[9]

---

8 "Crito . . . we owe Asclepius a cock. See that you all buy one, and don't forget." Plato, *Phaedo*, in *Euthyphro, Apology, Crito, Phaedo*, trans. Christopher Emlyn-Jones and William Preddy, LCL 36 (Cambridge, MA: Harvard University Press, 2017), 118a.

9 "You too, my child?" Suetonius, *Lives of the Caesars*, trans. John C. Rolfe, vol. 1, LCL 31 (Cambridge, MA: Harvard University Press, 1914), 182. More well-known is William Shakespeare's line, "*Et tu, Brutè?*" in *The Tragedy of Julius Caesar*, ed. Barbara A. Mowat and Paul Werstine, Folger Shakespeare Library (New York: Simon & Schuster, 1992), 3.1.85.

Doubtless Jesus's seven sayings from the cross are the most significant "last words" in history:

- "Father, forgive them, for they know not what they do" (Luke 23:34)
- "Truly, I say to you, today you will be with me in paradise" (Luke 23:43)
- "Woman, behold your Son! . . . Behold your mother!" (John 19:26–27)
- "My God, my God, why have you forsaken me?" (Matt. 27:46; Mark 15:34)
- "I thirst" (John 19:28)
- "It is finished" (John 19:30)
- "Father, into your hands I commit my spirit!" (Luke 23:46)

These sayings have rightly inspired countless paintings, poems, songs, and books.[10] Yet it is a misnomer to call Jesus's dying words his *last*, since he rose on the third day and spent forty days with his disciples before his ascension into heaven (Acts 1:2–3). The evangelists Matthew, Luke, and John each record examples of the risen Lord's teaching and instructions, the most well-known being the "Great Commission" in Matthew 28:18–20.[11] Everyone recognizes that a person's dying words are important, but Christ's dying words were not his last (Acts 1:3).

Jesus Opens the Scriptures (Luke 24:44–49)

Luke 24 records two examples of the risen Lord Jesus expounding the Scriptures for his disciples. First, Jesus meets two disciples and converses with them on the road to Emmaus, though they do not recognize him. These disciples tell their fellow traveler about Jesus's mighty words and deeds, as well as his shocking condemnation and crucifixion, which dashed their hopes that "he was the one to redeem Israel" (v. 21). Jesus then chides them for being slow to believe "all that the prophets have spoken" about how the Messiah must suffer these things and enter into glory (vv. 25–26). Then, "beginning with Moses and all the Prophets," Jesus interprets for these disciples "in all the Scriptures the things concerning

---

10 Recent examples include Andrew Peterson's song, "Last Words (Tenebrae)," in *Resurrection Letters: Prologue* (Franklin, TN: Centricity Music, 2018) and Jon Meacham's book *The Hope of Glory: Reflections on the Last Words of Jesus from the Cross* (New York: Convergent, 2020).

11 The longer ending of Mark also includes final instructions from Jesus before his ascension (Mark 16:15–18), though most commentators and textual scholars view these verses as a later addition to the Gospel.

himself" (v. 27)—though, of course, they still don't yet realize that their teacher is the risen Lord himself. Finally, when Jesus breaks bread with the two men, their eyes are "opened" to recognize him (vv. 30–31). They then recount how their hearts burned as Christ "opened" the Scriptures to them (v. 32).

Next, Jesus appears to his gathered disciples and overcomes their doubts by showing them his hands and feet and by eating fish (Luke 24:36–43). He summarizes what he taught them before his crucifixion, "that everything written about me in the Law of Moses and the Prophets and the Psalms must be fulfilled" (v. 44). Then Jesus opens their minds to understand the Scriptures (v. 45) and offers a threefold summary of their essential message: "Thus it is written, [1] that the Christ should suffer and [2] on the third day rise from the dead, and [3] that repentance for the forgiveness of sins should be proclaimed in his name to all nations, beginning from Jerusalem" (vv. 46–47). Jesus then identifies the disciples as "witnesses of these things" and promises to send the Spirit (vv. 48–49) before blessing them and ascending into heaven (v. 51).

Let's carefully consider Christ's climactic words in Luke 24:44–49, where he sums up the Scriptures and prepares his people to participate in his mission.

Review and Preview

Jesus's last words look back and also look ahead—they explain what happened to Jesus and anticipate the mission of his followers.[12] Christ speaks here with complete authority and definitively interprets the central events of the Gospel narrative—his crucifixion and resurrection—as fulfillments of his own and the Scriptures' predictions. Moreover, his biblical exposition in Luke 24:44–49 does not stop with his resurrection but includes the outpouring of the Spirit and the mission to all nations. Just as a movie trailer anticipates a blockbuster film, Luke 24:47–49 previews the coming attractions in Acts, where the disciples wait in Jerusalem, receive the promised Spirit, and powerfully proclaim Christ as his witnesses to the end of the earth (Acts 1:8).

Thus, at the end of Luke's Gospel, the risen Lord reviews his suffering and resurrection, and also previews the mission to all nations, showing that

---

12 See Robert C. Tannehill, *The Narrative Unity of Luke-Acts: A Literary Interpretation*, 2 vols. (Philadelphia: Fortress, 1986–1990), 1:294.

both of these follow the script of the Scriptures. This observation is crucial for the argument of this book: *the Messiah and his mission are the focus and fulfillment of the Old Testament.*

Double Fulfillment

The risen Lord also stresses the comprehensive fulfillment of the Scriptures. Note the following summary references to the Old Testament in Luke 24:

- "all that the prophets have spoken" (v. 25)
- "Moses and all the Prophets" (v. 27)
- "all the Scriptures" (v. 27)
- "the Law of Moses and the Prophets and the Psalms" (v. 44)
- "the Scriptures" (vv. 32, 45)
- "it is written" (v. 46)

New Testament and early Jewish writers regularly refer to the old covenant Scriptures using the shorthand phrase "the Law and the Prophets," and Luke uses a similar phrase in 24:27.[13] Jesus's appeal to "everything written about me in the Law of Moses and the Prophets and the Psalms" (v. 44) is the most expansive New Testament reference to the threefold division of the Hebrew canon—Law, Prophets, and Writings—with the Psalms representing the third division as the largest, most cited book.[14] "It is written" (*gegraptai*) occurs repeatedly in the New Testament and typically cites a specific passage from the Scriptures (*graphai*).[15] In verse 46, however, "it is written" does not introduce an Old Testament quotation but a threefold summary of the Scriptures' message. "All" and "everything" translate the same Greek word (*pas*) in verses 25, 27, and 44, and emphasize that the full range of the Scriptures, from beginning to end, has a singular focus *on Christ himself.*[16]

---

13 See also Matt. 5:17; 7:12; 11:13; 22:40; Luke 16:16; John 1:45; Acts 13:15; Rom. 3:21; 2 Macc. 15:9; 4 Macc. 18:10.

14 This threefold division of the Law, Prophets, and Writings is also reflected in early Jewish writings. For example, the prologue of Sirach refers to "the Law and the Prophets and the others that followed them," and 4Q397 in the Dead Sea Scrolls speaks of "the book of Moses, the books of the Prophets, and David" (21:10).

15 See, for example, Jesus's use of *gegraptai* in Luke 4:4 (citing Deut. 8:3); 4:8 (citing Deut. 6:13); 7:27 (citing Mal. 3:1 with Ex. 23:20); and 19:46 (citing Isa. 56:7).

16 "Luke is transparently concerned to communicate that the whole story of Scripture is a unified narrative, diverse but not disparate, testifying to and culminating in Christ," according to

In light of this remarkable claim, in what sense are the Scriptures "about" Jesus (Luke 24:44)? Daniel Block reasons that verse 27 means that Christ "explained those texts that spoke of him from all the Scriptures," not that all of Scripture refers or points to him.[17] Block affirms that there are "specific messianic prophecies" and that Jesus "embodies the fulfillment of the whole promise of the Hebrew Bible" as the biblical story finds its climax or telos in Christ.[18] However, Block's "Christotelic" approach does not adequately address the ways in which Jesus and the apostles cite the Law, Prophets, and Writings in relation to his messianic suffering, resurrection, and mission.[19] "All the Scriptures" likely refers not only to explicit messianic prophecies but also to patterns and prefigurements that anticipate the arrival of David's greater Son.[20] The Gospel of Luke and Acts (as well as other New Testament books) offer ample illustrations of Jesus's claims in Luke 24:27 and 44–47. The coming chapters will demonstrate that Jesus cites various biblical prophecies and patterns to explain the nature and necessity of his messianic identity and work, and his witnesses emulate their Lord's model of reading the Scriptures.

Moreover, Luke 24 shows that the surprising events of Jesus's death and resurrection transpire just as Jesus himself predicted for his followers (vv. 6–7, 44) *and* in accordance with "all that the prophets have spoken" (v. 25). Luke records three "passion predictions," in which Jesus foretells his coming suffering, rejection, and death (9:22, 44; 18:31–33). In 9:22 and 18:33, he also promises that he will rise "on the third day." Christ insists that these things "must" happen, employing the Greek word *dei* (9:22) and stressing that "everything that is written about the Son of Man by

---

Dane C. Ortlund, "'And Their Eyes Were Opened, and They Knew': An Inter-Canonical Note on Luke 24:31," *JETS* 53 (2010): 727.

17 Daniel I. Block, "Christotelic Preaching: A Plea for Hermeneutical Integrity and Missional Passion," *SBJT* 22.3 (2018): 12. Abner Chou makes a similar claim in *The Hermeneutics of the Biblical Writers: Learning to Interpret Scripture from the Prophets and Apostles* (Grand Rapids, MI: Kregel, 2018), 133.

18 Block, "Christotelic Preaching," 13.

19 Block's article inadequately deals with biblical typology, as noted by Peter J. Gentry, "'Christotelic Preaching': Reflections on Daniel Block's Approach," *SBJT* 22.3 (2018): 95–97. Tremper Longman III offers a more balanced "Christotelic" approach in "'What Was Said in All the Scriptures concerning Himself' (Luke 24:27)," in *Evangelical Scholarship, Retrospects and Prospects: Essays in Honor of Stanley N. Gundry*, ed. Verlyn D. Verbrugge (Grand Rapids, MI: Zondervan, 2017), 119–36.

20 See G. K. Beale, "Finding Christ in the Old Testament," *JETS* 63 (2020): 44–47.

the prophets will be accomplished" (18:31).[21] In Acts 3:22–23, the apostle Peter identifies Jesus as the prophet like Moses promised in Deuteronomy 18:15–19. Luke's Gospel repeatedly shows that Jesus's predictions come to pass because he is a true prophet, who speaks with divine authority in agreement with the Law and the Prophets. Jesus foresees his death and resurrection, and he reveals that these events will take place according to God's plan, following "the script of the Scriptures."[22] Thus, Jesus not only predicts the future accurately as a true prophet; he also fulfills prophecy as the messianic Savior and Lord.

Revelation and Recognition

Luke 24 stresses that people need spiritual sight to recognize Jesus's true identity as revealed in the Scriptures. The disciples' journey with Jesus on the road to Emmaus poignantly illustrates this crucial point. Even though Cleopas and his companion converse with Christ himself on the road, "their eyes were kept from recognizing him" (24:16). The passive voice of the Greek verb *ekratounto* ("were kept") means that someone or something prevents these disciples from grasping the true identity of their fellow traveler. Earlier in the Gospel, the disciples do not understand Jesus's predictions about his impending suffering, death, and resurrection because the meaning is "concealed" (9:45) and "hidden from them" (18:34). Some interpreters reason that Satan is the cause of the disciples' incomprehension.[23] Certainly the Gospel of Luke speaks of Satan's hostile aims toward the disciples and his involvement with Judas's betrayal (22:3, 31). However, in 10:21–22, Jesus joyously praises the Father because he conceals and reveals according to his gracious will. Thus, when the disciples "were kept" from recognizing Christ in 24:16 (and earlier in the narrative), the "divine passive" construction

---

21 For discussion of *dei* ("it is necessary") in Luke-Acts, see Charles H. Cosgrove, "The Divine ΔEI in Luke-Acts: Investigations into the Lukan Understanding of God's Providence," *NovT* 26 (1984): 168–90; and Brian J. Tabb, *Suffering in Ancient Worldview: Luke, Seneca, and 4 Maccabees in Dialogue*, LNTS 569 (London: Bloomsbury T&T Clark, 2017), 146–47, 161–62.

22 Cf. David P. Moessner, "The 'Script' of the Scripture in the Acts of the Apostles: Suffering as God's 'Plan' (βουλή) for the World for the 'Release of Sins,'" in *History, Literature, and Society in the Book of Acts*, ed. Ben Witherington III (New York: Cambridge University Press, 1996), 218–50; and Brigid C. Frein, "Narrative Predictions, Old Testament Prophecies and Luke's Sense of Fulfilment," *NTS* 40 (1994): 29–30.

23 For example, John Nolland, *Luke*, 3 vols., WBC 35A–C (Dallas: Word, 1989–1993), 2:514, 3:1201.

signals that *God* is ultimately the one who prevents the disciples from initially grasping Jesus's true identity.[24]

These disciples journeying to Emmaus need the risen Lord to remove the blinders, which happens as he reveals himself and the true meaning of the Scriptures. When Jesus breaks bread with Cleopas and the other disciple, "their eyes were opened, and they recognized him" (Luke 24:31).[25] They marvel over how Jesus "opened" the Scriptures to them (v. 32). Then, in the next scene with the larger group of disciples, Luke explains that Jesus himself "opened their minds to understand the Scriptures" (v. 45).[26] Thus, we see that Jesus brings *clarity* to the Bible's central message and gives his disciples the spiritual *capacity* to grasp his teaching. The word translated as "opened" (*dianoigō*) is used three times (vv. 31, 32, 45) to highlight our dual need for *revelation* and *receptivity*. We need Jesus to open God's word to us and to open us to the word.[27]

Identity and Empowerment

Jesus also gives his disciples a new identity and promises them divine power to accomplish their mission. Immediately after previewing the disciples' mission to all nations in accordance with Scripture (Luke

---

24 Walter L. Liefeld and David W. Pao, "Luke," in *Luke–Acts*, ed. Tremper Longman III and David E. Garland, EBC 10, rev. ed. (Grand Rapids, MI: Zondervan, 2007), 345; James R. Edwards, *The Gospel according to Luke*, PNTC (Grand Rapids, MI: Eerdmans, 2015), 716–17; Darrell L. Bock, *Luke*, 2 vols., BECNT (Grand Rapids, MI: Baker, 1994–1996), 2:1909–10; and Joseph A. Fitzmyer, *The Gospel according to Luke*, AB 28–28A (Garden City, NY: Doubleday, 1981–1985), 2:1568. For a dissenting interpretation, see Joel B. Green, *The Gospel of Luke*, NICNT (Grand Rapids, MI: Eerdmans, 1997), 390–91, 845n16.

25 Luke 24:31 likely alludes to Genesis 3:7 with the similar wording "and their eyes were opened, and they knew" (*diēnoichthēsan hoi ophthalmoi, kai egnōsan*). For support for this connection and its biblical-theological implications, see Ortlund, "And Their Eyes Were Opened, and They Knew," 717–28.

26 Matthew Bates proposes an alternative rendering of Luke 24:45: "Then Jesus exposited the Scriptures so that the disciples could understand their meaning," in which the Greek phrase *diēnoixen autōn ton noun* does not refer to Jesus opening the disciples' minds but expounding the "mind" of the Scriptures. Matthew W. Bates, "Closed-Minded Hermeneutics? A Proposed Alternative Translation for Luke 24:45," *JBL* 129 (2010): 539. However, the traditional interpretation of this verse is preferred based on the natural reading of the Greek word order and Luke's use of *dianoigō* to convey divine illumination or enablement in Luke 24:31 ("their eyes were opened") and Acts 16:14 ("the Lord *opened* her heart"). For a similar critique of Bates's reading, see Mark Batluck, "Visions of Jesus Animate Israel's Tradition in Luke," *ExpTim* 129 (2018): 413–14.

27 For a complementary emphasis, see Johnson, *Walking with Jesus*, 17–20.

24:47), Christ declares, "You are witnesses of these things" (v. 48). Jesus's words here likely allude to Isaiah 44:8: "Do not hide yourselves; have you not heard from the beginning, and did I not declare to you? *You are witnesses*, whether there is any god except me."[28] This anticipates the Lord's promise in Acts 1:8: "*You will be my witnesses* in Jerusalem and in all Judea and Samaria, and to the end of the earth." Note that Jesus does not here emphasize their *activity* of bearing witness but their *identity* as his witnesses. Peter stresses that he and the other apostles are witnesses of the resurrection (Acts 1:22; 2:32; 3:15; 5:32; 10:39, 41). They have seen the risen Christ with their own eyes, and so they act as his "authorized delegates."[29] "Witness" is a legal term in both the Old and New Testaments for someone who testifies in court to what he has seen.[30] The disciples are not just spectators to important events but must speak truthfully about what they have seen and heard. As Jesus's witnesses, the apostles testify to the facts of the Messiah's life, death, and resurrection, and they demonstrate that these things took place just as God promised in the Scriptures.[31]

Jesus promises to send the Spirit to empower his witnesses for their mission. Luke 24:49 records his final instructions to his followers: "And behold, I am sending the promise of my Father upon you. But stay in the city until you are clothed with power from on high." Once again, we see that Jesus's teaching looks back to the Old Testament and looks forward to the book of Acts. Jesus calls the Spirit "the promise of my Father" to stress the fulfillment of the ancient prophecy that God would pour out his Spirit in the last days when he would accomplish salvation for his people.[32] Jesus reiterates this command to "wait for the promise of the Father" and stresses again that the disciples will receive heavenly empowerment (Acts 1:4, 8). Jesus's promise is soon realized at Pentecost, when Peter explains

---

28 This is my translation of Isaiah 44:8 LXX. See also Isaiah 43:10, 12. For further discussion, see chap. 6, pp. 136–41.

29 Andrew C. Clark, "The Role of the Apostles," in *Witness to the Gospel*, ed. I. Howard Marshall and David G. Peterson (Grand Rapids, MI: Eerdmans, 1998), 178.

30 See, for example, Deut. 19:15–16; Ruth 4:9–11; Matt. 26:65; Heb. 10:28; *NIDNTTE*, 3:234–45.

31 See Allison A. Trites, *The New Testament Concept of Witness*, SNTSMS 31 (Cambridge: Cambridge University Press, 1977), 144–45.

32 "From on high" in Luke 24:49 probably alludes to the restoration prophecy of Isa. 32:15 ("until the Spirit is poured upon us from on high").

that the coming of the Spirit fulfills prophecy (Joel 2:28–32) and that the risen Lord himself is the one who pours out the Spirit (Acts 2:16–21, 33). Thus, Jesus provides his followers with supernatural power to carry out the mission. He also provides them with a pattern for interpreting the Scriptures.

Message and Model

Jesus's last words according to Luke are both *programmatic* and *paradigmatic*. That is, they express the plan for the disciples' mission and they offer a new pattern for them to follow. The apostles' preaching in Acts shows that they *teach* just what they *learned* from their Lord. They proclaim a *message* of salvation in Jesus's name, and they do so following Jesus's own *model* of expounding the Scriptures in light of his saving death, victorious resurrection, and universal mission. For example, in Acts 4:11, Peter boldly identifies Jesus as "the stone that was rejected by you, the builders, which has become the cornerstone," drawing on the same biblical text (Ps. 118:22) that Jesus cites in Luke 20:17. Likewise, Jesus stresses that he fulfills Isaiah 53:12 as he prepares for his arrest and execution (Luke 22:37), and in Acts 8:30–35, Philip proclaims the good news about Jesus to the Ethiopian eunuch reading Isaiah 53. Jesus does not simply claim that the Old Testament is about him in Luke 24:25–27 and 44–47, but his various appeals to Scripture throughout the Gospel of Luke illustrate a pattern of Bible reading that his disciples imitate in the book of Acts. This leads to a final point about Jesus's last words in Luke 24.

Messiah and Mission

Jesus claims that the Law, Prophets, and Writings find their central focus and climactic fulfillment in his death and resurrection *and* in his mission. Jesus's summary of the Scriptures does not stop with the Messiah's death and resurrection, but also anchors the mission to the nations in what is written.

On the road to Emmaus, Jesus interprets "in all the Scriptures *the things concerning himself*," emphasizing that he had to suffer and then enter into glory (Luke 24:27). Then for his gathered disciples he states "that everything written *about me* in the Law of Moses and the Prophets and the Psalms must be fulfilled" (v. 44). Thus, after the divine Son rises, he instructs his followers to see everything in his light.[33]

Jesus explains, "Thus it is written, that the Christ should suffer" (Luke 24:46). "Suffer" likely serves as shorthand for Christ's entire passion, including his betrayal by Judas, rejection by the Jewish leaders, shameful treatment and torture by the Romans, and ultimately death by crucifixion, just as he predicted (9:22; 17:25). This broad interpretation of "suffer" is suggested by the parallel summary of the Lord's teaching in 24:7 ("the Son of Man must be delivered into the hands of sinful men and be crucified") and verse 26, where "suffer these things" relates to the two disciples' summary of Jesus's condemnation and crucifixion in verse 20.

"The Christ should . . . on the third day rise from the dead" (Luke 24:46) again recalls Jesus's initial prediction of his suffering and resurrection in 9:22. "The third day" also echoes two earlier references in Luke 24 to the timing of the resurrection. The angel reminds the women at the empty tomb that Jesus said that he must rise "on the third day" (v. 7). Next, Cleopas and the other disciple recount to Jesus (whom they do not yet recognize) that "it is now the third day since these things happened" (v. 21).

Jesus continues his summary of what "is written" into Luke 24:47: "*and that repentance for the forgiveness of sins should be proclaimed in his name to all nations, beginning from Jerusalem*."[34] The first note of hope for the nations in Luke's Gospel comes when Simeon cradles the messianic child and calls Jesus "a light for revelation to the Gentiles" (2:32).[35] The closing scene of this Gospel clarifies that this hope is realized by preaching in the Messiah's name.

---

33 Here I adapt the closing line of C. S. Lewis, "Is Theology Poetry?," in *The Weight of Glory, and Other Addresses*, rev. ed. (San Francisco: HarperCollins, 1980), 140 ("I believe in Christianity as I believe that the Sun has risen, not only because I see it, but because by it I see everything else"). Richard Hays similarly writes, "*We interpret Scripture rightly only when we read it in light of the resurrection, and we begin to comprehend the resurrection only when we see it as the climax of the scriptural story of God's gracious deliverance of Israel.*" *Reading with the Grain of Scripture* (Grand Rapids, MI: Eerdmans, 2020), 47, emphasis original.

34 Cf. Thomas S. Moore, "The Lucan Great Commission and the Isaianic Servant," *BSac* 154 (1997): 60.

35 Note that "nations" in Luke 24:47 and "Gentiles" in 2:32 translate the same Greek term, *ethnē*. Simeon's prophetic words allude to Isa. 42:6 and 49:6, and receive focused attention in chap. 4, pp. 86–89.

This proclamation calls specifically for *repentance*, which involves not simply a change of one's mind but a complete change of one's allegiance and actions—"the true turning of our life to God."[36] Note that the response of repentance leads to "forgiveness of sins." While John the Baptist preaches a baptism of repentance unto forgiveness in Israel (Luke 3:3; cf. 1:77), the risen Lord explains that his followers' preaching will now have a Christological focus "in his name" and a universal scope "to all nations" (24:47). This verse effectively previews the mission of Jesus's witnesses, who call Jews and Gentiles to repent and believe in the exalted Lord and Messiah. Thus, Jesus explains that his death, resurrection, and universal mission follow the script of the Scriptures, offering a hermeneutical example for his disciples to follow.[37]

Thus far I have reflected on how the risen Lord expounds the Scriptures. In Luke 24:44–47, Jesus explains the Bible's central *message* about his suffering and resurrection and the mission to all nations, and he provides a *model* of biblical interpretation for his disciples to emulate after Emmaus. Let's now examine Paul's speech in Acts 26:22–23, which echoes Jesus's threefold summary of the Scriptures.[38]

Paul's Summary of the Scriptures (Acts 26:22–23)

Crucially for the argument of this book, Paul follows the Lord's lead by linking the mission to the nations with the expectation of the Scriptures. Acts 26:1–23 records Paul's defense before the Jewish king Agrippa II and the Roman governor Porcius Festus. He recounts how he zealously persecuted Christians until the risen Lord revealed himself to Paul and commissioned him as his witness.[39] Paul stresses his obedience to Christ and rehearses how the Jews seized and threatened him in the temple. He concludes his defense in verses 22–23 by summarizing his essential message:

---

36 John Calvin, *Institutes of the Christian Religion*, ed. John T. McNeill, trans. Ford Lewis Battles, Library of Christian Classics (Philadelphia: Westminster John Knox, 1960), 3.3.5. See further the recent study by Michael J. Ovey, *The Feasts of Repentance: From Luke–Acts to Systematic and Pastoral Theology*, NSBT 49 (London: Apollos, 2019).

37 See also Wright, *The Mission of God*, 30.

38 Parallels between Luke 24:44–47 and Acts 26:22–23 are also noted by Richard J. Dillon, "Easter Revelation and Mission Program in Luke 24:46–48," in *Sin, Salvation and the Spirit*, ed. Daniel Durken (Collegeville, MN: Liturgical, 1979), 247.

39 Acts 9, 22, and 26 recount Paul's conversion and call with varying emphases. For discussion of these accounts, see Tabb, *Suffering in Ancient Worldview*, 149–51.

To this day I have had the help that comes from God, and so I stand here testifying both to small and great, saying nothing but what the prophets and Moses said would come to pass: that the Christ must suffer and that, by being the first to rise from the dead, he would proclaim light both to our people and to the Gentiles.

Paul's speech contains a number of parallels with the risen Lord's teaching in Luke 24.

Paul appeals to "the prophets and Moses" (Acts 26:22) as the supreme authority for his teaching and insists that his words agree fully with the Scriptures. Paul's shorthand summary of the Old Testament canon parallels Jesus's interpretation of "Moses and all the Prophets" in Luke 24:27. Moreover, Paul asks the king, "Do you believe the prophets? I know that you believe" (Acts 26:27), recalling the Lord's rebuke that the two disciples were slow "to believe all that the prophets have spoken" (Luke 24:25).

Paul also expresses confidence that the words of Scripture "would come to pass" (Acts 26:22). The same Greek phrase (*mellō ginesthai*) also occurs in Luke 21:36 and Revelation 1:19 to express future realities that will soon take place. Earlier in Paul's defense, he declares that he is accused "because of my hope in the promise made by God to our fathers," a hope that motivates faithful Israelites in their daily worship (Acts 26:6–7). This expectation that God will surely fulfill his promises parallels Jesus's assertion that "everything written about me in the Law of Moses and the Prophets and the Psalms must be fulfilled" (Luke 24:44).

Additionally, the language of testimony and witness in Acts 26 recalls Jesus's declaration that his disciples are "*witnesses* [*martyres*] of these things" (Luke 24:48). This is noteworthy because Paul is not an eyewitness to Christ's resurrection like Peter, John, and the other apostles who ate fish with the risen Lord before his ascension. Nevertheless, in his defense, Paul insists that the Lord Jesus appointed him "as a servant and *witness* [*martyra*] to the things in which you have seen me and to those in which I will appear to you" (Acts 26:16). Thus, he stands before the king "testifying" (*martyromenos*) to what the Scriptures promised (v. 22), fulfilling Christ's promise that the former persecutor would carry his name before "kings" (9:15). These parallels show that Jesus's foundational words in Luke 24:44–49 do not concern only the Twelve but also have bearing for other "witnesses" who participate in Christ's mission among all nations.

Further, Paul's summary of his message in Acts 26:22–23 precisely parallels Jesus's own exposition in Luke 24:46–47 (see Table 1.1 below).[40] Both passages stress the comprehensive fulfillment of the Scriptures, the necessity of Christ's suffering, and the promise that he will rise again. While Luke 24:46 specifies the timing of Christ's resurrection "on the third day," Acts 26:23 clarifies how his past resurrection relates to the future resurrection hope for all God's people. By stating that Jesus was "the first to rise from the dead," Paul demonstrates his earlier claim "that God raises the dead" (26:8). Not only does Christ's past resurrection guarantee the future resurrection of others at the end of history (cf. 1 Cor. 15:23; 1 Thess. 4:14), but it means that the blessings of the age to come have broken into the present.

Thus, Jesus and Paul both summarize the scriptural hope of the Messiah and the mission to the nations. Luke 24:47 establishes the Christological focus of his disciples' preaching (in Jesus's name), their central message (repentance for the forgiveness of sins), and the universal scope of their mission (to all nations). Acts 26:23 states that *the risen Messiah himself* "would proclaim light both to our people and to the Gentiles." Earlier in his defense, Paul explains that Jesus sent him to the Gentiles "so that they may turn from darkness to light and from the power of Satan to God" (v. 18). The focus on "light" in verse 23 recalls Isaiah's prophecy that the Lord's "servant" would be "as a light for the nations" and bring salvation to "the end of the earth" (Isa. 49:6). Simeon alludes to precisely this prophecy when he identifies Jesus as "a light for revelation to the Gentiles" (Luke 2:32). Moreover, Paul and Barnabas cite Isaiah 49:6 as biblical support for their outreach to the Gentiles (Acts 13:46–47).[41] Thus, Jesus's witnesses identify with and participate in the mission of Jesus, the Lord's "servant," as they proclaim the message of salvation in his name to all nations.

---

40 Ben Witherington III rightly draws attention to "considerable parallels" between Acts 26:22–23 and Luke 24:44–48, in *The Acts of the Apostles: A Socio-Rhetorical Commentary* (Grand Rapids, MI: Eerdmans, 1998), 747. However, he overlooks the final parallel in the proclamation to the nations.

41 Acts 13:46–47 receives extended discussion in chap. 6, pp. 149–55.

	Luke 24:44–47	Acts 26:22–23
Old Testament Fulfillment	"everything written about me in the Law of Moses and the Prophets and the Psalms must be fulfilled"	"what the prophets and Moses said would come to pass"
Messiah's Suffering	"the Christ should suffer" (*pathein ton christon*)	"the Christ must suffer" (*ei pathētos ho christos*)
Messiah's Resurrection	the Christ should "on the third day rise from the dead" (*anastēnai ek nekrōn*)	the Christ must be "the first to rise from the dead" (*ex anastaseōs nekrōn*)
Mission to the Nations	"repentance for the forgiveness of sins should be proclaimed in his name to all nations [*ethnē*], beginning from Jerusalem"	"he would proclaim light both to our people and to the Gentiles" [*ethnesin*]

Table 1.1. The Messiah and Mission in Luke 24 and Acts 26

Definitions and Presuppositions

Before looking carefully at how Jesus and his disciples read the Bible messianically and missiologically, it is necessary to define several key terms and explain some of the essential presuppositions that inform such an interpretation of the Scriptures.

First, let's briefly reflect on the *mission* of Christ and his church. *Mission* (derived from the Latin word *mittō*, meaning "send") typically conveys a task that an individual or group is sent to carry out. In contemporary usage, *missions* refers to specific efforts of the Christian church and missions agencies to bear witness to Christ across boundaries such as language, culture, and ethnicity, while *mission* is a broader category that may describe all the church's activity to further God's kingdom.[42] Eckhard Schnabel employs the terms *mission* and *missions* interchangeably for the

---

42 A. Scott Moreau, Gary R. Corwin, and Gary B. McGee, *Introducing World Missions: A Biblical, Historical, and Practical Survey*, 2nd ed. (Grand Rapids, MI: Baker Academic, 2015), 17. For a historical overview of the terms *mission* and *missions*, see Craig Ott and Stephen J. Strauss, *Encountering Theology of Mission: Biblical Foundations, Historical Developments, and Contemporary Issues* (Grand Rapids, MI: Baker Academic, 2010), xiv–xviii.

activity of a faith community that calls other people to share its distinctive beliefs and way of life.[43]

Many scholars rightly argue that the church's mission is grounded in the unfolding mission of God in the world. For example, Christopher Wright responds to the common sentiment that "mission is what *we* do" by defining the church's mission as "*our committed participation as God's people, at God's invitation and command, in God's own mission within the history of God's world for the redemption of God's creation.*"[44] The Son of God takes center stage in the biblical story of God's mission to make himself known, save his people, and restore all things. Thus, Christ's mission "is the fundamental mission in the Scriptures."[45]

Jesus's mission refers to the work that he came to accomplish as the Savior, Lord, and Messiah. Luke's Gospel summarizes this mission in several ways. Jesus is "a light for revelation to the Gentiles" (Luke 2:32), referencing the servant's calling in Isaiah 49:6. Christ himself declares that he is "anointed . . . to proclaim good news" and "sent . . . to proclaim liberty [*kēryxai . . . aphesin*]" (Luke 4:18), fulfilling Isaiah 61:1. Moreover, he explains that he "came to seek and to save the lost" (Luke 19:10)—the very thing that God himself resolved to do for his people in Ezekiel 34:16, 22.[46] The risen Lord expresses the mission of his followers in similar terms: they must proclaim (*kērychthēnai*) repentance for the forgiveness (*aphesin*) of sins in his name to all nations, just as it is "written" in the Scriptures (Luke 24:46–47), and they will be his witnesses "to the end of the earth" (Acts 1:8), alluding to the same servant prophecy (Isa. 49:6) applied to Jesus himself in Luke 2:32. These and other passages show that Christ's own mission is the basis for his people's mission among the nations.[47]

Additionally, this book focuses on clear examples when Jesus and his followers refer to the authoritative Scriptures. *Quotation* and *citation* refer

---

43 Eckhard J. Schnabel, *Early Christian Mission*, 2 vols. (Downers Grove, IL: InterVarsity Press, 2004), 1:11.

44 Wright, *The Mission of God*, 21–23, emphasis original. Similarly, "Missions should never be conceptualized apart from the *missio dei*," according to Timothy C. Tennent, *Invitation to World Missions: A Trinitarian Missiology for the Twenty-First Century* (Grand Rapids, MI: Kregel, 2010), 59.

45 Köstenberger and Alexander, *Salvation to the Ends of the Earth*, 256.

46 For detailed exposition of these and other passages, see chap. 4.

47 The book's final chapter reflects on the message, mission, and motivation of Jesus's followers who participate in the Lord's work to the end of the earth.

to explicit biblical appeals that are usually signaled by an introductory formula, such as "it is written" or "the prophet said." An *allusion* is a brief, intentional reference to the Scriptures.[48] The basic key for discerning an allusion is to recognize a clear parallel in wording between the New Testament text and a specific Old Testament passage.[49]

For example, Luke 3:4–6 features a lengthy introductory formula ("As it is written in the book of the words of Isaiah the prophet") and then an extended *quotation* of Isaiah 40:3–5 that closely follows the Greek translation of Isaiah.[50] Jesus's words at the Last Supper offer an example of an *allusion* to the Old Testament: "This cup that is poured out for you is the new covenant in my blood" (Luke 22:20). While Christ does not explicitly reference "the Scriptures" or "the prophets" in this passage, the phrase "the new covenant" unmistakably alludes to the well-known prophecy of Jeremiah 31:31: "Behold, the days are coming, declares the LORD, when I will make *a new covenant* with the house of Israel and the house of Judah."[51] Since this is the only time in the Old Testament when the term *new covenant* occurs, we can confidently conclude that this parallel is not merely a coincidence but that Jesus intentionally uses language from Jeremiah to explain the significance of his sacrificial death.

Next, it is important to state here five fundamental beliefs or presuppositions that guide how Jesus and his followers interpret the Bible.[52] First, they believe the Scriptures—the Law, Prophets, and Writings—to be the holy, inspired word of God, supremely truthful and authoritative in every way.

---

48 These definitions and criteria for New Testament references to the Old Testament closely follow G. K. Beale, *Handbook on the New Testament Use of the Old Testament: Exegesis and Interpretation* (Grand Rapids, MI: Baker Academic, 2012), 29–34.

49 Beale offers a more extensive and technical explanation as follows: "The telltale key to discerning an allusion is that of recognizing an incomparable or unique parallel in wording, syntax, concept, or cluster of motifs in the same order or structure. When both unique wording (verbal coherence) and theme are found, the proposed allusion takes on greater probability." *Handbook on the New Testament Use of the Old Testament*, 31–32.

50 The Greek Old Testament is commonly called the Septuagint and abbreviated LXX, based on the tradition that seventy men translated the Pentateuch from Hebrew into Greek. See Karen H. Jobes and Moisés Silva, *Invitation to the Septuagint*, 2nd. ed. (Grand Rapids, MI: Baker Academic, 2015), 17.

51 Old Testament verse numbers sometimes differ between Hebrew, Greek, and English Bibles. In this case, Jeremiah 31:31 in Hebrew and English editions is 38:31 in the Septuagint.

52 For a complementary summary with extended explanations of these presuppositions, see Beale, *Handbook on the New Testament Use of the Old Testament*, 95–102.

The claim "thus it is written" clearly invokes the binding authority of the sacred book for Jesus's Jewish followers and foes alike. Second, because the Scriptures are from God, they reflect consistent patterns or correspondences between God's work in the past, present, and future. This is the foundational conviction underlying "typology," the study of Old Testament people, events, or institutions (types) that correspond to and prophetically prefigure later and greater fulfillments (antitypes) within biblical history.[53] Third, New Testament authors affirm the biblical principle of corporate solidarity, in which one individual represents the many. The Old Testament includes many examples of corporate solidarity, such as the high priest entering the most holy place to make atonement for all Israel, David acting as the people's champion against the giant, or the kings of Israel and Judah leading the nation to sin. The New Testament authors claim that Jesus the Messiah is the true representative for God's people. Fourth, the New Testament authors believe that Jesus's death, resurrection, and gift of the Holy Spirit have begun "the last days" that were foretold by the prophets and will be consummated in the future when Jesus returns. The term *inaugurated eschatology* is a standard way to express this presupposition that the last days have begun already but are not yet fully realized.[54] Fifth, the New Testament authors understand Jesus to be the focus and fulfillment of the Scriptures. This is precisely what the risen Lord claims in Luke 24:27, 44. The next six chapters of this book examine various examples of how Jesus and the apostles unpack the centrality of the Messiah and his mission, guided by these foundational biblical-theological beliefs about the authority, unity, and fulfillment of God's word in the last days.

Proposal and Plan

This book proposes that the risen Christ supplies us with corrective lenses to see that the Messiah's death, resurrection, and mission are like the big letters on the Bible's "eye chart." Luke 24:44–47 summarizes the essential message of the Scriptures and offers disciples a hermeneutical model or

---

53 This definition is adapted from Peter J. Gentry and Stephen J. Wellum, *God's Kingdom through God's Covenants: A Concise Biblical Theology* (Wheaton, IL: Crossway, 2015), 39.

54 For an excellent introduction to inaugurated eschatology, see Benjamin L. Gladd and Matthew S. Harmon, *Making All Things New: Inaugurated Eschatology for the Life of the Church* (Grand Rapids, MI: Baker Academic, 2016).

lens for reading the Bible with the proper focus. Readers do not need to guess in what sense the Scriptures are "about" Christ and the mission to the nations because Jesus and his first followers offer various examples of Christological and missiological readings of the Old Testament.

The plan for the remaining chapters of this book is as follows. Chapter 2 examines Christ's suffering, rejection, and death in Luke's Gospel, which both the Scriptures and Jesus himself foretell. Chapter 3 considers how Jesus predicts and explains the necessity of his resurrection from the dead. Chapter 4 focuses on Luke's presentation of the Messiah's mission and the hope for the nations and the outcasts. Chapters 5–6 turn attention to the book of Acts, exploring how the apostles and their associates proclaim Jesus as the suffering Savior and risen Lord according to the Scriptures and how they expound the biblical basis for their mission to all nations. Chapter 7 expands beyond Luke-Acts to consider how Matthew, John, Paul, and Peter explain the biblical rationale for the Messiah's suffering, resurrection, and mission. The concluding chapter summarizes the book's argument and highlights how the Scriptures' focus on the Messiah and his mission relate to the church's message, mission, and motivation for gospel witness.

2

The Rejected Cornerstone

The Messiah's Suffering in Luke

And he strictly charged and commanded them to tell this
to no one, saying, "The Son of Man must suffer many
things and be rejected by the elders and chief priests and
scribes, and be killed, and on the third day be raised."

LUKE 9:21–22

MACBETH, THE LEAD CHARACTER in Shakespeare's famous tragedy, takes destiny into his own hands. "Brave Macbeth" is a battlefield hero, who wields his sword in service to King Duncan.[1] Then the witches prophesy that Macbeth "shalt be king hereafter,"[2] planting a sinister seed that flowers in the dark soil of his ambition. His friend Banquo reminds him that "the instruments of darkness tell us truths" but ultimately betray us "in deepest consequence,"[3] yet Macbeth does not heed this warning. Not willing to wait for chance to crown him, Macbeth forces fate by slaying Duncan to secure Scotland's crown. Bloodshed begets bloodshed, and the ambitious Macbeth becomes a tragic tyrant king who gains the whole world yet forfeits his soul.[4]

---

1 William Shakespeare, *Macbeth*, ed. Barbara A. Mowat and Paul Werstine, Folger Shakespeare Library (New York: Simon & Schuster, 2010), 1.2.18.
2 Shakespeare, *Macbeth*, 1.3.53.
3 Shakespeare, *Macbeth*, 1.3.136–38.
4 Peter J. Leithart, *Brightest Heaven of Invention: A Christian Guide to Six Shakespeare Plays* (Moscow, ID: Canon, 2006), 165.

Contrast David, who is anointed by the prophet yet patiently waits years to succeed Saul as Israel's king. Even when Saul threatens David's life and forces him to flee, the giant slayer refuses to stretch out his hand against Saul, the Lord's anointed (1 Sam. 24:6; 26:11). David does not exalt himself or force fate, but endures adversity while trusting God to "exalt the horn of his anointed" at the proper time (2:10). The son of Jesse is the anti-Macbeth and a preview of the greater David, who embraces his divine destiny even unto death.

A Strange Script

Jesus predicts his coming suffering, rejection, and death multiple times in Luke's Gospel. The first passion prediction comes immediately after Jesus asks the disciples, "Who do the crowds say that I am? . . . Who do you say that I am?" Peter confesses that he is "the Christ of God" (Luke 9:18–20). The disciples have seen Jesus still the storm (8:24), drive out demons (8:27–33), raise the dead (8:49–56), and feed the masses (9:12–17). They recognize that Jesus is not merely a prophet of old or John the Baptist returned; he is the one whom John and the prophets foretold. Peter, acting as the spokesman for the twelve, correctly identifies Christ and probably expects commendation. Surprisingly, Jesus responds with a sharp and sober word: "And he strictly charged and commanded them to tell this to no one, saying, 'The Son of Man must suffer many things and be rejected by the elders and chief priests and scribes, and be killed, and on the third day be raised'" (9:21–22). A *suffering* Christ? That's not the script that the disciples have in mind. Jesus reiterates similar themes in 17:25, warning his followers that "he must suffer many things and be rejected by this generation."

Jesus makes his second passion prediction in Luke 9:44, following his transfiguration.[5] As the crowds marvel at his mighty deeds, Jesus again addresses his disciples: "Let these words sink into your ears: The Son of Man is about to be delivered into the hands of men."

Luke 18:31–33 is Christ's most detailed prophecy of his suffering and resurrection:

See, we are going up to Jerusalem, and everything that is written about the Son of Man by the prophets will be accomplished. For he will be de-

---

5   I discuss the transfiguration scene (Luke 9:28–36) in chap. 3, pp. 69–72.

livered over to the Gentiles and will be mocked and shamefully treated and spit upon. And after flogging him, they will kill him, and on the third day he will rise.

These passion predictions emphasize the necessity and nature of Christ's suffering, as well as the disciples' incomprehension and the cost of following Jesus.

First, Jesus stresses the *necessity* of his suffering. The Greek word *dei*, translated "must," in Luke 9:22 and frequently elsewhere, conveys the idea of divine necessity of God's plan coming to pass—a plan that is rooted in the divine Scriptures.[6] For example, Jesus says that he *must* preach the gospel to other towns, he *must* suffer many things, wars and tumults *must* take place before the end, and the Scripture *must* be fulfilled in him.[7] Divine necessity defines and drives Christ's mission, and he states plainly that his passion is God's plan.

Jesus also specifies the *nature* of his coming suffering. He "will be rejected" (*apodokimasthēnai*) by the Jewish leaders and also by his generation (Luke 9:22; 17:25). The Greek verb *apodokimazō* means "to regard as unworthy/unfit and therefore to be rejected."[8] These two predictions of rejection anticipate Christ's climactic explanation of the parable of the wicked tenants: "The stone that the builders *rejected* [*apedokimasan*] has become the cornerstone" (Luke 20:17).[9] Jesus warns that he will also be scorned, shamefully treated, spat upon, and scourged before being killed (18:32). Such verbal and physical abuse corresponds closely to Isaiah's prophecies concerning God's righteous servant.[10]

Further, Luke makes clear that the disciples do not truly understand Jesus's passion predictions:

> But they did not understand this saying, and it was concealed from them, so that they might not perceive it. And they were afraid to ask him about this saying. (9:45)

---

6 See Cosgrove, "The Divine ΔEI in Luke-Acts," 174; and Tabb, *Suffering in Ancient Worldview*, 146–47.

7 Luke 4:43; 17:25; 21:9; 22:37; see also 24:7, 26, 44.

8 BDAG, 110.

9 Jesus's use of Ps. 118:22 in Luke 20:17 is discussed below, pp. 46–48.

10 See below, pp. 50–56.

But they understood none of these things. This saying was hidden from them, and they did not grasp what was said. (18:34)

The evangelist highlights the disciples' ignorance and fear, but he also explains *why* they fail to comprehend Christ's coming fate. The passive verbs in Luke 9:45 ("was concealed") and 18:34 ("was hidden") likely indicate God's plan to conceal these things from Jesus's disciples for a time.[11] The disciples do not—indeed, *cannot*—discern the deeper truths about Jesus's coming suffering until the risen Lord opens their minds to understand the Scriptures (24:45).[12]

Finally, Jesus instructs his disciples to likewise expect and embrace adversity.[13] Immediately after predicting his own suffering, Jesus calls his followers to lives of costly discipleship: "If anyone would come after me, let him deny himself and take up his cross daily and follow me" (Luke 9:23). In the ancient world, cross bearing was bound up with crucifixion, the most shameful and painful form of public execution. Thus, Jesus's summons to bear one's cross is a call to "voluntary *self-stigmatization*."[14]

Jesus offers three reasons why his disciples must demonstrate supreme loyalty to him and deny themselves each day (Luke 9:24–26; see also 14:26–33). He explains that a person can "save" his life only by losing it through daily cross bearing. The future tense verbs "will lose" and "will save" in 9:24 suggest that Jesus has final salvation or judgment in view, not just temporal preservation of life.[15] Further, his rhetorical question in verse 25 supports the summons to self-denial by underscoring the futility of gaining "the whole world" at the cost of losing oneself. Jesus powerfully pictures this point in the parable of the rich fool, who stored up great wealth for himself yet was not rich toward God (12:16–21). Finally, Christ asserts

---

11   This is the view of many commentators, including Fitzmyer, *The Gospel according to Luke*, 1:814; and Edwards, *The Gospel according to Luke*, 289. Alternatively, Joel Green claims that "it is doubtful that imperception can be attributed to divine intent." *The Gospel of Luke*, 390.

12   François Bovon, *Luke 2: A Commentary on the Gospel of Luke 9:51–19:27*, trans. Christine M. Thomas, Hermeneia (Minneapolis: Fortress, 2013), 578. See chap. 1 for an extended discussion of Luke 24.

13   This paragraph and the next summarize material from Tabb, *Suffering in Ancient Worldview*, 165–66.

14   Sverre Bøe, *Cross-Bearing in Luke*, WUNT 2/278 (Tübingen: Mohr Siebeck, 2010), 152, emphasis original.

15   Bøe, *Cross-Bearing in Luke*, 135.

that the Son of Man will reject whoever is ashamed of him and his words (9:26; cf. 12:8–9), a sober warning that relates particularly to his teaching about his own suffering and the cost of discipleship (9:22–23).

The Suffering Messiah Fulfills the Scriptures

In *The Voyage of the Dawn Treader*, Caspian—the king of Narnia—comes to the Lone Islands in search of seven lords who were loyal to his father.[16] When Caspian arrives, traffickers capture him (unaware of who he is) and sell him at the slave market. There he is bought by Bern—one of the seven lost lords—who recognizes Caspian and intends to free him. Caspian learns that Gumpas, the governor of the Lone Islands, is a scoundrel who feigns allegiance to the king of Narnia but really promotes his own agenda and profits from the slave trade. So Caspian and his allies board Bern's boat and travel around to the island where the governor resides. They raise the king's banner, draw their swords, and march toward the governor's house. When they arrive, they find Gumpas to be a rude, self-absorbed, spineless bureaucrat. Caspian sacks the governor and appoints Bern as the Duke of the Lone Islands. In Lewis's story, Caspian endures shameful treatment before revealing his true identity, liberating the Lone Islands, and ousting the imposters who are not loyal to the crown. Gumpas and his cronies are like the wicked tenants who despise the vineyard's owner, his servants, and even his son, until they are destroyed and the vineyard is entrusted to others (Luke 20:9–16). As Jesus explains, the rejected stone is the foundational cornerstone (20:17).

Jesus repeatedly declares that he must suffer to fulfill God's plan. Luke's Gospel presents multiple examples of the scriptural script that Jesus follows. Christ is the dishonored prophet, whose message falls on deaf ears (Isa. 6:9). He is the rejected stone chosen by God as the cornerstone (Ps. 118:22). He is the last Passover lamb, whose shed blood secures the new covenant promise (Jer. 31:31). He is the suffering servant, who is numbered with the transgressors (Isa. 53:12). And he is the righteous King, who responds to suffering by entrusting his spirit to the Father (Ps. 31:5).

---

16 C. S. Lewis, *The Voyage of the Dawn Treader*, The Chronicles of Narnia (New York: HarperCollins, 1952).

The Dishonored Prophet (Luke 8:9–10)

Jesus's rejection in Nazareth proves the proverb: "No prophet is acceptable in his hometown" (Luke 4:24). During a typical Sabbath gathering, Jesus reads the Isaiah scroll and surprisingly declares the fulfillment of Scripture before a rapt audience.[17] The Nazareth synagogue regulars speak well of Jesus and marvel at his "gracious words," but their opinion of "Joseph's son" quickly changes, and they drive him out of town and nearly off a cliff (Luke 4:16–29). Though Jesus proclaims "the year of the Lord's favor," he soon falls out of favor with his friends and family. This scene in Jesus's hometown offers a preview of coming attractions in the Gospel narrative.[18] It reveals both *who* Jesus is—the Spirit-anointed Messiah who brings good news to the poor and fulfills prophecy—and *how* his own people will reject him as they did the prophets of old.

The rejected prophet theme recurs several chapters later, when Jesus explains to his disciples why he teaches in parables:

And when his disciples asked him what this parable meant, he said, "To you it has been given to know the secrets of the kingdom of God, but for others they are in parables, so that 'seeing they may not see, and hearing they may not understand.'" (Luke 8:9–10)

Christ here alludes to the prophet's commissioning in Isaiah 6:9:

Go, and say to this people:

"Keep on hearing, but do not understand;
keep on seeing, but do not perceive."[19]

Isaiah 1–5 repeatedly establishes Israel's idolatry, hardness of heart, and lack of wisdom. Though there are flickers of hope, the dominant note

---

17 Jesus's quotation of Isa. 61 is considered further in chap. 4, pp. 94–101.

18 The programmatic function of Luke 4 is noted by Scott S. Cunningham, *"Through Many Tribulations": The Theology of Persecution in Luke-Acts*, JSNTSup 142 (Sheffield: Sheffield Academic, 1997), 58–59; and David E. Garland, *Luke*, ZECNT (Grand Rapids, MI: Zondervan, 2011), 189.

19 The parallel account in Matt. 13:10–15 includes a lengthy quotation of Isa. 6:9–10 and refers to "the prophecy of Isaiah" being fulfilled.

throughout these chapters is promised judgment on God's rebellious people. The Lord then charges his prophet to blind the people's eyes, stop up their ears, and harden their hearts (6:9–13). Isaiah's parabolic proclamation confirms the Israelites in their idolatrous rebellion against God.[20] Elsewhere, Isaiah refers to the people's malfunctioning eyes and ears as an ironic yet fitting judgment for their worship of idols who neither see nor hear. The people come to resemble the blind and deaf deities that they revere.[21]

The parable of the sower is fundamentally about hearing the word of God.[22] Jesus concludes the parable with this enigmatic exhortation: "He who has ears to *hear*, let him *hear*" (Luke 8:8). He repeats the word *hear* four times in verses 12–15 when explaining this parable. Jesus then urges his followers, "Take care then how you *hear*" in verse 18, using the same Greek verbs *blepō* ("take care" or "see") and *akouō* ("hear") from Isaiah 6:9. Finally, in Luke 8:21 Jesus insists that his true family members "are those who *hear* the word of God and do it." The point is that Jesus's teaching about the kingdom demands a response of obedience. True hearing results in fruit bearing (8:15).

Jesus alludes to Isaiah 6 to explain why his ministry is met with rejection. He continues the pattern of God's prophets who faithfully proclaimed God's word to a people who refused to listen. Throughout the Old Testament, Israel persecuted and killed the prophets sent to her by God, so unsurprisingly, the Christ whom the prophets proclaimed faces a similar fate.[23] Luke 8:10 is a clear example of typological fulfillment of the Old Testament: Isaiah's call to speak God's word to those who are spiritually blind and deaf foreshadows the later and greater ministry of Jesus, who not only proclaims the secrets of God's kingdom but also fulfills the Scriptures (4:21). There is also an important redemptive-historical development from Isaiah to Jesus. Isaiah prophesied imminent judgment followed by

---

20 Rikk E. Watts, "Mark," in *Commentary on the New Testament Use of the Old Testament*, ed. G. K. Beale and D. A. Carson (Grand Rapids, MI: Baker Academic, 2007), 152.

21 See Isa. 42:16–20; 43:8–12. For extended discussion of Isa. 6, see G. K. Beale, *We Become What We Worship: A Biblical Theology of Idolatry* (Downers Grove, IL: IVP Academic, 2008), 36–70.

22 Klyne Snodgrass, *Stories with Intent: A Comprehensive Guide to the Parables of Jesus*, 2nd ed. (Grand Rapids, MI: Eerdmans, 2018), 152. This emphasis is most explicit in Mark's account of the parable, which begins with the command "Listen!" (Mark 4:3).

23 See Luke 4:24; 6:22–23; 11:49–50; 13:33–34; 20:9–18; Acts 7:52; and Cunningham, *"Through Many Tribulations,"* 59–65, 158.

glorious salvation, when blind eyes will be opened, and deaf ears will be unstopped (Isa. 35:5). Jesus not only reveals the secrets of God's kingdom, but he also opens deaf ears and gives sight to the blind. These miracles of reversal signal that the promised time of salvation has come (Luke 7:21–23; 18:42). While great crowds gather to listen to Jesus's teaching, most fail to truly hear and believe his message, and even his closest disciples cannot grasp that their master must suffer many things according to God's plan (9:45; 18:34). As Jesus opens the eyes of the blind beggar in 18:35–43, the disciples need Jesus to give them spiritual sight to grasp how his suffering fulfills the Scriptures and brings salvation.

The Rejected Cornerstone (Luke 20:17)

When Jesus predicts that he must suffer rejection and death, he sets his face toward Jerusalem (Luke 9:22, 51). For ten long chapters Jesus journeys toward "the city that kills the prophets" (13:34). A crowd of disciples cheers his arrival as "the King who comes in the name of the Lord" (19:38, invoking Ps. 118:26), while the Pharisees protest their praise and the priests, scribes, and leading men of Israel plot his demise (Luke 19:39, 47). After Jesus drives out the sellers and begins teaching daily in the temple (19:45, 47), the Jewish leaders question his authority (20:1–8). Jesus then tells the people a parable, which his opponents rightly perceive to be "against them" (20:19).

The parable of the wicked tenants, recounted in all three Synoptic Gospels, explains the redemptive-historical context and consequences of Christ's imminent rejection and death. The parable's setting—"a vineyard"—alludes to Isaiah 5:1–7, the song concerning the vineyard that yielded wild grapes despite its fertile ground and choice vines. The prophet explains that the Lord's vineyard "is the house of Israel" and laments that God looked for justice and righteousness but instead found bloodshed and an outcry (Isa. 5:7). While scholars have interpreted this parable in various ways, it is most plausible that Jesus deliberately draws on Isaiah's imagery "to retell Israel's story with a new twist," confronting the Jewish religious authorities and clarifying his own mission.[24] As in Isaiah, the vineyard symbolizes Israel, whose owner is God. The tenants are Israel's rulers, and the servants whom

---

24 Snodgrass, *Stories with Intent*, 276; cf. N. T. Wright, *Jesus and the Victory of God*, Christian Origins and the Question of God 2 (Minneapolis: Fortress, 1997), 178.

the owner sends are the prophets (compare Luke 11:49; 13:34). The son whom the tenants cast out and kill clearly refers to Jesus, since the heavenly voice identifies him as "my beloved son" in 3:22. The others to whom God will give the vineyard are probably Christ's apostles.[25]

At the climax of the parable, Jesus clarifies his point by appealing to what is "written" in Psalm 118:22: "The stone that the builders rejected has become the cornerstone" (Luke 20:17).[26]

This Old Testament quotation is no optional add-on but is the key that unlocks this parable's significance.[27] Psalm 118 is a thanksgiving hymn that was sung by pilgrims coming to Jerusalem's temple and recited during the Passover celebration.[28] The psalm opens and concludes with the same refrain: "Oh give thanks to the LORD, for he is good; for his steadfast love endures forever!" (vv. 1, 29). The psalmist recounts that the Lord has heard his prayers for help and has become his "salvation" (vv. 14, 21). God has accomplished his marvelous work of redemption through rejection, which prompts the faithful to rejoice and pray in anticipation of God's coming salvation (vv. 22–26). The rejected stone in the psalm likely refers to a royal figure who is oppressed by others but vindicated by God and called blessed "from the house of the LORD" (v. 26).[29]

Jesus also quotes Psalm 118:26 when he laments over Jerusalem: "Behold, your house is forsaken. And I tell you, you will not see me until you say, 'Blessed is he who comes in the name of the Lord!'" (Luke 13:35). His prediction is fulfilled when the crowd praises him at the triumphal entry (19:38).[30] This makes clear that *Jesus* is the King who comes in God's name. He then weeps over Jerusalem's imminent destruction and drives out sellers from

---

25 The account in Matt. 21:41 specifies that the owner will "let out the vineyard to other tenants who will give him the fruits in their seasons."

26 Ps. 118:22 is numbered 117:22 in the Septuagint—Luke 20:17 follows the Greek version of the psalm word-for-word. Luke 20:18 supplements this quotation of Ps. 118:22 with an additional "stone" saying that combines Isa. 8:14–15 and Dan. 2:34–35. See David W. Pao and Eckhard J. Schnabel, "Luke," in *Commentary on the New Testament Use of the Old Testament*, 362–65.

27 Snodgrass, *Stories with Intent*, 290.

28 Wright, *Jesus and the Victory of God*, 498; and Nancy L. DeClaissé-Walford, Rolf A. Jacobson, and Beth LaNeel Tanner, *The Book of Psalms*, NICOT (Grand Rapids, MI: Eerdmans, 2014), 864.

29 G. K. Beale, *The Temple and the Church's Mission: A Biblical Theology of the Dwelling Place of God*, NSBT 17 (Downers Grove, IL: InterVarsity Press, 2004), 184.

30 C. Kavin Rowe, *Early Narrative Christology: The Lord in the Gospel of Luke*, BZNW 139 (Berlin: de Gruyter, 2006), 164.

the Lord's house, which has become "a den of robbers" (vv. 41–46). The parable of the wicked tenants confirms and clarifies the point of Jesus's temple cleansing: God is bringing judgment on Israel's rulers, who are "the tenants" in the parable and "the builders" in the psalm.[31] Moreover, these rulers have rejected God's "beloved son," the coming king and the temple cornerstone.

The parable of the wicked tenants presents a crucial perspective on Christ's identity and mission.[32] He is not simply another prophet sent to Israel, but the "beloved son" of the Father. As the Son, he will face scorn, suffering, and death, just as he predicted and as God planned. Yet the Scriptures specify that the rejected stone is ironically the precious cornerstone, whom God will vindicate.[33] For those who see and celebrate Jesus's divine identity and saving mission, "This is the Lord's doing; it is marvelous in our eyes" (Ps. 118:23).

The Last Passover Lamb (Luke 22:19–20)

Jesus reveals the saving purpose of his suffering over a sacred supper with his disciples. Meal scenes in the Gospels illustrate the character of God's kingdom and the nature of Jesus's ministry.[34] Jesus challenges the customs and sensibilities of the Jewish leaders by feasting with tax collectors and sinners (Luke 5:33; 7:34; 15:2). The Lord's surprising table fellowship offers a preview of the heavenly banquet where the repentant will dine while the proud will be denied. The climactic meal scene comes in Luke 22, where Jesus celebrates the Passover with his disciples and explains its symbolic significance in terms of his own passion. There is a notable play on words in Greek between *pascha* ("Passover") and *paschō* ("suffer"). Luke explains that "the Passover lamb had to be sacrificed" on the day of Unleavened Bread (22:7), and this need to slay the lamb parallels and prepares for Christ's own necessary suffering.[35] As Jesus says to his disciples, "I have earnestly desired to eat this Passover [*pascha*] with you before I suffer [*pathein*]" (v. 15).

---

31 Peter and John declare before the Sanhedrin: "This Jesus is the stone that was rejected by you, the builders, which has become the cornerstone" (Acts 4:11). This use of Ps. 118 is discussed further in chap. 5, pp. 109–11.

32 Snodgrass, *Stories with Intent*, 298.

33 See J. Ross Wagner, "Psalm 118 in Luke-Acts: Tracing a Narrative Thread," in *Early Christian Interpretation of the Scriptures of Israel: Investigations and Proposals*, ed. Craig A. Evans and James A. Sanders, JSNTSup 148 (Sheffield: Sheffield Academic, 1997), 170–71.

34 Michael Ovey helpfully explores how feasts function as "type scenes" in Luke's Gospel, in *The Feasts of Repentance*, 12.

35 Green, *The Gospel of Luke*, 755.

Jesus assigns new symbolic meaning to the bread and wine of this sacred meal in Luke 22:19–20:

> And he took bread, and when he had given thanks, he broke it and gave it to them, saying, "This is my body, which is given for you. Do this in remembrance of me." And likewise the cup after they had eaten, saying, "This cup that is poured out for you is the new covenant in my blood."[36]

Jesus yearns that he and his disciples might share the Passover, a solemn meal that memorialized Israel's exodus from bondage, when the Lord struck down Egypt's firstborn but passed over the houses of his people (Ex. 12:26–27). Jesus identifies the bread and cup of this holy feast with his own body and blood that would be broken and shed for others at the cross. Thus, the Passover meal and the saving event it memorialized serve as types foreshadowing Jesus's last supper and sacrificial death.[37]

Luke's account of Christ's words of institution includes several distinctive emphases when compared with the parallel accounts in Matthew 26:26–29 and Mark 14:22–25.[38] First, Jesus states that his blood is poured out "for many" in Matthew and Mark, likely recalling the work of God's servant in Isaiah 53:12.[39] But in Luke, Jesus asserts that both his body and blood are given "for you." This phrase highlights the particularity and personal nature of Jesus's substitutionary death for his disciples.

Second, according to Matthew and Mark, Christ declares, "This is my blood of the covenant," precisely recalling Moses's pronouncement when the Sinai covenant is confirmed.[40] However, in Luke's account, Jesus identifies the Passover cup as "the new covenant in my blood"

---

36 One important Greek manuscript (Codex Bezae) abbreviates Christ's words of institution to the phrase "This is my body," omitting the reference to the cup and the explanation of the redemptive significance of his death found in all other known Greek manuscripts. For a recent defense of the traditional reading of Luke 22:19–20 that is included in all major English translations, see Benjamin R. Wilson, *The Saving Cross of the Suffering Christ: The Death of Jesus in Lukan Soteriology*, BZNW 223 (Berlin: de Gruyter, 2016), 68–78.

37 Wilson, *The Saving Cross of the Suffering Christ*, 81–82.

38 For detailed discussion, see I. Howard Marshall, *Last Supper and Lord's Supper* (Grand Rapids, MI: Eerdmans, 1980), chap. 2.

39 R. T. France, *Jesus and the Old Testament*, repr. ed. (Vancouver: Regent College, 1998), 120–23.

40 "And Moses took the blood and threw it on the people and said, 'Behold the blood of the covenant that the LORD has made with you in accordance with all these words'" (Ex. 24:8).

(Luke 22:20). The distinctive phrase "new covenant" (*kainē diathēkē*) occurs only once in the Old Testament, in Jeremiah 31:31 (38:31 LXX): "Behold, the days are coming, declares the LORD, when I will make *a new covenant* with the house of Israel and the house of Judah." This covenant is unlike the Sinai covenant, which Israel broke, because God promises to write his law on people's hearts and to "forgive their iniquity" and "remember their sin no more" (31:32–34). The Septuagint version of Jeremiah specifies that God will gather his people from the farthest part of the earth "at the feast of Passover" and then make a new covenant with them.[41] The lengthy citation of Jeremiah 31:31–34 in Hebrews 8:8–12 and other New Testament references to "a new covenant" confirm this allusion to Jeremiah's prophecy in Luke 22:20.[42] The Lord's first covenant with Israel was closely tied to the exodus deliverance and memorialized in the Passover celebration. Jesus initiates the new covenant by his own vicarious death and commemorates this great saving act with a covenant meal.[43]

Jesus's words at the Last Supper signal that his substitutionary death brings about a new era in God's relationship with his people based on God's gracious forgiveness of their sins.[44] At this meal, Christ also stresses the coming fulfillment of God's kingdom (Luke 22:16, 18) and promises that the disciples will eat and drink at *his* table in the kingdom given him by God (vv. 29–30). Christ shares bread and wine with and promises to die for the very disciples who betray, misunderstand, and fail him.[45]

The Suffering Servant (Luke 22:37)

The Old Testament repeatedly promised *that* God would rescue his people, but *how* would he do so?[46] Some Jews longed for a great monarch in David's line, who would slay the wicked, save Israel, and rule with righteousness,

---

41 Jer. 38:8, 31 LXX. See Wilson, *The Saving Cross of the Suffering Christ*, 80.

42 The other New Testament references to a "new covenant" are 1 Cor. 11:25; 2 Cor. 3:6; Heb. 8:13; 9:15; 12:24.

43 For a similar point, see Guy Prentiss Waters, *The Lord's Supper as the Sign and Meal of the New Covenant*, SSBT (Wheaton, IL: Crossway, 2019), 89.

44 Wilson, *The Saving Cross of the Suffering Christ*, 89–90.

45 Wilson, *The Saving Cross of the Suffering Christ*, 94.

46 This paragraph is adapted from Brian Tabb, "God's Answer to Human Suffering: The Cross of Christ and Problem of Pain," Desiring God, May 21, 2020, http://www.desiringgod.org/. Used with permission.

fulfilling prophecies such as Isaiah 11:1–10 and Psalm 2:9.[47] Others hoped for a messianic priest who would make atonement for sin or a great prophet to instruct Israel in God's ways.[48] *No one* expected a suffering Savior. But soon after Isaiah prophesies that God's "arm" will bring salvation (52:10), he declares that God's servant will be high and lifted up yet also despised and rejected (52:13; 53:3). The prophet asks, "To whom has the arm of the LORD been revealed?" (53:1). The implied answer to this rhetorical question is *no one*—no one realizes that this inglorious servant will bring about God's glorious salvation.[49]

Jesus's most emphatic citation of Scripture in Luke's Gospel comes on the night of his betrayal. He tells his disciples, "This Scripture must be fulfilled in me: 'And he was numbered with the transgressors.' For what is written about me has its fulfillment" (Luke 22:37). Jesus here quotes from the final verse of Isaiah's famous prophecy of the suffering servant:

> Therefore I will divide him a portion with the many,
> and he shall divide the spoil with the strong,
> because he poured out his soul to death
> and *was numbered with the transgressors*;
> yet he bore the sin of many,
> and makes intercession for the transgressors. (Isa. 53:12)

Let's first consider the context of this servant passage and then examine how Jesus fulfills Isaiah's prophecy.

Isaiah 52:13–53:12 is the fourth "Servant Song" in the book, bringing to a climax the description of the Lord's chosen servant who will be endowed with the Spirit (42:1), called to be "a light for the nations" (49:6), yet treated with disgrace (50:6). This final servant passage clarifies how

---

47 For example, consider Psalms of Solomon 17:21–24: "See, Lord, and raise up for them their king, the son of David, to rule over your servant Israel in the time known to you, O God. Undergird him with the strength to destroy the unrighteous rulers . . . in wisdom and in righteousness to drive out the sinners from the inheritance . . . to shatter all their substance with an iron rod; to destroy the unlawful nations with the word of his mouth." James H. Charlesworth, ed., *The Old Testament Pseudepigrapha*, 2 vols. (Garden City, NY: Doubleday, 1983–1985).

48 See John J. Collins, *The Scepter and the Star: The Messiahs of the Dead Sea Scrolls and Other Ancient Literature* (New York: Doubleday, 1995), 102–23.

49 For a similar point, see Paul R. House, *Isaiah*, 2 vols., Mentor (Ross-Shire, UK: Christian Focus, 2019), 2:492.

the servant's suffering fits into the Lord's mission among the nations.[50] Isaiah proclaims good news of peace, happiness, and salvation as the Lord returns to Zion to comfort and redeem his people and show his saving power before all the nations (52:7–10), recalling the glorious hope of the new exodus in 40:1–11. Then the Lord draws attention to his servant, who "shall be high and lifted up" (52:13), which parallels Isaiah's early vision of the Lord on his throne (6:1; cf. 57:15). Yet this exalted servant is also marred beyond recognition (52:14) and despised and rejected by people (53:3) while bearing others' sins (53:4–5, 11). The Lord's servant suffers silently, humbly, and unjustly (53:7–8). He is a righteous one numbered with transgressors, and he will see light and make others righteous (53:11–12).

It is noteworthy that this Servant Song opens and concludes with God's perspective on "my servant" (52:13; 53:11). The intervening verses are presented in the first-person plural:

Who has believed what he has heard from *us*? (53:1)

He was despised, and *we* esteemed him not. (53:3)

Surely he has borne *our* griefs
   and carried *our* sorrows;
yet *we* esteemed him stricken. (53:4)

But he was pierced for *our* transgressions;
   he was crushed for *our* iniquities;
upon him was the chastisement that brought *us* peace,
   and with his wounds *we* are healed. (53:5)

All *we* like sheep have gone astray;
   we have turned—every one—to his own way;
and the LORD has laid on him
   the iniquity of *us* all. (53:6)

---

50 Andrew T. Abernethy, *The Book of Isaiah and God's Kingdom: A Thematic-Theological Approach*, NSBT 40 (Downers Grove, IL: InterVarsity Press, 2016), 151.

Thus, the singular divine perspective at the beginning and end of this passage reveals that this suffering servant has not failed but succeeded in his mission.[51]

Old Testament scholars vigorously debate the original identity of this servant and the meaning of his suffering. R. N. Whybray goes so far as to claim that "the supposed references to the Servant's vicarious suffering and death and resurrection are illusory."[52] However, others explain that the servant's suffering on behalf of others makes this passage truly unique.[53] Some identify the servant in Isaiah 52:13–53:12 as the prophet (as in 42:1–9; 49:1–6; and 50:4–11), who embodies the essence of servanthood.[54] Still others interpret the servant as the righteous remnant of the covenant community.[55] However, the exalted description of the servant in 52:13 and his vicarious suffering to atone for others' sins strongly suggest that the servant is a messianic figure. Jesus and his followers do not interpret Isaiah 53 as a type or analogy for the Lord's suffering and vindication, but as a clear biblical script that he fully executes.[56]

Jesus forcefully claims that he fulfills Isaiah's prophecy. Notice the double stress on the *fulfillment* of what is written in Luke 22:37. "Must be fulfilled" translates the Greek verb *teleō*, which connotes finishing, accomplishing, or bringing something to an end.[57] "Fulfillment" renders the Greek noun *telos*, which typically means an end or goal. Jesus also uses *teleō* in Luke 18:31—"See, we are going up to Jerusalem, and everything that is written about the Son of Man by the prophets *will be accomplished*"—and in his final word from the cross in John 19:30—"It *is finished.*" Jesus unmistakably identifies himself as the one about whom

---

51   Bernd Janowski, "He Bore Our Sins: Isaiah 53 and the Drama of Taking Another's Place," in *The Suffering Servant: Isaiah 53 in Jewish and Christian Sources*, ed. Bernd Janowski and Peter Stuhlmacher, trans. Daniel P. Bailey (Grand Rapids, MI: Eerdmans, 2004), 61.

52   R. N. Whybray, *Isaiah 40–66*, NCB (Grand Rapids, MI: Eerdmans, 1975), 171. For a response to Whybray, see Abernethy, *The Book of Isaiah and God's Kingdom*, 151–55.

53   Janowski, "He Bore Our Sins," 48–74; and Shalom M. Paul, *Isaiah 40–66: Translation and Commentary*, ECC (Grand Rapids, MI: Eerdmans, 2012), 398.

54   John Goldingay, *The Message of Isaiah 40–55: A Literary-Theological Commentary* (London: T&T Clark, 2005), 467. See Whybray, *Isaiah 40–66*, 171.

55   Paul, *Isaiah 40–66*, 398.

56   Craig S. Keener, *Acts: An Exegetical Commentary*, 4 vols. (Grand Rapids, MI: Baker Academic, 2012–2015), 2:1586.

57   See BDAG, 997–98.

Isaiah speaks by claiming that this text "is written *about me*" and will be accomplished "*in me*" (Luke 22:37),[58] declaring that he must finish the mission of the Lord's servant in Isaiah 53.

Jesus's emphatic appeal to Isaiah 53:12 at this crucial juncture in the Gospel narrative suggests that this prophecy serves as a heading for Luke's account of Jesus's passion.[59] Moreover, Isaiah 53 is effectively "the hermeneutical key" for understanding the theological significance of Jesus's suffering and death.[60] This is confirmed by repeated allusions to Isaiah's servant passages elsewhere in Luke.[61] Jesus warns that he will be "delivered over," as the Lord's servant "was given over to death" (Isa. 53:12 NETS).[62] Similarly, he predicts that he will be spat upon, treated shamefully, and scourged in Luke 18:32–33, just as the servant declares in Isaiah 50:6:

> I have given my back to *scourges*
>   and my cheeks to blows,
> but I did not turn away my face
>   from the shame of *spittings*. (NETS)

Pilate orders Jesus to be *punished* in Luke 23:16, 22, which parallels the servant's "*punishment* that brought us peace" (Isa. 53:5 NIV). At the climax of the crucifixion scene, the centurion declares that Jesus is *dikaios*—"innocent" (Luke 23:47 ESV) or "righteous" (NIV)—which recalls Isaiah's description of "the righteous one, my servant" who will "make many to be accounted righteous" (Isa. 53:11).

We have seen *that* Jesus fulfills Isaiah 53:12, but *when* is Jesus "numbered with the transgressors"? Interpreters have suggested several possible fulfillments of Isaiah 53:12 within Luke's Gospel, such as Jesus's arrest, his condemnation instead of Barabbas, his crucifixion between two criminals,

---

58 Philip the evangelist similarly proclaims the good news about Jesus from Isa. 53 in Acts 8:30–35. See chap. 5, pp. 116–19.

59 Wilson, *The Saving Cross of the Suffering Christ*, 99.

60 Pao and Schnabel, "Luke," 385; for a similar point, see William J. Larkin, "Luke's Use of the Old Testament as a Key to His Soteriology," *JETS* 20 (1977): 331.

61 For a similar list of allusions to Isa. 53, see Peter Mallen, *The Reading and Transformation of Isaiah in Luke-Acts*, LNTS 367 (London: T&T Clark, 2008), 121n80.

62 *Paradidōmi* ("betray" or "deliver over") occurs in Luke 9:44; 18:32; 22:4, 6, 21–22, 48; 23:25; 24:7; Acts 3:13; Isa. 53:6, 12 LXX.

or the disciples' reliance on swords.[63] However, none of these four options includes verbal parallels with Luke 22:37 or a clear signal about prophetic fulfillment. It is more likely that the whole narrative of Christ's passion fulfills his prediction rather than one single event.[64]

The prophet Isaiah chides the people of Judah as "transgressors" or "rebels," who have sinned and forsaken the Lord, and who therefore deserve judgment.[65] Yet the righteous servant is "numbered with the transgressors," experiences rejection and suffering, and is considered smitten by God (Isa. 53:12). God's servant is not merely treated *as* a rebel; he acts *on behalf of* rebels. This servant is "stricken for the transgression of my people," bears the sin of many, and intercedes for rebels (vv. 8, 12). Luke's Gospel insists that Jesus is *innocent* even though he is unjustly treated as a transgressor. Pilate and Herod conclude that Jesus is not guilty of the charges leveled against him (Luke 23:4, 14–15, 22), though the governor ultimately grants the Jews' demands to release the murderer Barabbas and execute the innocent Jesus (vv. 24–25). Then one of the criminals crucified with Jesus acknowledges his own just punishment but insists that "this man has done nothing wrong" (v. 41). Finally, the centurion who witnesses Jesus's death declares, "Certainly this man was righteous [*dikaios*]" (v. 47 AT).

Jesus's quotation of Isaiah 53:12 presents his passion as the decisive fulfillment of the servant's mission; it also serves as the basis for his instructions to his disciples in Luke 22:36–37: "But now let the one who has a moneybag take it, and likewise a knapsack. And let the one who has no sword sell his cloak and buy one. *For* I tell you that this Scripture must be fulfilled in me." Christ's directive "now" contrasts with his earlier instructions that the disciples take no provisions for their journey (9:3). Jesus's rather enigmatic words to his followers underscore difficult trials before them—one disciple will betray Christ, another will deny him, and Satan demanded to sift the disciples like wheat (22:21, 31, 34). I. Howard Marshall rightly explains, "The reason why the disciples must be ready for the worst is that their Master also faces the worst."[66] However, the disciples once again misunderstand

63 For an overview and discussion of these options, see Pao and Schnabel, "Luke," 388.

64 Larkin, "Luke's Use of the Old Testament," 331.

65 See Isa. 1:2, 28; 46:8; 48:8; 59:12–13; 66:24.

66 I. Howard Marshall, *The Gospel of Luke: A Commentary on the Greek Text*, NIGTC (Grand Rapids, MI: Eerdmans, 1978), 825.

Jesus's point and fail to grasp the necessity of his suffering and their solidarity with him. They produce two swords, yet they show themselves utterly unprepared to face "the power of darkness" (vv. 38, 53), as evidenced by their inability to remain awake in prayer and their resort to violence in the garden (vv. 46, 50).[67] Christ does not bring salvation by slaying his foes but by suffering in the stead of sinners.

The Righteous King (Luke 23:46)

This chapter has established that Jesus predicts his rejection and death, and has explained that he fulfills Old Testament patterns and promises through suffering. Now let's examine Luke's account of Christ's crucifixion, which presents Jesus as a righteous ruler who maintains trust in God unto death.[68]

The crucifixion scene in Luke 23 includes several allusions to psalms of David.[69] In verses 34–35, the Roman soldiers "cast lots to divide his garments" while the Jewish rulers stand by mocking the crucified king of the Jews. This scene recalls specific details from Psalm 22:

> All who see me mock me;
> > they make mouths at me; they wag their heads; . . .
> they divide my garments among them,
> > and for my clothing they cast lots. (vv. 7, 18)[70]

In Matthew 27:46 and Mark 15:34, Jesus cites the opening cry of lament in Psalm 22:1, "My God, my God, why have you forsaken me?" In Luke, Jesus typologically fulfills this psalm of David by enduring scorn while entrusting himself to God. The soldiers offer Jesus sour wine (*oxos*) while ridiculing his kingship (23:36), alluding to David's lament in Psalm 69:21 (68:22 LXX): "For my thirst they gave me sour wine to drink." The rulers, soldiers, and even a crucified criminal mock Jesus, calling him to save himself; neverthe-

---

67 "Typically, the disciples fail to understand how to respond to this persecution," according to Cunningham, "*Through Many Tribulations*," 150.

68 I discuss various Old Testament allusions and proposed Jewish and Greco-Roman parallels to the Lukan passion narrative in Brian J. Tabb, "Is the Lukan Jesus a 'Martyr'? A Critical Assessment of a Scholarly Consensus," *CBQ* 77 (2015): 280–301.

69 See the summary by Joshua W. Jipp, *The Messianic Theology of the New Testament* (Grand Rapids, MI: Eerdmans, 2020), 99–100.

70 Ps. 22 (English) is Ps. 21 LXX. All four Gospels include allusions to or quotations of this psalm.

less, he suffers according to the script of this psalm to demonstrate that he is indeed "the Christ of God, his Chosen One" (Luke 23:35).[71]

The most explicit Old Testament reference in Luke's account of Jesus's death comes in 23:46: "Father, into your hands I commit my spirit!" Matthew 27:50 and Mark 15:37 record that Jesus utters a loud cry with his dying breath, but Luke specifies that Christ's final cry from the cross is a prayer drawn from Psalm 31:5 (30:6 LXX): "Into your hands I commit my spirit." This psalm of David expresses confidence and trust in the faithful God who is a rock and refuge for the righteous (vv. 1–4).[72] Because the Lord sees his suffering and knows his distress (v. 7), the psalmist asks his God to rescue him from his adversaries (vv. 15–16). He then calls the faithful to "be strong" and "take courage" as they wait for the Lord (v. 24).

It is striking that Jesus does not lament or seek deliverance as David does (Ps. 31:15–16). Rather, the greater David dies a shameful death at the hands of his enemies, who scornfully call him to save himself. His quotation of Psalm 31:5—part of "a quintessential royal psalm of the righteous king's hope in God"[73]—fittingly answers his adversaries' taunts in Luke 23:35–37. Christ confidently commits himself to the hands of God with David's words on his lips as he submits to his Father's will (v. 46).[74] The empty tomb in Luke 24 shows that the Father does not let his righteous Son be put to shame but preserves him even through death (Ps. 31:17, 23).

Immediately following Jesus's dying prayer, Luke records the response of a centurion: "He glorified God and said, 'Surely this man was righteous'" (Luke 23:47 AT). In the parallel account in Mark 15:39, the soldier exclaims, "Truly this man was the Son of God!"[75] Luke's version of this scene includes two unique emphases. First, the centurion "glorified God." Elsewhere in Luke's writings, people glorify God after witnessing miraculous healings (Luke 5:25–26; 7:16; 13:13; 17:15; 18:43) or when they learn about God's

---

71 "His Chosen One" in Luke 23:35 may allude to Ps. 89 (88 LXX), where the Lord calls the Davidic king "my chosen one" (v. 3) and "one chosen from the people" (v. 19), as suggested by Joshua W. Jipp, "Luke's Scriptural Suffering Messiah: A Search for Precedent, a Search for Identity," CBQ 72 (2010): 261. This title may also allude to God's chosen servant in Isa. 42:1, according to Green, The Gospel of Luke, 821.

72 Cf. Anna M. Schwemer, "Jesu letzte Worte am Kreuz (Mk 15,34; Lk 23,46; Joh 19,28ff)," TBei 29 (1998): 20–21.

73 Jipp, "Luke's Scriptural Suffering Messiah," 262.

74 Schwemer, "Jesu letzte Worte am Kreuz," 22.

75 Similarly, in Matt. 27:54, the centurion says, "Truly this was the Son of God!"

saving purposes (Luke 2:20; Acts 11:18; 21:20). The use of this phrase in Luke 23:47 suggests that "the centurion has seen God at work" in Christ's death.[76] Second, the soldier here proclaims Jesus to be *dikaios*, typically translated as "innocent" (ESV, NASB, NRSV) or "righteous" (CSB, KJV, NIV). Understood in the former sense, Luke 23:47 is the climactic statement of Jesus's innocence of all wrongdoing.[77] However, in the nearby context, the cognate word *dikaiōs* in verse 41 clearly means "justly," and verse 50 describes Joseph positively as "a good and righteous man" (*anēr agathos kai dikaios*). Further, Peter, Stephen, and Paul each call the risen Christ "the Righteous One" (Acts 3:14; 7:52; 22:14). Notably, *dikaios* also is used for the suffering king in Psalm 31:18 and for the Lord's suffering servant in Isaiah 53:11—passages that Jesus himself quotes in Luke 23:46 (Ps. 31:5) and 22:37 (Isa. 53:12). Luke's narrative clearly shows that Jesus is guiltless of the spurious charges leveled against him, but here the centurion goes further and reverently confesses that he is *righteous*—indeed, *the righteous one*. While the Jewish leaders and crowd call for Jesus to be crucified, surprisingly it is a Gentile outsider at the cross who discerns God at work and recognizes Jesus's truly righteous status.

Conclusion

We've seen that Jesus consistently foretells his own suffering, rejection, and death, which "must" take place according to the script of the Scriptures. Christ alludes to Isaiah 6:9 to show that he continues the pattern of God's prophets who are rejected by a people who see and hear yet do not truly understand God's revealed word (Luke 8:10). While the crowds welcome him with the words of Psalm 118:26, "Blessed is the King who comes in the name of the Lord!" (Luke 19:38), Jesus explains that he is also the rejected stone who will be the cornerstone of God's new temple (Luke 20:17; Ps. 118:22). Moreover, he is the last Passover lamb, whose broken body and shed blood secure the new covenant between God and his people (Luke 22:19–20; Jer. 31:31). On the night of his betrayal, Jesus emphatically stresses that

---

76 Robert J. Karris, "Luke 23:47 and the Lucan View of Jesus' Death," *JBL* 105 (1986): 67.

77 Cf. Luke 23:4, 14, 15, 22, 41. Darrell Bock reasons that "the centurion could merely be reflecting on Jesus being innocent or on the result of such innocence, namely, that he is righteous." *A Theology of Luke and Acts*, Biblical Theology of the New Testament (Grand Rapids, MI: Zondervan, 2012), 200.

he is the suffering servant who will be "numbered with the transgressors" (Isa. 53:12, cited in Luke 22:37). Finally, Jesus speaks the words of Psalm 31:5 from the cross to express confident trust in his Father (Luke 23:46). His shameful crucifixion proves that he is no messianic pretender but the righteous ruler in David's line who suffers according to the divine script.

Time and again, Jesus's followers misunderstand their Master's teaching about his necessary suffering and its implications for discipleship. They do not—indeed, *cannot*—grasp God's plan for the Son's suffering until the risen Lord opens their minds to understand the Scriptures. These disciples not only fail to understand Jesus's message but also betray, deny, and desert him when he moves toward Calvary. It is for these unworthy friends that Jesus willingly offers his body and blood.

3

Hope on the Third Day

The Messiah's Resurrection in Luke

But he said to them, "How can they say that the Christ is David's son?
For David himself says in the Book of Psalms, 'The Lord said to
my Lord, "Sit at my right hand, until I make your enemies your
footstool."' David thus calls him Lord, so how is he his son?"

LUKE 20:41–44

MANY STORIES IN LITERATURE include a great reversal, though few
are as dramatic as the one in Alexander Dumas's classic tale *The Count of
Monte Cristo*. The story begins when nineteen-year-old Edmond Dantès is
torn away tragically from his bride and sent without trial to waste away in
the infamous Château d'If. After languishing in prison for fourteen years,
Edmond plots a daring escape, praying, "Since none but the dead pass
freely from this dungeon, let me assume the place of the dead!"[1] When his
dear friend Faria dies, Edmond secretly takes Faria's place in the body bag,
and the jailers carry the supposed corpse outside and throw him into the
ice-cold sea—"the cemetery of the Château d'If."[2] Edmond then rips open
the sack with his knife, frees himself from the heavy weight tied around
his feet, and swims to safety. Afterward, he discovers the fabulous treasures

---

1 Alexander Dumas, *The Count of Monte Cristo*, trans. David Coward, OWC (Oxford: Oxford
   University Press, 1990), 172.
2 Dumas, *The Count of Monte Cristo*, 175.

hidden on the island of Monte Cristo and reinvents himself as the wealthy Count of Monte Cristo. Edmond Dantès is considered as good as dead by his family and beloved Mercédès, and receives a criminal's unceremonious burial, yet he emerges alive from the waters of death.

The biblical story likewise includes numerous reversals. Abraham obeys God's call to sacrifice his beloved son on Mount Moriah, but on the third day of their journey, as the patriarch raises his knife, God provides a ram to sacrifice instead of Isaac. Joseph's jealous brothers throw him into a pit, sell him into slavery, and report his death to their father, yet Joseph is later exalted as ruler over Egypt and providentially preserves his family through famine. The disobedient prophet Jonah is thrown into the sea and swallowed by a great fish; three days later, he is spat out to fulfill his mission in Nineveh. During the Babylonian captivity, God preserves Hananiah, Mishael, and Azariah when they are thrown into a fiery furnace and delivers Daniel from the lions' den. The Lord also promises to restore Israel's fortunes after exile, a reversal likened to a valley of dry bones coming to life.[3] As C. S. Lewis explains, "Death and Resurrection are what the story is about; and had we but eyes to see it, this has been hinted on every page, met us, in some disguise, at every turn."[4]

The Resurrection Debate (Luke 20:27–40)

There was a lively debate among Jewish people around the time of Christ as to whether or not God would one day raise up the dry bones of his people. The sage Jesus Ben Sira reasoned that "there is no coming back" from death, while the philosopher Philo explained that at death the incorruptible soul is removed from the mortal body.[5] However, standard Jewish teaching in Jesus's day affirmed a future resurrection.[6] It's important to clarify that the Jewish doctrine of resurrection did not simply mean a belief in "life after death" or "immortality," but "the *reversal* or *undoing* or *defeat* of death," the "newly embodied life" of God's people at the end of the present age that "would constitute the age to come."[7]

---

3   These examples summarize Gen. 22; 37–50; Jonah 1–3; Dan. 3; 6; and Ezek. 37.

4   C. S. Lewis, *Miracles: A Preliminary Study*, repr. ed. (New York: Simon & Schuster, 1966), 131.

5   See Sir. 38:21; Philo, *Questions and Answers on Genesis*, trans. Ralph Marcus, LCL 380 (Cambridge, MA: Harvard University Press, 1953), 3.11.

6   N. T. Wright, *The Resurrection of the Son of God*, Christian Origins and the Question of God 3 (Minneapolis: Fortress, 2003), 129.

7   Wright, *The Resurrection of the Son of God*, 201, 205, emphasis original.

Meanwhile, all non-Jews rejected any notion of bodily resurrection. Apollo's words in the ancient Greek tragedy *Eumenides* reflect the standard Greek view: "But when a man has died, and the dust has soaked up his blood, there is no rising again [*anastasis*]."[8] While the writers of pagan antiquity described the deceased as shadows, stars, or disembodied souls, "resurrection was not among the available options."[9]

Within Judaism, the Pharisees and Sadducees staked out the key positions in the resurrection controversy. The Jewish historian Josephus explains that the Pharisees held "that souls have power to survive death and that there are rewards and punishments under the earth for those who have led lives of virtue or vice."[10] Alternatively, the Sadducees disagreed with the Pharisees in their views of fate, the afterlife, ritual purity, and other matters.[11] Josephus records that the Sadducees believed "that the soul perishes along with the body"[12] and thus rejected "the persistence of the soul after death, penalties in the underworld, and rewards."[13] Similarly, Luke explains, "For the Sadducees say that there is no resurrection, nor angel, nor spirit, but the Pharisees acknowledge them all" (Acts 23:8).

This longstanding Jewish debate about resurrection sets the table for the Sadducees' sparring with Jesus in Luke 20. After earlier confrontations between Jesus and the chief priests, scribes, and elders (vv. 1–26), the Sadducees bring to Jesus a resurrection riddle (vv. 27–33).[14] Luke introduces the Sadducees as "those who deny that there is a resurrection" (v. 27), which signals that they do not pose a genuine question to

---

8   Aeschylus, *Eumenides*, in *Oresteia: Agamemnon, Libation-Bearers, Eumenides*, trans. Alan H. Sommerstein, LCL 146 (Cambridge, MA: Harvard University Press, 2009), 647–48.

9   Wright, *The Resurrection of the Son of God*, 38.

10   Josephus, *Jewish Antiquities*, trans. H. St. J. Thackeray et al., 9 vols., LCL (Cambridge, MA: Harvard University Press, 1930–1965), 18.14.

11   See Acts 23:6; Josephus, *Jewish War*, trans. H. St. J. Thackeray and Ralph Marcus, 3 vols., LCL (Cambridge, MA: Harvard University Press, 1927–1930), 2.162–66; *Jewish Antiquities*, 13.171–73; and Günter Stemberger, "Sadducees," in *The Eerdmans Dictionary of Early Judaism*, ed. John J. Collins and Daniel C. Harlow (Grand Rapids, MI: Eerdmans, 2010), 1179–81.

12   Josephus, *Jewish Antiquities*, 18.16.

13   Josephus, *Jewish War*, 2.165. The Sadducees' views are discussed further in Wright, *The Resurrection of the Son of God*, 131–39.

14   This section expands Brian J. Tabb and Steve Walton, "Exodus in Luke-Acts," in *Exodus in the New Testament*, ed. Seth Ehorn and Sarah Whittle, LNTS (London: Bloomsbury T&T Clark, forthcoming).

Jesus but seek "to make fun of the idea of resurrection and so to disprove it."[15] They piously appeal to what "Moses wrote," summarizing the law's instructions concerning levirate marriage in Deuteronomy 25:5. Then the Sadducees present a hypothetical situation in which one woman has seven husbands (six by levirate marriage) but no children, and they ask whose wife she will be "in the resurrection" (Luke 20:33). In the Sadducees' here-and-now worldview, to "raise up" (*exanistēmi*) a child to preserve the family name (v. 28) is as close as they come to belief in "resurrection" (*anastasis*, vv. 27, 33).[16]

N. T. Wright states that Christ's response to the Sadducees is "far and away the most important passage about resurrection in the whole gospel tradition."[17] Jesus explains,

> The sons of this age marry and are given in marriage, but those who are considered worthy to attain to that age and to the resurrection from the dead neither marry nor are given in marriage, for they cannot die anymore, because they are equal to angels and are sons of God, being sons of the resurrection. (Luke 20:34–36)

Thus, Jesus explains that there is no marriage and no death in the age of resurrection. His argument assumes a common Jewish division of time into two epochs—the present age and the age to come (cf. Luke 18:30). "This age" and "that age" correspond to two groups of people: "the sons of this age" on the one hand and "sons of God, being sons of the resurrection" on the other. The expression "sons of" does not refer to biological descent but to people's outlook on life expressed in their character and actions.[18] In the present age, people marry, raise up children, and die. But the coming age "is marked by resurrection,"[19] which means that people do not die and thus they do not marry (or remarry) in order to raise up progeny.

15 Wright, *The Resurrection of the Son of God*, 131.

16 For a similar point, see Kevin L. Anderson, *'But God Raised Him from the Dead': The Theology of Jesus' Resurrection in Luke-Acts*, Paternoster Biblical Monographs (Bletchley: Paternoster, 2006), 132.

17 Wright, *The Resurrection of the Son of God*, 415.

18 Green, *The Gospel of Luke*, 720.

19 Brandon D. Crowe, *The Hope of Israel: The Resurrection of Christ in the Acts of the Apostles* (Grand Rapids, MI: Baker Academic, 2020), 111.

In what sense does Jesus conceive of the sons of the resurrection being "equal to the angels" (Luke 20:36) or "like angels in heaven" (Mark 12:25)? Joseph Fitzmyer suggests that they are like angels in that they are "disembodied spirits who do not marry."[20] This interpretation is incorrect for two reasons. First, "resurrection" simply does not convey disembodied spiritual existence, as Christ emphatically makes clear to his disciples in Luke 24:39: "Touch me, and see. For a spirit does not have flesh and bones as you see that I have." Second, it is crucial to see that the claim "because they are equal to angels" explains Jesus's immediately preceding statement, "for they cannot die anymore" (20:36). The sons of resurrection are not equal to angels in every respect. Rather, "they become like the angels in that they are given the privilege of dwelling in the divine presence forever."[21]

Jesus further refutes the Sadducees by arguing that "even Moses showed" that God raises the dead and that "he is not God of the dead, but of the living" (Luke 20:37–38). He appeals to "the passage about the bush" in Exodus 3, where God reveals himself to Moses and calls him to bring his people out of Egypt. This foundational passage "combines three traditions that define Israel: the patriarchs, the exodus, and Sinai."[22] At this theophany on "the mountain of God" (Ex. 3:1), the Lord discloses his name and his purposes to deliver his people out of Egypt and into the promised land. In Luke 20:37, Jesus cites Exodus 3:15: "Say this to the people of Israel: 'The LORD, the God of your fathers, the God of Abraham, the God of Isaac, and the God of Jacob, has sent me to you.'"[23]

The Lord's self-identification as the God of the patriarchs long after their deaths suggests that they must still be alive in some sense, since the living God "does not maintain a covenant relationship with corpses, but with living persons."[24] Jesus draws out this implication in Luke 20:38: "Now he is not God of the dead, but of the living, for all live to him."[25] Jesus is not here

---

20 Fitzmyer, *The Gospel according to Luke*, 2:1305. He appeals to Jewish parallels such as 2 Bar. 51:10 and Philo, *On the Sacrifices of Cain and Abel*, in *Philo, Volume II*, trans. F. H. Colson and G. H. Whitaker, LCL 227 (Cambridge, MA: Harvard University Press, 1929), 1.5.

21 Anderson, *'But God Raised Him from the Dead,'* 136.

22 Pao and Schnabel, "Luke," 368.

23 Ex. 3:15 reiterates God's self-revelation in Ex. 3:6. The wording in Mark 12:26 reflects Ex. 3:6, as noted in Tabb and Walton, "Exodus in Luke-Acts."

24 Anderson, *'But God Raised Him from the Dead,'* 137.

25 The early Jewish work 4 Maccabees similarly affirms that the patriarchs and other faithful Jews "do not die to God but live to God" (7:19; cf. 16:25).

arguing that the patriarchs have already experienced bodily resurrection; rather, they "live" to God beyond the reach of death in "an intermediate state," awaiting the future resurrection.[26] The Lord's covenant love for Abraham's family that led him to deliver them from Egypt "can only mean that Abraham will be forever with God," thus ensuring the resurrection.[27] Jesus thus affirms the abiding authority of Exodus 3 and bases the hope of future resurrection squarely on God's identity, reputation, and secure promise to his covenant people.[28]

Jesus does not predict his own resurrection on the third day when responding to the Sadducees' question. Rather, he affirms the distinction between the present age and the coming age, closely linking the resurrection with the reality of new creation.[29] However, Jesus earlier identifies himself as "the cornerstone" (Luke 20:17), implying that he will be vindicated after rejection. Moreover, in verses 41–44, Jesus cites Psalm 110:1, a text that the apostles cite as proof of the risen Lord's exaltation to God's right hand (Acts 2:33–35). Thus, by framing his teaching about the age to come with references to his own vindication, the Son of God implies that he will be the first son of the resurrection, whose experience of life beyond death will usher in the promised new age.

The Risen Messiah Fulfills the Scriptures

When I was a college student, I periodically made the eight-hundred-mile-drive between Wheaton, Illinois, and my hometown of Norman, Oklahoma. The route was straightforward: take Interstate 355 south out of the Chicago suburbs, merge onto I-55 through Springfield to St. Louis, travel west on I-44 for hundreds of miles until picking up the turnpike between Tulsa and Oklahoma City, then wrap up the journey on I-35. I did not have a smartphone or personal GPS device to guide me, but I

---

26 Wright, *The Resurrection of the Son of God*, 426. He adds that Jesus "speaks about YHWH's past word to Moses, in order to indicate a present reality (the patriarchs are still alive), in order thereby to affirm the future hope (they will be raised to newly embodied life)."

27 John J. Kilgallen, "The Sadducees and Resurrection from the Dead: Luke 20:27–40," *Bib* 67 (1986): 488–89.

28 Mitchell L. Chase rightly asserts, "The stories of Abraham, Isaac, and Jacob were stories of God preserving the Abrahamic line." However, he concludes that Jesus cites Ex. 3:6 to demonstrate God's life-giving power toward the patriarchs, especially in overcoming barrenness. "The Genesis of Resurrection Hope: Exploring Its Early Presence and Deep Roots," *JETS* 57 (2014): 469–70.

29 Anderson, *'But God Raised Him from the Dead,'* 139.

had a few Rand McNally maps, and I looked for the plentiful signs on the highway to guide me through the great states of Illinois, Missouri, and Oklahoma to my intended destination. But on one of these road trips, I inadvertently took a wrong turn and didn't realize my mistake until I was well into Arkansas! I failed to heed the familiar signs and ended up in the wrong state, far from home.

Throughout the Bible, "signs" are deeds that display divine glory and power, and demand a response. God commands Moses to perform many signs before Pharaoh and the people, yet Pharaoh refuses to heed God's word. Israel experiences the Lord's salvation from Egypt and provision in the wilderness; nevertheless, the people do not trust in their God "in spite of all the signs" (Num. 14:11). In the Gospels, the Jewish leaders ask Jesus to show them "a sign from heaven" immediately after he feeds thousands with a few loaves and fish and casts out demons (Mark 8:1–12; Luke 11:14–16). These signs reveal Jesus's glory and offer divine confirmation of his true identity (John 2:11; Acts 2:22), yet time and again Jesus's contemporaries fail to heed the signs and so reject the Lord. John explains, "Though he had done so many signs before them, they still did not believe in him" (John 12:37).

Jesus not only performs signs that signal the inbreaking of God's glorious kingdom in his ministry; he *is* himself a sign. Simeon holds the child Jesus in his arms and prophesies that he will be "a *sign* that is opposed" (Luke 2:34). Jesus later promises to give his sign-hungry generation no sign except for "the sign of Jonah" (11:29). Those with eyes to see this sign rightly recognize Jesus as greater than King Solomon and the prophet Jonah (vv. 31–32), since he not only preaches with wisdom and authority but also overcomes death on the third day.

Jesus teaches that the Messiah must rise from the dead on the third day according to the Scriptures (Luke 24:46). While Jesus predicts on multiple occasions that he will rise on the third day, he does not state exactly *how* his resurrection fulfills the Scriptures.[30] Daniel Marguerat rightly suggests that Luke 24 anticipates the specific scriptural arguments for Christ's resurrection in the book of Acts, where the apostles appeal to various Old Testament prophecies and promises as they proclaim Jesus as the risen and exalted Lord

---

30 For a similar point, see Richard B. Hays, *Echoes of Scripture in the Gospels* (Waco, TX: Baylor University Press, 2016), 223.

of all.[31] Yet Jesus provides subtle clues concerning the biblical rationale for his resurrection already in Luke's Gospel. We've seen that Jesus explains that the God of Abraham, Isaac, and Jacob is "God . . . of the living" (Luke 20:38; cf. Ex. 3:6). The remainder of this chapter considers Jesus's enigmatic appeal to "the sign of Jonah" (Luke 11:29), his transfiguration and "exodus" (9:28–36), the biblical precedents for resurrection on "the third day" (9:22; 18:33), and his riddle about the Messiah as David's son and his Lord (20:41–44). But first, we turn to Simeon's foundational prophecy about the Christ child.

The Falling and Rising of Many (Luke 2:34)

Only Luke records the meeting between Simeon and the infant Jesus in the temple. Luke 2:25 presents Simeon as "righteous and devout, waiting for the consolation of Israel." Three times the narrator highlights the role of the Holy Spirit, who is present with Simeon and has revealed that he will see the promised Messiah (vv. 25–27). This old saint not only sees Christ but cradles him in his arms (v. 28).

Simeon's prophetic words in Luke 2:29–35 explain the biblical-theological significance of Jesus's arrival and also preview the coming division within Israel that he will bring. In the next chapter, we will consider Simeon's words in verses 29–32, which express how God has begun to fulfill Old Testament hopes for consolation, salvation, and revelation for Israel and for the Gentiles.[32] Here, let's briefly examine Simeon's warning to Mary in verses 34–35.

Simeon prophesies that the Christ child is "appointed for the fall and rising of many in Israel" (Luke 2:34).[33] The Greek word *ptōsis* ("fall") often refers to calamity and divine judgment in the Scriptures.[34] Jesus uses similar language in 20:18 to explain the consequences of rejecting him as the Lord's chosen cornerstone: "Everyone who *falls* on that stone will be broken to

---

31 Daniel Marguerat, "Quand la résurrection se fait clef de lecture de l'histoire (Luc-Actes)," in *Resurrection of the Dead : Biblical Traditions in Dialogue*, ed. Geert Van Oyen and Tom Shepherd, BETL 249 (Leuven: Peters, 2012), 190.

32 Simeon's prophecy alludes to Isa. 40:5 and 52:10 ("see . . . salvation") and 49:6 ("light . . . nations"); Mallen discusses these and other possible Old Testament allusions in *The Reading and Transformation of Isaiah in Luke-Acts*, 65–66. I will consider the allusions to Isaiah in Luke 2:29–32 in chap. 4, pp. 86–89.

33 This paragraph summarizes the argument in Tabb, *Suffering in Ancient Worldview*, 159–60.

34 Cf. Matt. 7:27; Nah. 3:3; Zech. 14:12, 18; Isa. 17:1; 51:17, 22; Jer. 6:15 LXX.

pieces, and when it *falls* on anyone, it will crush him."[35] Some interpreters understand "falling" to be an image of judgment, while "rising" pictures divine blessing.[36] While this reading is possible and is popular among commentators, the word *anastasis* (translated "rising" in 2:34) consistently refers to "resurrection" in its other forty-one New Testament occurrences.[37] Wright explains, "Luke does not . . . reduce the meaning of 'resurrection' to a metaphor for present events, but sees circles of meaning radiating out from the centre which is Jesus's own actual resurrection."[38]

Thus, Simeon's prophecy means that "Israel as a whole is going to 'fall' and 'rise again' in and through him."[39] This reading fits well with the earlier reference to Israel's consolation in Luke 2:25. However, Isaiah 26:19 contrasts the eternal destinies of the wicked and righteous in terms of "falling" and "rising": "The dead *shall rise*, and those who are in the tombs *shall be raised* ... but the land of the impious *shall fall*" (NETS).[40] Moreover, Jesus declares that he has come to bring division, even between families (Luke 12:51–53). Thus, Simeon's prophecy likely foreshadows that the Messiah will bring about a fundamental division within Israel, one that has ultimate eschatological implications of judgment and resurrection.

Jesus's Transfiguration and "Exodus" (Luke 9:28–36)

"Who do you say that I am?" Jesus's question to his disciples in Luke 9:20 lingers as he teaches about his necessary suffering, death, and resurrection, the cost of discipleship, and his coming in glory (vv. 21–26). This question about Jesus's identity receives an emphatic answer eight days later when the Lord takes three disciples up on the mountain for prayer (v. 28). Christ's transfiguration on the mountain plays a pivotal role in the Gospel narrative. This scene serves as an initial fulfilment of his promise that some of his

---

35 Jesus's statement alludes to Isa. 8:14–15 and explains his citation of Ps. 118:22 in Luke 20:17; see chap. 2, pp. 46–48.

36 For example, Cunningham, *"Through Many Tribulations,"* 46.

37 Consider the following examples: Luke 14:14 ("the *resurrection* of the just"); Acts 2:31 ("the *resurrection* of the Christ"); Acts 23:8 ("the Sadducees say that there is no *resurrection*"); and 1 Cor. 15:42 ("the resurrection of the dead"). Fitzmyer acknowledges that *anastasis* "usually means 'resurrection,'" yet he concludes that the meaning in Luke 2:34 is "rather more generic." *The Gospel according to Luke*, 1:429.

38 Wright, *The Resurrection of the Son of God*, 436.

39 Wright, *The Resurrection of the Son of God*, 650.

40 See also Ps. 20:8: "They collapse and *fall*, but we *rise* and stand upright."

disciples "will not taste death until they see the kingdom of God" (v. 27). It also prepares for Jesus's journey to Jerusalem (v. 51) and the "exodus" that he would soon accomplish (v. 31). In short, Jesus's transfiguration anticipates his resurrection glory and clarifies his identity and mission.

Luke 9:28–36 includes a number of Old Testament allusions—especially to the book of Exodus—that show the biblical theological significance of Jesus's transfiguration.[41] First, Jesus goes up on the mountain (v. 28) just like Moses at Sinai.[42] In Luke's Gospel and throughout Exodus (beginning at 3:1), the mountain is a place of divine presence and revelation.

Second, the alteration in Jesus's facial appearance (Luke 9:29) may recall "the appearance of the glory of the LORD" on the mountain (Ex. 24:17) or perhaps the radiance of Moses's face after talking with God (34:29–30).[43] The disciples see Jesus's glory in Luke 9:32, which parallels various displays of divine glory in Exodus that culminate in Moses's request, "Show me your glory" (Ex. 33:18), and the glory of God filling the tabernacle (40:34–35).[44]

Third, a cloud overshadows the disciples on the mountain in Luke 9:34. The cloud represents God's glorious presence with the people of Israel during their exodus from Egypt, at Mount Sinai, and during their journey through the wilderness.[45] Luke's description of the cloud alludes specifically to the close of Exodus: when divine glory fills the tabernacle, not even Moses can enter the tent "because *the cloud was overshadowing it*" (Ex. 40:29 NETS).[46] Additionally, the disciples enter into the cloud (Luke 9:34), just as Moses does on Mount Sinai (Ex. 24:18). Moreover, the voice coming from the cloud in Luke 9:35 parallels God's call to Moses "out of the midst of the cloud" (Ex. 24:16).

Fourth, according to Luke 9:30–31, Moses and Elijah appear in glory and speak with Jesus about "*his departure*, which he was about to accomplish in Jerusalem." Matthew and Mark also record the presence of Moses and Elijah

---

41 This section adapts material from Tabb and Walton, "Exodus in Luke-Acts," chap. 5.

42 See Ex. 19:3; 24:13, 18; 34:4; cf. Deut. 5:5; 10:3 LXX.

43 Interpreters debate whether this text alludes to Moses's glory-charged face. If Luke intended such a parallel, he did so to indicate "contrast as well as comparison" between Jesus and Moses, as noted by Mark L. Strauss, *The Davidic Messiah in Luke-Acts: The Promise and Its Fulfillment in Lukan Christology*, JSNTSup 110 (Sheffield: Sheffield Academic, 1995), 270.

44 See also Ex. 16:7, 10; 24:16–17.

45 Ex. 13:21–22; 14:19–20, 24; 16:10; 19:9, 16; 24:15–16, 18; 40:36–37.

46 Ex. 40:35 in Hebrew and English Bibles.

at the transfiguration, but Luke uniquely records that they discuss Jesus's "departure" (*exodos*). In the Septuagint, the term *exodos* refers to Israel's "departure" from Egypt in Exodus 19:1 and elsewhere.[47] Philo, Josephus, the author of Hebrews, and other Jewish and Christian writers also refer to this well-known event as "the exodus" (*hē exodos*).[48] This usage of the word *exodos* elsewhere strongly suggests that Luke 9:31 does not refer to Jesus's journey to Jerusalem (v. 51) but to his "departure" from this world at death and his subsequent ascension.[49] Additionally, Luke 9:31 describes Jesus's departure in Jerusalem "as a fulfillment event" using the Greek term *plēroō* ("accomplish"),[50] which refers to the fulfillment of the Scriptures in Luke 24:44. Thus, the "exodus" of Jesus recalls Israel's departure from Egypt, and the fulfillment language suggests that Jesus is accomplishing a greater work of salvation in accord with God's plan.[51]

Fifth, the heavenly voice says, "This is my Son, my Chosen One; listen to him!" (Luke 9:35). This declaration of Jesus's sonship parallels the heavenly message at his baptism: "You are my beloved Son; with you I am well pleased" (3:22). It also weaves together three significant Old Testament threads.[52] "My Son" probably alludes to the Lord's decree in Psalm 2:7: "You are my Son." Additionally, "my Chosen One" recalls the description of the Lord's chosen servant in Isaiah 42:1, who is anointed with God's Spirit to bring justice to the nations. Finally, the command to the disciples—"Listen to him!"—probably alludes to Moses's promise that God "will raise up for you a prophet like me . . . it is to him you shall listen" (Deut. 18:15).[53] Peter

---

47 Num. 33:38; 1 Kings 6:1; Pss. 105:38 [104:38 LXX]; 114:1 [113:1 LXX].

48 Philo, *On Moses*, in *Philo, Volume VI*, trans. F. H. Colson, LCL 289 (Cambridge, MA: Harvard University Press, 1935), 1.105; 2.248; Josephus, *Jewish Antiquities*, 2.309, 312, 320, 325; 5.72; *Testament of Simeon* 9:1; *Testament of Benjamin* 12:4; Aristobulus 1:17; and Heb. 11:22.

49 See Nolland, *Luke*, 2:499; and François Bovon, *Luke 1: A Commentary on the Gospel of Luke 1:1–9:50*, trans. Christine M. Thomas, Hermeneia (Minneapolis: Fortress, 2002), 376. I disagree with the interpretation of Sharon H. Ringe, "Luke 9:28–36: The Beginning of an Exodus," *Semeia* 28 (1983): 94.

50 Michael Wolter, *The Gospel according to Luke*, trans. Wayne Coppins and Christoph Heilig, 2 vols., Baylor-Mohr Siebeck Studies in Early Christianity (Waco, TX: Baylor University Press, 2016–2017), 1:393.

51 See Bock, *Luke*, 1:869; and Susan R. Garrett, "Exodus from Bondage: Luke 9:31 and Acts 12:1–24," *CBQ* 52 (1990): 656.

52 Bock, *A Theology of Luke and Acts*, 179.

53 "A typological reference to Moses is present in the command," according to Pao and Schnabel, "Luke," 312.

identifies the risen Lord as the prophet like Moses in Acts 3:22–23, warning that anyone who does not listen to him will be destroyed. Likewise, Paul proclaims that God has fulfilled his word in Psalm 2:7 "by raising Jesus" (Acts 13:33).[54] The heavenly voice confirms Jesus's true identity, while the Old Testament allusions suggest that Jesus's transfiguration offers a sneak preview of his resurrection glory.

Cumulatively, these Old Testament parallels recall the Lord's glorious revelation to Moses and highlight the greater glory of Jesus's transfiguration. But Jesus is not simply Moses 2.0; the heavenly voice declares him to be God's *Son*, the chosen servant whose word must be heeded (Luke 9:35). He shares in the divine glory and accomplishes the divine will through his "exodus." Jesus sets his face to go to Jerusalem in verse 51, where he "will suffer many things" and "be delivered into the hands of men" (vv. 22, 44). However, his transfiguration on the mountain confirms that Jesus speaks with divine authority as God's Son and anticipates the exalted glory that Jesus will attain by dying, rising, and ascending into heaven.[55] As Jesus asks the disciples on the Emmaus Road, "Was it not necessary that the Christ should suffer these things and enter into his glory?" (Luke 24:26).

The Sign of Jonah (Luke 11:29–30)

Christ's contemporaries clamor for "signs" that demonstrate heavenly power, yet they fail to see the power and presence of God at work in his ministry (Luke 11:14–16, 20). Jesus offers these sign-seeking skeptics only "the sign of Jonah" (Luke 11:29; Matt. 12:39; 16:4). While the queen of the South and the Ninevites "will rise up at the judgment with the men of this generation and condemn them" because they responded favorably to Solomon's wisdom and Jonah's preaching, respectively, Jesus's generation fails to recognize the one who is far greater than Solomon or Jonah (Luke 11:31–32; cf. Matt. 12:41–42).

In Matthew 12:40, Jesus explains this "sign of Jonah" by drawing a typological comparison between Jonah's three days and nights in the fish's belly and his own three days and nights "in the heart of the earth" (cf. Jonah 1:17).[56] Thus, the prophet's vindication after three days offers a scriptural

---

54 I discuss the use of Ps. 2:7 in Acts in chap. 5, pp. 128–33.

55 Strauss, *The Davidic Messiah in Luke-Acts*, 263.

56 R. T. France, *The Gospel of Matthew*, NICNT (Grand Rapids, MI: Eerdmans, 2007), 491.

analogy that anticipates the Son of Man's coming resurrection on the third day (Matt. 16:21).

Jesus offers a more concise and enigmatic explanation of this sign in Luke 11:30: "For as Jonah became a sign to the people of Nineveh, so will the Son of Man be to this generation." Interpreters have variously identified the sign of Jonah as (1) the Son of Man's "Parousia," his future "coming" in judgment; (2) his end-time preaching; (3) his coming vindication after suffering; or (4) some combination of these views.[57] In favor of the first view, Jesus elsewhere refers to the Son of Man's "coming in a cloud" (Luke 21:27; cf. Dan. 7:13), which will happen at an unexpected hour (Luke 12:40). However, Christ's coming is the time of reckoning, not the occasion for repentance.[58] The sign of Jonah serves as a warning that demands a response ahead of the future day of judgment. In favor of the second view, interpreters observe that Luke's account does not refer to Jonah's three days and nights in the fish's belly, as Matthew's does, but explicitly says that Jonah's *preaching* moves Nineveh to repent (Luke 11:32). Fitzmyer explains, "His preaching is the only sign that will be given to this generation; indeed, the note of irony is unmistakable, since this sign is already being given."[59] Yet note the future tense verb *estai* ("will be") in 11:30: Jesus does not appeal to a sign already given, but declares that the Son of Man *will be* a sign. Because the sign is still to come, it does not primarily refer to Jesus's preaching ministry. Rather, this "sign" most likely denotes Jesus's coming vindication after his suffering.[60] The only fitting response to this sign is repentance, as Peter explains in Acts 2:38.

Luke 11:16 records that some people continuously seek from Jesus "a sign from heaven" in order to test him, yet Jesus does not say that *he will give* a sign but that *he will be* a sign to "this evil generation" (vv. 29–30). This recalls Simeon's prophecy: "Behold, this child is appointed . . . for a *sign* that is opposed" (2:34). While some, like Simeon and the prophetess

---

57 For a complementary survey of scholarship, see Hans F. Bayer, *Jesus' Predictions of Vindication and Resurrection: The Provenance, Meaning, and Correlation of the Synoptic Predictions*, WUNT 2/20 (Tübingen: Mohr Siebeck, 1986), 138–42.

58 See Bayer, *Jesus' Predictions of Vindication and Resurrection*, 139; and Michael W. Andrews, "The Sign of Jonah: Jesus in the Heart of the Earth," *JETS* 61 (2018): 111.

59 Fitzmyer, *The Gospel according to Luke*, 2:933.

60 Pao and Schnabel, "Luke," 324. "The new 'sign of Jonah' refers to the attestation of the message by divine vindication of the Son of Man," according to Bayer, *Jesus' Predictions of Vindication and Resurrection*, 142.

Anna, respond rightly to Jesus as the sign embodying God's promised salvation (2:30, 38), many others observe Jesus's deeds and hear his teaching yet respond with hostile antagonism. As Jesus says, "seeing they may not see" (8:10), demanding a heavenly sign yet denigrating the divine Son who is greater than Solomon and Jonah. Indeed, "neither will they be convinced if someone should rise from the dead" (16:31). Thus, while Matthew 16 typologically ties "the sign of Jonah" to Jesus's death and resurrection, Luke's account stresses that Jesus himself will be the sign, highlighting his divinely appointed destiny to suffer and rise on the third day.

The Third Day (Luke 18:33 and 24:46)

The Lord Jesus repeatedly predicts that he must suffer many things and be killed, but he also foretells that "on the third day he will rise" (Luke 18:33; cf. 9:22). Matthew and Mark likewise record the Lord's predictions of his resurrection "on the third day" or "after three days."[61] In John's Gospel, Jesus enigmatically predicts his resurrection in three days when he cleanses the temple and declares, "Destroy this temple, and in three days I will raise it up" (John 2:19). John clarifies that Jesus was not speaking of the temple of gold and stone but "the temple of his body" (2:21).[62]

Luke also records four references to "the third day" that have no parallel in the other Gospels. When Jesus hears that Herod seeks to kill him, he retorts, "Go and tell that fox, 'Behold, I cast out demons and perform cures today and tomorrow, and *the third day* I finish my course'" (Luke 13:32). Jesus thus effectively summarizes his entire mission in terms of "three days," culminating in his willing death in Jerusalem (v. 33).[63] "Today and tomorrow, and the third day" is an idiomatic reference to a brief time period. Some scholars discern here an allusion to Hosea 6:2: "After two days he will revive us; on the third day he will raise us up."[64]

---

61 See Matt. 16:21; 17:23; 20:19; Mark 8:31; 9:31; 10:34. In Matt. 27:63, the priests and Pharisees state Jesus's claim: "After three days I will rise."

62 For discussion of the "sign" of the temple cleansing in John 2:18–22, see Andreas J. Köstenberger, "The Seventh Johannine Sign: A Study in John's Christology," *BBR* 5 (1995): 87–103.

63 See Stephen G. Dempster, "From Slight Peg to Cornerstone to Capstone: The Resurrection of Christ on 'the Third Day' according to the Scriptures," *WTJ* 76 (2014): 405–6.

64 See, for example, Edwards, *The Gospel according to Luke*, 406. For a cautious assessment of this possible Old Testament allusion in Luke 13:32, see Karl Lehmann, *Auferweckt am dritten Tag nach der Schrift, früheste Christologie, Bekenntnisbildung und Schriftauslegung im Lichte von 1 Kor. 15, 3–5* (Freiburg: Herder, 1969), 156–62.

However, the only verbal parallel between these texts is the common word "third" (*tritos*). Further, "third day" carries different connotations as the day of death in Luke 13:32 and of resurrection in Hosea 6:2. Jesus here summarizes his three-day mission in terms of exorcism, healing, and death as a rejected prophet. While Christ does not directly refer to resurrection in Luke 13:32, he has already stated clearly that he will rise on "the third day" after his death (9:22).

Luke's remaining references to "the third day" all fittingly come in chapter 24. At Christ's empty tomb, two angels inform the perplexed women that they are looking for the living Lord in the wrong place.[65] They do not prove the Lord's resurrection but proclaim that he "has risen" (v. 6). The dazzling witnesses urge the women to "remember" Jesus's teaching "that the Son of Man must be delivered into the hands of sinful men and be crucified and *on the third day rise*" (vv. 6, 7).[66] This summary effectively reiterates Jesus's predictions in Luke 9:44 ("The Son of Man is about to be delivered into the hands of men") and 18:33 ("on the third day he will rise"). The angels thus confirm that everything has happened just as Jesus foretold. Moreover, the Greek term *dei* ("must") once again affirms the necessity of Christ's suffering and resurrection according to God's plan.[67] The angels' testimony prompts the women to remember Jesus's words and report to the apostles, who initially do not believe their "idle tale" (24:8–11).

The next mention of the "third day" comes on the Emmaus road. Cleopas and his companion recount the shocking crucifixion of Jesus, the one they had hoped would "redeem Israel" (Luke 24:20–21). Then they muse that "it is now *the third day* since these things happened" and report the testimony of those who visited the empty tomb (vv. 21–24). These disciples did not "see" Christ at the grave (v. 24), and ironically, they fail to recognize that their traveling companion is the risen Lord and to remember his promise of resurrection on the third day.

Finally, after appearing to his disciples and eating with them (Luke 24:36–43), the risen Lord reminds them of his prior teaching that the Scriptures

---

65 The "two men . . . in dazzling apparel" (Luke 24:4) are identified as "angels" in v. 23.

66 For additional parallels, see Anderson, *'But God Raised Him from the Dead,'* 163; and Frein, "Narrative Predictions," 30.

67 The divine *dei* is discussed briefly in chap. 2, pp. 40–43. "In Luke, Jesus' resurrection is God's doing and is a part of his overall plan," according to Charles H. Talbert, "The Place of the Resurrection in the Theology of Luke," *Interpretation* 46 (1992): 21.

must be fulfilled and opens their minds to understand (vv. 44–45). He then declares, "Thus it is written, that the Christ should suffer and *on the third day rise from the dead*" (v. 46). The empty tomb, the angels' testimony, and Christ's appearances to the disciples all confirm that the Lord's suffering and resurrection fulfill prophecies in the Old Testament and Jesus's own predictions.[68]

The apostle Paul similarly affirms that Christ *"was raised on the third day in accordance with the Scriptures"* (1 Cor. 15:4). So it is clear *that* Jesus rose from the grave on the third day, but interpreters have long been perplexed about *how* exactly the Scriptures speak to Christ's resurrection on that day.[69]

The most explicit scriptural support for the third day resurrection in the Gospels is the enigmatic sign of Jonah, discussed above. The early church fathers proposed other Old Testament proofs. Tertullian cites Hosea 6:1–2 as a prophecy of Christ's resurrection on the third day.[70] Cyprian likewise appeals to Hosea 6:2 and the sign of Jonah, and adds a more allusive reference to the Lord coming down on Sinai on the third day (Ex. 19:11).[71] Lactantias also explains that "Hosea . . . testified of His resurrection," and he appeals to Psalm 16:8 and 3:5, though neither refers to the third day.[72] Similarly, Augustine writes, "Further on still, Osee [Hosea] foretold the resurrection of Christ on the third day, but in the mysterious way that is proper to prophecy. He says: 'He shall heal us after two days, and on the third day we shall rise up again.'"[73] Even though Jesus and the apostles do not directly cite Hosea 6:2, many interpreters since Tertullian have concluded that this prophecy is at least one of the key Scripture passages that anticipate Christ's resurrection on the third day.[74]

---

68 Frein, "Narrative Predictions," 31.

69 S. Vernon McCasland expresses skepticism about the biblical underpinnings of the "third day" tradition, in "The Scripture Basis of 'on the Third Day,'" *JBL* 48 (1929): 135.

70 Tertullian, *An Answer to the Jews*, 13, in *ANF*, 3:171; and *Against Marcion*, 4.43, in *ANF*, 3:422.

71 Cyprian, *Three Books of Testimonies against the Jews*, 2.25, in *ANF*, 5:525.

72 Lactantius, *Divine Institutes*, 4.19, in *ANF*, 7:122.

73 Augustine, *The City of God*, ed. Hermigild Dressler, trans. Gerald G. Walsh et al., 3 vols., The Fathers of the Church 8, 14, 24 (Washington, DC: The Catholic University of America, 1950–1954), 18.28.

74 See the recent studies by Lidija Novakovic, *Raised from the Dead according to Scripture: The Role of Israel's Scripture in the Early Christian Interpretations of Jesus' Resurrection*, JCTCRS 12 (London: Bloomsbury T&T Clark, 2012), 125–33, 175; and Dempster, "From Slight Peg to Cornerstone to Capstone," 371–409.

Hosea 5 diagnoses Israel as proud and faithless, and warns of coming judgment. The people are desperately sick and wounded, yet they seek help from Assyria's king, who cannot "cure" or "heal" them (v. 13). In response, the LORD promises to "tear" them like a lion and go away until they acknowledge their sin and seek him (vv. 14–15; cf. 3:5). Scholars debate whether 6:1–3 expresses the prophet's hope for Israel's future repentance and restoration[75] or the people's shallow response of "self-appeasement" in the face of coming danger.[76] The Greek translation of Hosea presents these verses as the people's words that they will speak when they seek the Lord in tribulation.[77] Their only hope is to return to the God who has torn and struck them down, but who also will heal and bind up their wounds (6:1). This echoes the divine declaration in Deuteronomy 32:39:

> See now that I, even I, am he,
>> and there is no god beside me;
> *I kill and I make alive;*
>> *I wound and I heal;*
> and there is none that can deliver out of my hand.

The "return" to the Lord in Hosea 6:1 reiterates the prophecy in 3:5 that the people will "return and seek the LORD their God, and David their king . . . in the latter days." Hosea 6:2 expresses hope that the Lord will "revive" (*ḥyh*) and "raise up" (*qwm*) his people, that they might "live [*ḥyh*] before him." Scholars commonly argue that this text suggests "restoration from sickness rather than resurrection from death."[78] However, when the Hebrew verbs *ḥyh* ("revive") and *qwm* ("raise up") occur together elsewhere in the Old Testament, "the meaning clearly relates to resurrection, not simply healing."[79]

75 Douglas K. Stuart, *Hosea–Jonah*, WBC 31 (Waco, TX: Word, 1987), 107–8.

76 Hans Walter Wolff, *Hosea: A Commentary on the Book of the Prophet Hosea*, ed. Paul D. Hanson, trans. Gary Stansell, Hermeneia (Philadelphia: Fortress, 1974), 117.

77 See W. Edward Glenny, *Hosea: A Commentary Based on Hosea in Codex Vaticanus*, SCS (Boston: Brill, 2013), 109–10.

78 Paul R. Williamson, *Death and the Afterlife: Biblical Perspectives on Ultimate Questions*, NSBT 44 (Downers Grove, IL: InterVarsity Press, 2017), 79; cf. Wolff, *Hosea*, 117; and A. A. Macintosh, *A Critical and Exegetical Commentary on Hosea*, ICC (Edinburgh: T&T Clark, 2014), 220–22.

79 John Day, *Yahweh and the Gods and Goddesses of Canaan*, JSOTSup 265 (Sheffield: Sheffield Academic, 2002), 119; cf. Jon D. Levenson, *Resurrection and the Restoration of Israel: The*

Perhaps the clearest parallel is Isaiah 26:19: "Your dead *shall live*; their bodies *shall rise*." Thus, Hosea depicts Israel's repentance and restoration to the Lord after exile as life after death on the third day.[80] This anticipates God's grand promise several chapters later:

> I shall ransom them from the power of Sheol;
>> I shall redeem them from Death.
> O Death, where are your plagues?
>> O Sheol, where is your sting? (Hos. 13:14)[81]

Hosea 6:2 is the only Old Testament text to link resurrection and the third day, and offers a very close parallel to Jesus's teaching that the Messiah should rise on the third day:

> "And on the third day we will rise up" (*en tē hēmera tē tritē anastēsometha*, Hos. 6:2 LXX).

> "And on the third day he will rise" (*tē hēmera tē tritē anastēsetai*, Luke 18:33).

> "And on the third day rise from the dead" (*kai anastēnai ek nekrōn tē tritē hēmera*, Luke 24:46).

Given this clear verbal agreement, it is reasonable to conclude that Hosea 6:2 is one of the Scripture passages that anticipated Christ's resurrection on the third day. Of course, Hosea describes Israel's *collective* return from exile as a resurrection on the third day, but Jesus predicts and explains his *individual* resurrection on the third day. This illustrates the biblical principle of corporate solidarity, in which the individual acts on behalf of the nation. Thus, when Jesus rises on the third day, "the true Israel in him rises to life."[82]

Ultimate Victory of the God of Life (New Haven: Yale University Press, 2006), 206; and Stuart, *Hosea–Jonah*, 108.

80 Dempster, "From Slight Peg to Cornerstone to Capstone," 397–98.

81 For detailed discussion of parallels between Hos. 5–6 and 13–14, see Day, *Yahweh and the Gods and Goddesses of Canaan*, 119–20.

82 Jason S. DeRouchie, "Why the Third Day? The Promise of Resurrection in All of Scripture," Desiring God, June 11, 2019, http://www.desiringgod.org/.

Stephen Dempster offers a sweeping survey of the Old Testament hope of resurrection and the biblical pattern of a three-day "ordeal."[83] For example, he observes that on "the third day" Abraham passes the test and receives back Isaac, God provides water for Israel in the wilderness (Ex. 15:25–26), King Hezekiah is healed of lethal illness (2 Kings 20:5–6), and Queen Esther successfully intercedes on behalf of the Jewish nation (Est. 4:16).[84] Hosea's promise of resurrection after exile "on the third day" fits this wider biblical pattern, which "finally reaches its zenith in the death of the Messiah and his resurrection on the third day."[85] Thus, Jesus's empty tomb on Sunday morning confirms his predictions (Luke 9:22; 18:33; 24:7) and fulfills Hosea 6:2 as the true Israel embodies "the hope of Israel" (Acts 28:20) as he is raised up on the third day.

David's Son and David's Lord (Luke 20:41–44)

Having answered the Sadducees' resurrection riddle, Jesus poses his own riddle about the Messiah's identity in Luke 20:41–44. In this passage, Jesus asks two questions that frame a quotation of Psalm 110:1: "How can they say that the Christ is David's son?" (v. 41) and "David thus calls him Lord, so how is he his son?" (v. 44). The belief that the Messiah would descend from David derives from God's covenant promises to David in 2 Samuel 7:12–16. The opening chapters of Luke's Gospel hail Jesus as David's son, who is born in David's town and heir to David's throne.[86] Jesus does not here dispute the Messiah's Davidic ancestry. Rather, he appeals to a Davidic psalm to show that the Christ is not *merely* David's "son" but his "Lord" as well. Thus, "son of David" is not the exclusive or decisive category for the Messiah's identity.[87]

The New Testament cites or alludes to Psalm 110:1 more often than any other Old Testament text.[88] Interpreters typically classify Psalm 110 as a

---

83 Dempster, "From Slight Peg to Cornerstone to Capstone," 397. For a complementary survey, see Michael Russell, "On the Third Day, according to the Scriptures," *RTR* 67 (2008): 1–17.

84 Dempster, "From Slight Peg to Cornerstone to Capstone," 387–89, 396, 402.

85 Dempster, "From Slight Peg to Cornerstone to Capstone," 407.

86 See Luke 1:32–33, 69; 2:4, 11. Sarah Harris, *The Davidic Shepherd King in the Lukan Narrative*, LNTS 558 (London: Bloomsbury T&T Clark, 2016).

87 See Darrell L. Bock, *Proclamation from Prophecy and Pattern: Lucan Old Testament Christology*, JSNTSup 12 (Sheffield: JSOT Press, 1987), 132; and Green, *The Gospel of Luke*, 724.

88 Gerhard Dautzenberg, "Psalm 110 im Neuen Testament," in *Liturgie und Dichtung: Ein interdisziplinäres Kompendium*, ed. Hansjakob Becker and Reiner Kaczynski, Pietas liturgica 2

"royal psalm"[89] and outline it in two parts that correspond to the divine speeches in verse 1 ("The LORD says") and verse 4 ("The LORD has sworn").[90] The style and content of these divine sayings resemble the oracles of the Old Testament prophets.[91] In Psalm 110, Yahweh commands David's Lord, "Sit at my right hand" and "Rule in the midst of your enemies!" (vv. 1–2). The Lord sends forth the royal scepter to shatter kings in his wrath (vv. 2, 5), recalling the comprehensive authority of the royal son that God sets on Zion in Psalm 2. In Psalm 110:4, the Lord also distinctively swears that his king is also a priest.[92]

All three Synoptic Gospels record Jesus's riddle about David's Lord, each with its own emphases. Matthew 22:41–42 specifies that Jesus questions the Pharisees about the Christ before turning to Psalm 110, while Mark 12:37 notes that the crowd "heard him gladly." Further, according to Matthew 22:43, David speaks "in the Spirit" when calling his son "Lord" (similarly Mark 12:36). In Luke 20:42, Jesus introduces his appeal to Scripture with the explanatory conjunction "for" (*gar*) and specifies that "David himself says *in the Book of Psalms*." The only other explicit mention of "Psalms" in the Gospels comes in Luke 24:44, where the risen Christ explains to the disciples "that everything written about me in the Law of Moses and the Prophets and *the Psalms* must be fulfilled."[93] This repetition of "Psalms"

(Sankt Ottilien: EOS Verlag, 1983), 141; and Martin Hengel, "Sit at My Right Hand!," in *Studies in Early Christology* (Edinburgh: T&T Clark, 1995), 133. "No other psalm has in research evoked as many hypotheses and discussions as Psalm 110," according to Hans-Joachim Kraus, *Psalms: A Commentary*, trans. H. C. Oswald, 2 vols. (Minneapolis: Augsburg, 1988–1989), 2:345.

89 DeClaissé-Walford, Jacobson, and Tanner, *Psalms*, 834. They list Pss. 2, 18, 20, 21, 45, 72, 89, 101, 132, and 144 as the other "royal psalms."

90 Willem A. VanGemeren, *Psalms*, rev. ed., EBC 5 (Grand Rapids, MI: Zondervan, 2008), 479; Frank Lothar Hossfeld and Eric Zenger, *Psalms 3: A Commentary on Psalms 101–150*, trans. Linda Maloney, Hermeneia (Minneapolis: Fortress, 2011); Tremper Longman III, *Psalms: An Introduction and Commentary*, TOTC 15–16 (Downers Grove, IL: InterVarsity Press, 2014), 2:381; and Walter Brueggemann and William H. Bellinger Jr., *Psalms*, NCBC (Cambridge: Cambridge University Press, 2014), 479.

91 James L. Mays, *Psalms*, Interpretation (Philadelphia: Westminster John Knox, 1994), 350.

92 The book of Hebrews cites Ps. 110:4 to declare that Jesus is an eternal priest (Heb. 5:6; 7:17, 21). For discussions of Melchizedekian priesthood in the Old Testament and in Hebrews, see respectively Joshua G. Mathews, *Melchizedek's Alternative Priestly Order: A Compositional Analysis of Genesis 14:18–20 and Its Echoes throughout the Tanak*, BBRSup 8 (Winona Lake, IN: Eisenbrauns, 2013); and Jared Compton, *Psalm 110 and the Logic of Hebrews*, LNTS 537 (London: Bloomsbury T&T Clark, 2015).

93 See also Acts 1:20 ("in the Book of Psalms) and 13:33 ("in the second Psalm").

suggests that Jesus's appeal to Psalm 110:1 in Luke 20:42 directly anticipates his comprehensive summary of the Scriptures in Luke 24:44.

The exchange concludes with a lingering Christological quandary: "David thus calls him Lord, so how is he his son?" (Luke 20:44). Readers must not miss the irony here: it is the Lord (*kyrios*) himself who quotes this psalm and poses this question.[94] During his trial, Jesus asserts to his accusers that "from now on the Son of Man shall be seated at the right hand of the power of God" (22:69). Jesus's declaration of his future heavenly authority ties together the biblical threads of the Son of Man coming with the clouds of heaven (Dan. 7:13; cf. Luke 21:27) with David's Lord seated at God's right hand (Ps. 110:1).[95]

Jesus's riddle from Psalm 110:1 finds resolution in the apostles' preaching in Acts. In his foundational Pentecost sermon, Peter cites the same psalm as the climactic proof that the risen Christ has been exalted to God's right hand (Acts 2:33–35; cf. 5:31).[96] Thus, while Jesus does not explicitly predict his resurrection and heavenly ascension in Luke 20:41–44, his apostles explain that the Messiah's resurrection and lordship "are indissolubly bound together."[97] How is David's son shown to be David's Lord also? By rising from the dead according to the Scriptures.

Conclusion

Jesus engages the debates of his day about the hope of the resurrection and the identity of the Davidic Messiah (Luke 20:27–44). He refuses to perform miracles on demand for sign-seeking skeptics, and instead offers only "the sign of Jonah," becoming a sign himself through his suffering and vindication as the Son of Man (11:29–32). Christ's transfiguration on the mountain previews his resurrection glory (9:28–36), and he promises his followers that he will rise on the third day, yet they cannot grasp the true meaning

---

94 Rowe, *Early Narrative Christology*, 172.

95 There is significant scholarly discussion around Jesus's favorite title, "Son of Man," which most likely recalls the famous prophecy in Dan. 7:13. See, for example, France, *Jesus and the Old Testament*, 135–48; Darrell L. Bock, "The Use of Daniel 7 in Jesus' Trial, with Implications for his Self-Understanding," in *'Who Is This Son of Man?': The Latest Scholarship on a Puzzling Expression of the Historical Jesus*, ed. Larry W. Hurtado and Paul L. Owen, LNTS 390 (London: T&T Clark, 2011), 78–100; and Craig L. Blomberg, *A New Testament Theology* (Waco, TX: Baylor University Press, 2018), 46–48.

96 I discuss Acts 2:34–35 further in chap. 5, pp. 126–28.

97 Anderson, *'But God Raised Him from the Dead,'* 131.

of his words (18:33–34). Even on the third day after Jesus's crucifixion, his female friends are perplexed by the empty tomb as they mistakenly look for the living among the dead, and at first the disciples dismiss their report of resurrection as an idle tale (24:1–11). Cleopas and his companion recount Jesus's crucifixion and lament their dead dreams of redemption even as they unknowingly walk alongside the risen Lord (24:13–21). It is only at the end of Luke's Gospel that the disciples truly understand the reality and necessity of Christ's resurrection on the third day according to the Scriptures. The resurrection demonstrates that Jesus is not only David's son but also the Lord who reigns at God's right hand and ushers in the promised last days.

4

A Light for the Nations

Salvation and Mission in Luke

The Spirit of the Lord is upon me,
because he has anointed me
to proclaim good news to the poor.
He has sent me to proclaim liberty to the captives
and recovering of sight to the blind,
to set at liberty those who are oppressed,
to proclaim the year of the Lord's favor.

LUKE 4:18–19

ONCE THERE WAS A GREAT RULER whose followers hailed him as the savior of mankind, the one who brought good news for the world. His name was Gaius Julius Caesar Augustus. After his father, Gaius Octavius, died, he was adopted by his great-uncle, Julius Caesar, in 44 BC, and became emperor of Rome in 31 BC. In 27 BC, the Roman Senate bestowed on him the honorific "Augustus" to celebrate his military victories.[1] Augustus was considered the "Father of his Country"[2] because his long and accomplished

---

1 See Suetonius, *The Lives of the Caesars*, trans. John C. Rolfe, 2 vols., LCL 31, 38 (Cambridge, MA: Harvard University Press, 1914), 2.7; and D. S. Potter, "Augustus (Emperor)," in *The Anchor Yale Bible Dictionary* (New Haven: Yale University Press, 1992), 1:525. The Latin term "Augustus" is equivalent to "*Majesty or Imperial Majesty,*" according to Charlton T. Lewis and Charles Short, *Harper's Latin Dictionary*, rev. ed. (New York: Harper & Brothers, 1891), 205.

2 Suetonius, *Lives of the Caesars*, 2.58; cf. Augustus, *Res Gestae Divi Augusti*, trans. Frederick W. Shipley, LCL 152 (Cambridge, MA: Harvard University Press, 1924), 35.

reign until AD 14 marked a golden age of peace, economic prosperity, and literary and artistic achievement in Rome. A remarkable inscription in Priene, Greece, from 9 BC commemorated the "gospel" of Augustus's reign:

> Since Providence has put in order everything in our lives and has deep interest in our life, she has set everything in perfect order by giving us Augustus (for the great benefit of men) whom she filled with great virtue, so that he might benefit humankind, sending him as a savior [*sōtēr*] for us and our descendants, to end war and to put everything in the cosmos in order. He, by his appearance [*epiphania*], went beyond all our expectations and beyond all previous helpers, and not leaving to the future any hope of accomplishing more than what he has done; . . . the birthday of the God Augustus was the beginning of the good tidings [or "gospel," *euangelia*] for the world he established.[3]

During Augustus's celebrated reign, an angel of the Lord appeared in glory to some shepherds in Israel to announce "good news of great joy that will be for all the people. For unto you is born this day in the city of David a Savior [*sōtēr*], who is Christ the Lord" (Luke 2:10–11). Remarkably, it was Augustus's decree that brought Joseph and his betrothed to Bethlehem, where Mary gave birth to Jesus in the humblest of circumstances (vv. 1–7).

It is difficult to conceive of a starker contrast than that between a manger in Bethlehem and the halls of power in Rome, yet both Jesus and Augustus are hailed as savior figures whose reigns bring joyous "good news" and enduring "peace" for humanity (Luke 2:10, 14).[4] Augustus established the famed "Roman peace" by military conquest, political will, and financial investments, as foreign kings and their peoples pledged allegiance to Rome.[5] He died an honorable death at the age of seventy-six, received a splendid

---

3   The Priene Inscription, cited in David R. Cartlidge and David L. Dungan, *Documents and Images for the Study of the Gospels*, 3rd ed. (Minneapolis: Fortress, 2015), 4. Virgil similarly hails Augustus as "son of a god, who shall again establish a Golden Age." *Aeneid*, in *Eclogues. Georgics. Aeneid: Books 1–6*, trans. H. R. Fairclough and G. P. Goold, LCL 63 (Cambridge, MA: Harvard University Press, 1916), 6.792–93.

4   The term *euangelizomai* ("bring good news") is thus "completely redefined by the gospel story of Jesus," according to Garland, *Luke*, 123. Sarah Harris also notes the contrast between Augustus and Jesus in *The Davidic Shepherd King in the Lukan Narrative*, 70.

5   Augustus, *Res Gestae Divi Augusti*, 32.

funeral, and was venerated as a god. Alternatively, Jesus proclaimed good news for the poor, salvation for sinners, and the coming of God's kingdom. He held no political office, led no army, funded no public works, and received no state funeral after his dishonorable death by crucifixion. Yet after his resurrection on the third day, the Lord Jesus declared "that repentance for the forgiveness of sins should be proclaimed in his name to all nations, beginning from Jerusalem," in fulfillment of the sacred Scriptures (24:47).

The Messiah's Mission Fulfills the Scriptures

The Jews of Jesus's day remembered how their leaders had once made a pact with the Gentiles, abandoning the holy covenant and selling themselves to commit evil (1 Macc. 1:11–15). The pagan ruler Antiochus IV had forced Israel to give up its customs and adopt his religion under penalty of death, and he even set up a desolating sacrilege on the altar of burnt offering in 167 BC (1:41–50, 54). Then a great leader, Judas Maccabeus, fought valiantly against the tyrant and brought deliverance to Israel. Three years after Antiochus defiled Israel's sanctuary, Judas cleansed the temple and restored proper worship according to the law (4:36–59). The Jews celebrated the annual Feast of Dedication (Hanukkah) to commemorate the restoration of the temple and to remember how, as Josephus writes, "the right to worship appeared to us at a time when we hardly dared hope for it."[6] Similarly, many Jews in Jesus's day felt squeezed by Roman rule and longed for God to restore Israel's fortunes and put the Gentiles in their place. Yet Jesus's coming fulfilled the Old Testament hopes of salvation not just for Israel but for "all flesh" (Luke 3:6).

This chapter focuses on four key passages that draw upon the Old Testament Prophets to clarify Jesus's identity, mission, and saving work. First, Simeon identifies the Christ child as the Lord's servant who brings the light of salvation to the Gentiles (Luke 2:32; Isa. 49:6). Second, Luke cites Isaiah's prophecy of the new exodus to clarify the scope of God's saving work that begins with the Lord Jesus's arrival (Luke 3:4–6; Isa. 40:3–5). Third, Jesus announces that he is the Lord's Spirit-anointed agent sent to proclaim good news to the poor and oppressed (Luke 4:18–19; Isa. 61:1–2). Finally, Jesus presents his mission "to seek and to save the lost" in terms that recall God's own commitment as Israel's true shepherd (Luke 19:10; Ezek. 34:16, 22).

6   Josephus, *Jewish Antiquities*, 12.325.

Light for the Gentiles (Luke 2:29–32)

I begin this chapter on the Messiah's mission and the hope of the nations by returning to Simeon's meeting with the baby Jesus in the temple (Luke 2:25–35). Simeon's prophetic words in verses 29–35 explain the biblical-theological significance of Jesus's arrival, drawing deeply from the well of Isaiah to express how God has begun to fulfill his promises to bring consolation, salvation, and revelation for Israel and the nations.[7] This prophecy anticipates and explains facets of Jesus's identity, destiny, and mission that are developed throughout Luke's narrative and culminate in the risen Lord's summary of the Scriptures in 24:44–47.[8] Here I consider Simeon's preview of salvation for all peoples in 2:29–32.

The pious old man has waited long for Israel's "consolation," and now he sees salvation in the flesh and holds the hoped-for Christ in his wrinkled hands. Similarly, aged Anna of Asher's tribe is among those "waiting for the redemption of Jerusalem," and she thanks God and speaks to everyone about the Christ child (Luke 2:36–38). Together Simeon and Anna represent all those who patiently yet expectantly wait for God to save his people according to the ancient prophecies, and they are among the first to see the sunrise of salvation.[9]

Simeon identifies the Christ child as the one who will bring God's "salvation"—that is, "light" for the Gentiles and "glory" for Israel. This oracle is brimming with several important references to the book of Isaiah, which together identify Jesus as the messianic servant who carries out the promised new exodus salvation for God's people.

In Luke 2:30–32, Simeon declares,

My eyes have seen your salvation
    that you have prepared in the presence of all peoples,
a light for revelation to the Gentiles,
    and for glory to your people Israel.

---

7 Simeon's prophecy alludes to Isa. 40:5 and 52:10 ("see . . . salvation," NETS) and 49:6 ("light . . . Gentiles," NIV); Peter Mallen discusses these and other possible Old Testament allusions in *The Reading and Transformation of Isaiah in Luke-Acts*, 65–66.

8 The programmatic function of Simeon's prophecy is noted by Collin Blake Bullard, *Jesus and the Thoughts of Many Hearts: Implicit Christology and Jesus' Knowledge in the Gospel of Luke*, LNTS 530 (London: Bloomsbury T&T Clark, 2015), 66.

9 This "sunrise" image comes from Mal. 4:2 and Luke 1:78.

These words likely allude to Isaiah 40:3–5, the great prophecy of the new exodus in the wilderness. "Your *salvation*" parallels "the *salvation* of God" in verse 5,[10] and "you have *prepared*" recalls the command "*prepare* the way of the LORD" in verse 3. Further, Israel's "consolation" (*paraklēsis*) in Luke 2:25 likely refers to the "comfort" (*parakaleō*) announced three times in Isaiah 40:1–2 LXX.[11] While Simeon waits for God to comfort *Israel*, he explains that God has prepared his glorious salvation "in the presence of *all peoples*" (Luke 2:31). "All peoples" parallels "all flesh" in Isaiah 40:5 and includes both Jews and Gentiles together as beneficiaries of God's work of salvation. Luke 3:4–6 explicitly cites Isaiah 40:3–5 LXX to offer a biblical rationale for John's prophetic ministry in the wilderness. Simeon's words in Luke 2 anticipate this fuller quotation of Isaiah's famous prophecy in chapter 3, but there is more. Simeon *sees* God's salvation as he looks upon Christ—the very salvation that "all flesh" *will see*, according to Isaiah 40:5.[12] This Christ child is embodied salvation, swaddled in old Simeon's arms.

Simeon further identifies Jesus as "a light" bringing revelation to the Gentiles and glory to Israel (Luke 2:32). This verse stands in apposition to verse 30 and thus unpacks the meaning of God's "salvation" in terms of "light." Simeon's words here allude to Isaiah 49:6:

> It is too light a thing that you should be my servant
>> to raise up the tribes of Jacob
>> and to bring back the preserved of Israel;
> I will make you as *a light for the nations,*
>> that my salvation may reach to the end of the earth.[13]

The phrase "a light for the nations" also occurs in the initial Servant Song in 42:6. In Luke 2:32, this "light" has two expressed purposes: "for

---

10 The phrase "the salvation of God" occurs only in the LXX version of Isa. 40:5. See the discussion of this passage in the next section, pp. 90–94.

11 Holly Beers, *The Followers of Jesus as the "Servant": Luke's Model from Isaiah for the Disciples in Luke-Acts*, LNTS 535 (New York: Bloomsbury T&T Clark, 2015), 95–96.

12 "Luke has Simeon interpret his encounter with the promised messianic king as an encounter with the salvation of God itself," according to Wolter, *The Gospel according to Luke*, 1:140.

13 Most commentators recognize this allusion to Isa. 49:6, though Morna D. Hooker disputes it in *Jesus and the Servant: The Influence of the Servant Concept of Deutero-Isaiah in the New Testament* (London: SPCK, 1959), 84.

revelation to the Gentiles" and "for glory to your people Israel."[14] The first phrase, "revelation to the Gentiles," may recall another promise of future salvation in Isaiah 52:10 (NETS):

And the Lord shall *reveal* his holy arm
    before *all the nations*,
and all the ends of the earth shall see
    the *salvation* that comes from God.

The second purpose, "glory" for Israel, may also reflect Old Testament prophecies of restoration—particularly Isaiah 60:1–2, which closely links light and glory through poetic parallelism.[15]

Simeon's words introduce several images related to the prophetic hope of salvation—light, revelation, and glory—that are developed further in the Gospel narrative. Zechariah's earlier prophecy depicts salvation as a rising sun that illuminates those sitting in darkness (Luke 1:78–79), as Isaiah prophesied that light would come to people in darkness (Isa. 9:2; 42:6–7).[16] Later, Paul encounters the risen Lord as "a light from heaven" (Acts 26:13), and he describes conversion as turning from darkness to light, from Satan's power to God (26:18). Moreover, Paul depicts Christ himself proclaiming light to Israel and the nations (26:23). The Greek term *apokalypsis* ("revelation") in Luke 2:32 "always refers to divine revelation" in the New Testament.[17] Jesus explains that full divine disclosure is coming: "Nothing is covered up that will not be *revealed*, or hidden that will not be known" (12:2). Jesus himself reveals the secret thoughts of people's hearts (2:35), which sounds a note of judgment: "God is bringing a light of revelation to the Gentiles, but, figuratively, light must also reveal things hidden in darkness."[18] Moreover, while the Father conceals and reveals according to his gracious will, Jesus uniquely and truly reveals his Father to whomever he chooses (10:21–22). "Glory" is closely associated with God's own radiant presence (2:9; Acts 7:2, 55) and also with Jesus's resurrection, exaltation, and coming with power (Luke

---

14 The Greek syntax of Luke 2:32 is challenging. For an explanation of the interpretive options, see Alan J. Thompson, *Luke*, EGGNT (Nashville: Broadman & Holman, 2017), 51–52; and Bock, *Luke*, 1:244.

15 Pao and Schnabel, "Luke," 273.

16 Pao and Schnabel, "Luke," 265.

17 *NIDNTTE*, 2:615. See, for example, Rom. 16:25; 2 Cor. 12:1; Eph. 1:17; 1 Pet. 1:7; Rev. 1:1.

18 Bullard, *Jesus and the Thoughts of Many Hearts*, 80–81.

9:26; 21:27; 24:26). Thus, Israel's hope of "glory" is bound up with the radiance of the resurrected, reigning Lord Jesus.

Isaiah 49 identifies the Lord's servant as "Israel, in whom I will be glorified" (v. 3). However, this servant is not the nation but an individual who carries out God's plan to bring back, gather, and raise up the tribes of Israel (vv. 5–6).[19] Moreover, this servant has a global mission, which is anticipated by the opening call to the coastlands and peoples (v. 1) and made explicit by the servant's designation as "as a light for the nations" (v. 6; cf. 42:6).

Thus, by alluding to Isaiah 49:6, Simeon identifies Jesus as the promised servant who will bring about the new exodus salvation for Israel and all the nations.[20] At the same time, Jesus alludes to Isaiah 49:6 when he commissions his witnesses "to the end of the earth" in Acts 1:8. Moreover, Paul and Barnabas explain their outreach to the Gentiles by citing the Lord's command in Isaiah 49:6 (Acts 13:47).[21] This progressive application of Isaiah's servant prophecy to Jesus (Luke 2:32), then to the apostles (Acts 1:8), and finally to Paul and Barnabas (13:47) is significant to the biblical-theological argument of this book. Jesus fulfills Isaiah's servant prophecies as the promised Messiah, the agent of end-time salvation for God's people who is "chosen," "numbered with the transgressors," and "led to the slaughter" (Luke 9:35; 22:37; Acts 8:32).[22] Christ *is* the "light" of salvation in the flesh. As his witnesses proclaim forgiveness in his name among all nations and call people to turn from darkness to light, they are an extension of the risen Lord's own activity, for Paul explains that the Christ would suffer, rise, and "proclaim light both to our people and to the Gentiles" (Acts 26:23).

Simeon recognizes the Christ child to be the fulfillment of God's promises to save and comfort his people and to extend revelation even to the nations. This scene anticipates the appeal to Isaiah's prophecy of the new exodus salvation in Luke 3:4–6.

---

19 Scholars debate the identity of the servant in Isa. 49. I discuss this passage further in chap. 6, pp. 149–55.

20 "The Isaianic servant is the human agent" of the new exodus, according to Beers, *The Followers of Jesus*, 88–89.

21 I consider Acts 1:8 and 13:47 further in chap. 6, pp. 136–41, 149–55.

22 Luke 9:35 alludes to Isa. 42:1; Luke 22:37 cites Isa. 53:12; and Acts 8:32–33 quotes Isa. 53:7–8; these passages receive extended treatment in chaps. 2, 3, and 5. For a survey of other passages in Luke-Acts that portray Jesus as the Isaianic servant, see Dennis E. Johnson, "Jesus against the Idols: The Use of Isaianic Servant Songs in the Missiology of Acts," *WTJ* 52 (1990): 343–45.

Salvation for All Flesh (Luke 3:4–6)

"The word of God came to John the son of Zechariah in the wilderness" (Luke 3:2). This summary closely parallels Old Testament descriptions of the prophets receiving revelation from God,[23] and it fulfills Zechariah's prophecy that his son would be "the prophet of the Most High" (1:76). John's appearance also represents a key turn in redemptive history: he receives God's word around AD 29 following hundreds of years of prophetic silence.[24] John proclaims "a baptism of repentance for the forgiveness of sins," and Luke explains that John's prophetic activity fulfills prophetic hopes (3:3–4).

All four Gospels cite Isaiah 40 in connection with John's wilderness ministry, though Luke offers the most expansive quotation of this famous prophecy:

As it is written in the book of the words of Isaiah the prophet,

"The voice of one crying in the wilderness:
'Prepare the way of the Lord,
    make his paths straight.
Every valley shall be filled,
    and every mountain and hill shall be made low,
and the crooked shall become straight,
    and the rough places shall become level ways,
and all flesh shall see the salvation of God.'" (Luke 3:4–6)[25]

Zechariah's prophecy anticipates this link between Isaiah 40 and John's vocation in Luke 1:76–77:

And you, child, will be called the prophet of the Most High,
    for you will go before the Lord to prepare his ways,

---

23 For example, "the word of the LORD came" to Samuel (1 Sam. 15:10), Nathan (2 Sam. 7:4), Elijah (1 Kings 17:2, 8), Isaiah (2 Kings 20:4; Isa. 38:4), Jeremiah (Jer. 1:4, 11), Ezekiel (Ezek. 1:3; 3:16), Jonah (Jonah 1:1; 3:1), and other Old Testament prophets.

24 1 Macc. 9:27 refers to "the time that prophets ceased to appear" in Israel, and Josephus remarks about "the failure of the exact succession of prophets" from the time of Artaxerxes to his day. *Against Apion*, in *The Life, Against Apion*, trans. H. St. J. Thackeray, LCL 186 (Cambridge, MA: Harvard University Press, 1926), 1.41.

25 Luke cites the LXX version of Isa. 40:3–5. Matt. 3:3, Mark 1:3, and John 1:23 each quote only verse 3 of Isaiah's prophecy.

to give knowledge of salvation to his people
    in the forgiveness of their sins.

John's message of forgiveness may recall Isaiah's tender word of hope that Jerusalem's sin has been loosed (Luke 3:2; Isa. 40:2 LXX). The wider context of Luke's Gospel makes clear that God has sent the prophet John to prepare the way for *the Lord Jesus*, "the one who is to come" (Luke 7:19–20).[26] Simeon further signals that Jesus is the one who will bring "consolation" to Israel and usher in the "salvation" that God has prepared, just as Isaiah prophesied (Luke 2:25–30). Because of these and other textual links, David Pao calls this citation of Isaiah 40:3–5 "the hermeneutical key" for properly understanding Luke's Gospel and Acts.[27]

The message of coming salvation in Isaiah 40 offers comfort and hope following the announcement that Israel will be exiled to Babylon (39:5–8). Isaiah declares that the Lord will again reveal his glory and come to deliver his people in decisive fashion (40:3–5).

Isaiah 40:1–11 introduces many of the key themes of chapters 40–55,[28] and these verses are bursting with exodus imagery.[29] Consider five examples. First, the voice crying "in the wilderness" (Isa. 40:4) alludes to the wilderness setting for Moses's call (Ex. 3:1), Israel's journey out of Egypt "by the way of the wilderness" (13:18), and God's provision for Israel in the wilderness (16:32; Deut. 1:31; 2:7; 29:5). Second, "*the way* of the LORD" (Isa. 40:3) recalls how the Lord led his people "along *the way*" in the exodus and sent his angel to guard them "on *the way*" (Ex. 13:21; 23:20). "The way" expresses the Lord's saving presence with his people during the first exodus from Egypt and the coming exodus from exile.[30] The same God

---

26 "The structure and movement of the story prepares us to follow the way of the Lord of Israel as his coming is embodied in the life and person of the Lord Jesus," according to Rowe, *Early Narrative Christology*, 77.

27 David W. Pao, *Acts and the Isaianic New Exodus*, BSL (Grand Rapids, MI: Baker Academic, 2002), 38.

28 Isa. 40:1–11 is "the prologue" to chaps. 40–55, according to Pao, *Acts and the Isaianic New Exodus*, 45. The entirety of Isa. 40 "serves an introductory function," according to John N. Oswalt, *The Book of Isaiah*, 2 vols., NICOT (Grand Rapids, MI: Eerdmans, 1986–1998), 2:48.

29 "The theme of a second exodus unifies the message of Isaiah," according to L. Michael Morales, *Exodus Old and New: A Biblical Theology of Redemption*, ESBT (Downers Grove, IL: InterVarsity Press, 2020), 134.

30 Pao, *Acts and the Isaianic New Exodus*, 52.

who "makes a *way* in the sea" will one day do "a new thing" and "make a *way* in the wilderness and rivers in the desert" (Isa. 43:16, 19). Third, Isaiah highlights the Lord's comfort and shepherd-like care for Israel (40:1, 11; cf. 63:14), which Moses similarly emphasizes in his song at the Red Sea (Ex. 15:13). Fourth, Isaiah's description of the Lord's almighty arm (40:10; cf. 52:9–10) recalls God's promise to redeem Israel "with an outstretched arm" (Ex. 6:6; cf. 6:1; 15:16; Deut. 4:34; 7:19). Isaiah later appeals for the Lord's arm to "awake" and "put on strength," recalling that he "dried up the sea" so that his redeemed might safely pass. The prophet then announces a coming exodus-esque deliverance for God's people:

And the ransomed of the LORD shall return
and come to Zion with singing;
everlasting joy shall be upon their heads;
they shall obtain gladness and joy,
and sorrow and sighing shall flee away. (Isa. 51:11)

Finally, the Septuagint of Isaiah 40:5 (quoted in Luke 3:6) specifies that "all flesh shall see *the salvation of God*." This recalls the salvation God accomplishes at the exodus and introduces one of the signature emphases of Isaiah. Moses summons Israel to "see the salvation of the LORD" in Exodus 14:13, but Isaiah prophesies that "all flesh" and "all the ends of the earth" will see this glorious salvation (Isa. 40:5; 52:10). Thus, Israel's salvation from slavery in Egypt in the past fostered hope that one day the Lord would return to accomplish a greater exodus in the future, rescuing his people and revealing his glory among the nations.

It is noteworthy that Luke cites the Greek translation of Isaiah 40:3–5.[31] The ESV formally translates the Hebrew text of verse 5 this way:

And the glory of the LORD shall be revealed,
and all flesh shall see it together,
for the mouth of the LORD has spoken.

---

31 Luke customarily cites and alludes to the Greek translation of the Scriptures. For a detailed comparison of Luke 3:4–6 and the Greek and Hebrew versions of Isa. 40:3–5, see Pao, *Acts and the Isaianic New Exodus*, 38–39; and Dietrich Rusam, *Das Alte Testament bei Lukas*, BZNW 112 (Berlin: de Gruyter, 2003), 155–58.

The Septuagint offers a theologically significant expansion of the Hebrew text:

> And the glory of the Lord shall appear,
> and all flesh shall see *the salvation of God*,
> because the Lord has spoken. (AT)

Within the book of Isaiah, this declaration offers an ultimate answer to Hezekiah's predicament in 38:11 ("I said, No longer shall I see the salvation of God on the earth," NETS). It also anticipates further references to the glorious salvation that God's people will experience.[32] Luke 3:6 quotes Isaiah 40:5 LXX to highlight the crucial promise that "all flesh shall see the salvation of God." While salvation is a common theme throughout Luke and Acts, the specific Greek word *sōtērion* ("salvation") is infrequent in the New Testament, yet it occurs in two key places in Luke's writings.[33] First, when Simeon cradles the Christ child in his arms, he exclaims that "my eyes have seen your *salvation* [*sōtērion*]" (Luke 2:30). Then, at the end of Acts, Paul declares to the Jews in Rome, "Therefore let it be known to you that this *salvation* [*sōtērion*] *of God* has been sent to the Gentiles; they will listen" (Acts 28:28). Other references to Isaiah in Luke 2 and Acts 28 confirm that "salvation" in these texts recalls the prophetic hope of Isaiah 40:5 LXX and signals the surprising fulfillment of God's promise that "all flesh shall see the salvation of God."[34]

Early Jewish interpreters understood Isaiah's prophecy as a promise for Israel's restoration after exile,[35] and the Jews in the Qumran community actually moved into the wilderness to prepare for the Lord's work of salvation by carefully studying and keeping the Law.[36] However, while these Jews longed for God to accomplish a new exodus salvation for his people in the

---

32 See, for example, salvation references in Isa. 51:5–6, 8; 56:1; 59:17.

33 The other New Testament use of *sōtērion* comes in Eph. 6:17 ("take the helmet of *salvation*"), which alludes to Isa. 59:17.

34 See Pao, *Acts and the Isaianic New Exodus*, 39–40.

35 Consider, for example, Bar. 5:7 in the Apocrypha: "For God has ordered that every high mountain and the everlasting hills be made low and the valleys filled up to make level ground, so that Israel may walk safely in the glory of God."

36 See *The Rule of the Community* (1QS) in the Dead Sea Scrolls: "When such men as these come to be in Israel, conforming to these doctrines, they shall separate from the session of perverse men to go to the wilderness, there to prepare the way of truth, as it is written, 'In the wilderness prepare the way of the LORD, make straight in the desert a highway for our God' (Isaiah 40:3)."

future, Luke and the other evangelists announce that John's ministry in the wilderness and the coming of the Lord Jesus represent the fulfillment of Isaiah 40. Moreover, Luke makes clear that this salvation of God is good news for "all flesh"—including Gentiles who heed God's word (Acts 28:28). In fact, the book of Acts even refers to Christ's followers as "the Way" (e.g., 9:2), alluding to "the way of the LORD" in Isaiah 40:3 and identifying them as God's true people.[37]

Thus, Luke's extended quotation of Isaiah 40 signals that the time is at hand when "all flesh shall see the salvation of God" (Luke 3:6). In the next chapter, Jesus himself unrolls Isaiah's scroll in his hometown synagogue and announces that this ancient prophecy is fulfilled "in your hearing" (4:17–21).

Good News for the Poor (Luke 4:18–19)

Luke 4:16–30 contributes significantly to this chapter's focus on the Messiah's mission. This passage offers the first extended example of Jesus's public ministry. Further, his appeal to Isaiah 61:1–2 (combined with a line from 58:6) provides crucial definition for Jesus's identity and vocation to proclaim liberty, good news, and healing to the poor and oppressed in the Spirit's power. Luke's narrative also recounts that Jesus is misunderstood and opposed in his hometown, following the pattern of the rejected prophets of old and anticipating his future suffering and death.

After he is baptized in the Jordan and tempted in the wilderness, Jesus returns "in the power of the Spirit" to Galilee, where he teaches in the synagogues and is "glorified by all" (Luke 4:14–15). Jesus then comes to his hometown of Nazareth, where he stands up to read the Scriptures on the Sabbath (vv. 16–20). Luke skillfully narrates this scene using a series of parallel phrases that form a chiasm:

A into the synagogue (v. 16)
  B he stood up to read (v. 16)
    C the scroll was handed to him (v. 17)
      D he unrolled the scroll (v. 17)
        E "The Spirit of the Lord is upon me . . ." (vv. 18–19)

1QS 8:12–14, in *The Dead Sea Scrolls: A New Translation*, trans. Michael O. Wise, Martin G. Abegg, and Edward M. Cook (San Francisco: HarperSanFrancisco, 1996).

37 For references and discussion, see Pao, *Acts and the Isaianic New Exodus*, 59–68.

D¹ he rolled up the scroll (v. 20)

C¹ he gave the scroll back (v. 20)

B¹ he sat down (v. 20)

A¹ in the synagogue (v. 20)

This literary structure draws attention to the center of the chiasm: Jesus's declaration from Isaiah 61:1, "The Spirit of the Lord is upon *me*."[38] After reading Isaiah's prophecy, Jesus sits down and announces its fulfillment "today" (Luke 4:21). The people of Nazareth initially speak well of Jesus and marvel at his winsome words (v. 22). However, by calling him "Joseph's son," they show that they do not grasp Jesus's true identity. Their misunderstanding grows into malice (v. 28) when Jesus illustrates the proverb that no prophet is acceptable in his hometown (v. 24) with examples from the ministries of Elijah and Elisha to those outside of Israel (vv. 25–27). The Nazareth crowd thus despises Jesus and the good news he proclaims, driving him out of town (v. 29).

This passage hangs on Jesus's reading and application of Scripture, so let's look carefully at Luke 4:18–19:

The Spirit of the Lord is upon me,

　because he has anointed me

　　to proclaim good news to the poor.

He has sent me to proclaim liberty to the captives

　and recovering of sight to the blind,

　　to set at liberty those who are oppressed,

to proclaim the year of the Lord's favor.

This quotation follows Isaiah 61:1–2 LXX with several variations.[39] Notably, the line "to proclaim liberty to the captives" comes from an earlier related passage in Isaiah 58:6:

---

38 Edwards, *The Gospel according to Luke*, 134. See Charles H. Talbert, *Reading Luke: A Literary and Theological Commentary on the Third Gospel*, rev. ed., Reading the New Testament (Macon, GA: Smyth & Helwys, 2002), 57; and Wolter, *The Gospel according to Luke*, 1:199.

39 For detailed textual comparisons, see Pao, *Acts and the Isaianic New Exodus*, 71–74; and Stanley E. Porter, "Composite Citations in Luke-Acts," in *Composite Citations in Antiquity, Volume Two: New Testament Uses*, ed. Sean A. Adams and Seth M. Ehorn, LNTS 593 (London: Bloomsbury T&T Clark, 2018), 64.

Is not this the fast that I choose:
  to loose the bonds of wickedness,
  to undo the straps of the yoke,
to let the oppressed go free,
  and to break every yoke?[40]

Isaiah 60 describes the glorious future of God's people, whom the Lord will save (v. 16), beautify (v. 9), and vindicate (v. 14–15) in his time. Isaiah 61 introduces a messianic figure who comforts mourners and proclaims good news (vv. 1–3), prompting the redeemed to build up the ancient ruins (v. 4). The Lord promises everlasting joy and an everlasting covenant for his people (vv. 7–9). Then the chapter shifts back to the first person in verse 10, where the messianic figure from verse 1 rejoices as he puts on the garments of salvation and righteousness—the Lord's own clothing, according to 59:17.[41]

Most interpreters recognize the central role that the figure in Isaiah 61:1–3 plays in the final chapters of the book, though they variously identify this individual as the Davidic king (e.g., 11:1–5), the Lord's servant (e.g., 42:1–7), a prophetic messenger (e.g., 52:7), or some combination of these figures.[42] This individual's endowment with the divine Spirit (61:1) parallels the description of the royal Messiah in 11:2 and the Lord's servant in 42:1, each of whom is an agent of divine justice (11:4; 42:1, 4). Additionally, the speaker in 61:1 (NETS) proclaims release for captives and sight for the blind, which recalls the servant's task:

  to open the eyes of the blind,
  to bring out from bonds those who are bound
    and from the prison house those who sit in darkness. (42:7 NETS;
      cf. 49:9)[43]

---

40 Though the connection is less apparent in English, the shared words *aphesis* ("liberty") and *apostellō* ("send") in Greek link these verses. This combination of Isa. 61:1–2 and 58:6 may reflect the interpretive practice of *gezerah shavah* ("verbal analogy") or may follow a Jewish precedent for reading these texts together, according to Pao and Schnabel, "Luke," 289.

41 House, *Isaiah*, 2:635. See J. Alec Motyer, *Isaiah: An Introduction and Commentary*, TOTC 20 (Downers Grove, IL: InterVarsity Press, 1999), 430. Alternatively, "I" in verse 10 may refer to redeemed Zion, as argued by Oswalt, *The Book of Isaiah*, 2:574.

42 For a survey of interpretive options, see Abernethy, *The Book of Isaiah and God's Kingdom*, 161–62.

43 House, *Isaiah*, 2:637.

This individual also reverses Israel's injustice and apathy by carrying out the work that God calls his acceptable fast in Isaiah 58:6 (a text Jesus alludes to in Luke 4:18). Moreover, he is sent to bring healing to the brokenhearted (Isa. 61:1), which recalls the Lord's promises to heal his people's wounds (30:26; 57:18–19), as well as the servant's wounds that heal sinners (53:5). Thus, the figure in 61:1–3 "speaks in the voice and takes on the role of the servant."[44]

The first words Jesus reads from Isaiah's scroll—"The Spirit of the Lord is upon me" (Luke 4:18)—declare what the Gospel has already narrated: Jesus has been conceived by the Spirit (1:35), endowed with the Spirit at his baptism (3:22), led by the Spirit into the wilderness and out again (4:1, 14), and will baptize with the Spirit (3:16). Peter later explains that "God anointed Jesus of Nazareth with the Holy Spirit and with power" (Acts 10:38). So in his hometown, Jesus draws upon Isaiah's prophecy to assert that the divine Spirit rests on him.[45]

The rest of the Isaiah quotation summarizes the aims of Jesus's Spirit-anointed ministry. God sent him to proclaim (1) good news to the poor, (2) liberty to the captives and the oppressed, (3) recovery of sight to the blind, and (4) the Lord's favor. Let's consider how Jesus's ministry fulfills these purposes.

First, Jesus is "to proclaim good news to the poor" (Luke 4:18). Earlier in this Gospel, angels and the Baptist announce good news (1:19; 2:10; 3:18). Soon after he leaves Nazareth, Jesus declares, "*I must preach the good news of the kingdom of God to the other towns as well; for I was sent for this purpose*" (4:43). This gospel of the kingdom that Jesus proclaims likely recalls Isaiah's prophecy of heralds of good news declaring that "God reigns" and is coming to save his people (Isa. 40:9–11; 52:7). Later, Jesus tells John's wondering disciples to tell the imprisoned prophet "what you have seen and heard: the blind receive their sight, the lame walk, lepers are cleansed, and the deaf hear, the dead are raised up, *the poor have good news preached to them*" (Luke 7:22).[46] This verse clearly echoes Jesus's quotation from Isaiah

---

44 Beers, *The Followers of Jesus*, 44. "It seems likely that both Matthew and Luke would have identified Isa 61:1–2 as a Servant passage," according to Joseph Blenkinsopp, *Opening the Sealed Book: Interpretations of the Book of Isaiah in Late Antiquity* (Grand Rapids, MI: Eerdmans, 2006), 162.

45 See Max Turner, *Power from on High: The Spirit in Israel's Restoration and Witness in Luke-Acts*, JPTSup 9 (Sheffield: Sheffield Academic, 1996), 213.

46 These examples are representative, not exhaustive; the verb *euaggelizō* ("proclaim good news") occurs ten times in the Gospel of Luke and another fifteen times in Acts.

61:1–2, as well as other prophecies announcing the era of salvation, such as Isaiah 35:4–6. Jesus specifies that *the poor* receive good news (Luke 4:18; 7:22; cf. Isa. 61:1), which highlights this Gospel's significant emphasis on the poor, marginalized, and outcasts. These people humbly receive Jesus's mercy and welcome God's kingdom, while the rich and proud typically refuse to repent and follow Christ.[47] For example, Jesus asserts that the poor are blessed (Luke 6:20), he directs those planning a feast to "invite the poor" and other unlikely guests (14:13; cf. 14:21), and he singles out a poor widow as the consummate example of generosity (21:1–4). Moreover, Zacchaeus's offer to give half his possessions to the poor shows that salvation has indeed come to his house (19:8–9); his generosity also contrasts sharply with the rich man who shows no concern for Lazarus (16:19–21) and the ruler whose wealth keeps him from following Jesus (18:18–25). Luke's emphasis on the poor shows that "the gospel is truly for everyone."[48]

Second, Jesus's mission is to proclaim "liberty" to the captives and the oppressed. The word "liberty" occurs twice in this Isaiah citation and translates the Greek word *aphesis*, which means "the act of freeing and liberating" from confinement, obligation, or punishment.[49] The only occurrences of *aphesis* in Isaiah LXX come in 58:6 and 61:1, which explains the combined reference to these texts in Luke 4:18–19. Elsewhere in Luke's writings, *aphesis* consistently refers to "the forgiveness of sins" for those who repent and receive God's salvation.[50] This suggests that the liberty Jesus proclaims is not release from mere physical captivity or oppression, but from the deeper spiritual bondage to sin. Moreover, Jesus not only speaks of this liberty, like John the Baptist and other prophets; he also secures it as the messianic Savior, in whose name forgiveness is heralded. Jesus's announcement of *aphesis* at the beginning of his public ministry anticipates his teaching after Emmaus about repentance leading to forgiveness (*aphesis*) for all nations (24:47).[51]

---

47 For a careful study contrasting repentant and unrepentant characters in Luke's Gospel, see Ovey, *The Feasts of Repentance*, 11–34.

48 Bock, *A Theology of Luke and Acts*, 352.

49 BDAG, 155.

50 In addition to Luke 4:18, *aphesis* occurs in Luke 1:77; 3:3; 24:47; Acts 2:38; 5:31; 10:43; 13:38; 26:18.

51 This link between Luke 4:18 and 24:47 is also noted by Mallen, *The Reading and Transformation of Isaiah in Luke-Acts*, 80; and Moore, "The Lucan Great Commission," 51–52.

Third, Jesus announces that "the blind" will receive sight, which recalls prophecies of the coming age of salvation, when "the eyes of the blind shall be opened" (Isa. 35:5). Yet Isaiah also chides Israel and Judah for their metaphorical blindness and deafness toward God and his word—they see without perceiving and hear without understanding (6:9–10), and have come to resemble their idols, which cannot see, hear, speak, or save.[52] Thus, malfunctioning eyes and ears represent the people's spiritual condition before God, and only God can reverse their plight, bringing them out of darkness and granting them true sight and hearing (29:18). Jesus restores sight to many who are blind (Luke 7:21; cf. 18:35–43), signaling the inbreaking of the promised age of salvation. Yet he also explains that it is futile for one blind man to lead another (6:39); the parallel account in Matthew 15:12–14 calls the Pharisees "blind guides." Moreover, Jesus speaks in parables "so that seeing they may not see" (Luke 8:10).[53] Even his own disciples fail to grasp the sort of Messiah he truly is (18:31–34), and they need the Lord to remove their cataracts that they might truly see him and his purposes according to the Scriptures (24:45).

Fourth, God sends Jesus "to proclaim the year of the Lord's favor" (Luke 4:19). Isaiah's words may recall the Old Testament Year of Jubilee, a time of "liberty" (Lev. 25:10) that prescribed canceling debts, releasing bondservants, and returning property to its original owners.[54] Isaiah 49:8 similarly describes the day of salvation as "a time of favor."[55] The Old Testament prophets employ Jubilee imagery to describe the full-orbed liberty of the age of redemption and restoration.[56] The point of Jesus's quotation in Luke 4:19 is not to demand that the people of Nazareth return land and cancel debts, but to stress that he is the one sent by God to bring salvation.[57]

---

52 See also Isa. 29:9–10; 42:18–20; 43:8; 59:10. This link between the people's idolatry and their spiritual blindness and deafness is persuasively shown by Beale, *We Become What We Worship*, 41–51 (and throughout the book).

53 For discussion of this allusion to Isa. 6:9 and Luke's presentation of Jesus as the dishonored prophet, see chap. 2, pp. 44–46.

54 House, *Isaiah*, 2:637–38.

55 Paul cites Isa. 49:8 and proclaims that "now is the favorable time" in 2 Cor. 6:2.

56 See Chris Bruno, "Jesus Is Our Jubilee . . . But How? The OT Background and Lukan Fulfillment of the Ethics of Jubilee," *JETS* 53 (2010): 94, 98.

57 Bock, *Luke*, 1:410. Scholars have often noted that Jesus's citation of Isa. 61:1–2 concludes with "the Lord's favor," immediately before the prophet's reference to "the day of vengeance of our God." Luke's account omits this reference to divine judgment "to suppress . . . a negative aspect of

Jesus's recorded "sermon" on Isaiah is brief yet emphatic: "Today this Scripture has been fulfilled in your hearing" (Luke 4:21). Jesus's meaning is plain yet unprecedented: *he* is the one of whom Isaiah wrote, the Spirit is on *him*, *he* is anointed to proclaim good news and liberty. Jesus's stress on Scripture's fulfillment at the outset of his public ministry previews his climactic claim that "everything written about me in the Law of Moses and the Prophets and the Psalms must be fulfilled" (24:44).

Strikingly, immediately after proclaiming the Lord's *favor* (*dektos*), Jesus highlights that no prophet is *accepted* (*dektos*) in his hometown (Luke 4:24). He then reminds the people of Nazareth that God sent Elijah to minister to a Gentile widow and that Elisha healed the Syrian Naaman rather than Israel's lepers (vv. 25–27), summarizing 1 Kings 17:8–24 and 2 Kings 5:1–14. These familiar Old Testament stories illustrate the proverb in Luke 4:24 and serve as a warning to those who will soon spurn the Lord's anointed servant. They also anticipate events later in Jesus's ministry. The Lord also raises a widow's only son, recalling Elijah's miracle in Zarephath and prompting onlookers to identify him as "a great prophet" (7:11–16). Likewise, he heals ten lepers—including a Samaritan "foreigner" who demonstrates true faith (17:11–19). Jesus tells John's disciples that "lepers are cleansed . . . the dead are raised up, the poor have good news preached to them" (7:22), combining the language of Isaiah 61:1 (cited in Luke 4:18) with references to his miracles that parallel those of Elijah and Elisha (cited in 4:25–27). Further, Jesus's appeal to these two great Israelite prophets ministering to those outside Israel also points to the Old Testament hope that Gentiles would receive God's salvation and be included in his people.[58] In fact, it is Christ's very mention of the prophets' ministry to those outside of Israel that enrages the people of Nazareth (4:28).[59] As Simeon earlier identified Jesus as "a light for revelation to the Gentiles" (2:32), so also the Nazareth scene

---

the Isaianic message," according to Green, *The Gospel of Luke*, 209–10. But the Gospels include various references to coming judgment (including John the Baptist's warning in Luke 3:17). It is tenuous to speculate on what New Testament authors do not quote from their sources—Jesus's quotation also leaves out Isaiah's line "to comfort all who mourn," which is hardly negative! More likely, the quotation ends with "the Lord's favor" to stress the portion of Isa. 61 that Jesus "fulfills" in his first coming (note Luke 4:21).

58 See Pao, *Acts and the Isaianic New Exodus*, 78–84.

59 Jesus's rejection at Nazareth parallels Acts 22:21–22, where the Jewish crowd demands Paul's life as soon as he mentions his commission to the Gentiles.

in 4:16–30 "grounds the Gentile mission in the ministry and proclamation of Jesus from its very beginning."[60]

Thus, Jesus defines his mission according to Isaiah 61:1–2. He begins his public ministry with the stunning claim that *he* is the Lord's Spirit-anointed agent sent to proclaim good news to the poor and liberty to captives (Luke 4:18–19). Surprisingly, Christ heralds favor and forgiveness to those on the margins—the poor, captives, blind, and oppressed—while his Nazareth neighbors drive away "Joseph's son" (vv. 22–29). Jesus's message of liberty anticipates the preaching about forgiveness of sins that will go forth to the nations (24:47). This pivotal passage also prepares us for Christ's most explicit statement of his mission "to seek and to save the lost" in 19:10.

Seeking the Lost (Luke 19:10)

Jesus sets his face for Jerusalem in Luke 9:51, and for the next ten chapters he journeys toward the city that kills the prophets until he draws near as the coming king (19:28–40), the weeping prophet (vv. 41–44), and the Lord entering his house (vv. 45–46).[61] Jesus's encounter with Zacchaeus is perhaps the climactic scene of this lengthy travel narrative, as salvation comes to the house of a notorious tax collector whose life is radically changed by Jesus (vv. 1–10). This scene concludes with Jesus's summary of his mission: "For the Son of Man came to seek and to save the lost" (v. 10). The conjunction "for" signals that this statement explains why salvation has come to Zacchaeus (v. 9). This verse also effectively distills some of the major emphases of Jesus's teaching and mission in Luke's Gospel while alluding to God's promise to seek out and rescue the lost sheep of Israel (Ezek. 34:11–24).

As Jesus journeys through Jericho toward Jerusalem, he meets a man named Zacchaeus (Luke 19:1–2; cf. 18:31). Luke introduces him as a chief

---

60 Jeffrey S. Siker, "'First to the Gentiles': A Literary Analysis of Luke 4:16–30," *JBL* 111 (1992): 89.

61 Luke 9:51 is widely recognized as the beginning of Jesus's journey to Jerusalem, though interpreters debate where precisely this travel narrative concludes. I agree with François Bovon's assessment of the book's narrative structure: "Luke divides the life of Jesus into three literary units. Jesus is active chiefly in Galilee (4:14–9:50), he then teaches and performs healings on the way to Jerusalem (9:51 probably to 19:27), and he finally concludes his saving activity in Jerusalem with a last series of teachings in the temple, and his suffering, death, resurrection, and ascension (19:28–24:53)." *Luke 1*, 2.

tax collector, which reminds readers of Jesus's call of Levi the tax collector (5:27) and his parable of the proud Pharisee and the humble tax collector (18:9–14). While tax collectors in that day were "almost universally despised,"[62] Luke's Gospel presents them as examples of repentance and discipleship. But Zacchaeus is also "rich" (19:2), and Jesus warns that it is difficult for the wealthy to enter God's kingdom—as the rich young ruler illustrates (18:23, 25). The theme of seeking frames this poignant passage: Zacchaeus is *seeking* (*ezētei*) to see Jesus (19:3), but in the end we see that the Lord has come *to seek* (*zētēsai*) the lost—including Zacchaeus (v. 10). When Jesus insists that he "must" stay at the tax collector's house, Zacchaeus welcomes him with joy (vv. 5–6). However, onlookers grumble about Jesus receiving hospitality from "a sinner" (v. 7). The tax collector then declares to "the Lord" that he intends to give half his possessions to the poor and to restore fourfold what he has defrauded (v. 8). Jesus responds that salvation has come to his house "today" (v. 9).

Joel Green argues that this episode is not a conversion story, since Luke does not mention Zacchaeus's need to repent and exercise faith. Rather, he explains the reference to "salvation" in Luke 19:9 to indicate "Zacchaeus's vindication and restoration to the community of God's people."[63] However, the close link between verses 9 and 10 strongly suggests that "salvation" has come to Zacchaeus's house because Jesus is there, and he has come to seek and save "lost" people.[64] Jesus's previous dealings with sinners and tax collectors also establish a framework for understanding his encounter with a notorious "chief tax collector" and "sinner" (vv. 2, 7). Earlier, when the Pharisees and scribes grumble about his table fellowship with "tax collectors and sinners," Jesus responds, "I have not come to call the righteous but sinners to repentance" (5:30, 32). Luke doesn't use the word "repentance" in 19:1–10, but the tax collector's

---

62   Green, *The Gospel of Luke*, 669. The Roman statesman Cicero wrote that "those means of livelihood are rejected as undesirable which incur people's ill-will, as those of tax gatherers and usurers." *On Duties*, trans. Walter Miller, LCL 30 (Cambridge, MA: Harvard University Press, 1913), 1.150.

63   Green, *The Gospel of Luke*, 672.

64   Monique Cuany, "'Today, Salvation Has Come to This House': God's Salvation of God's People in Luke's Gospel," *CurTM* 45.4 (2018): 15n10. Jesus's healing of the blind beggar (Luke 18:35–43) and his encounter with Zacchaeus (19:1–10) offer two paradigms of what conversion entails, according to Talbert, *Reading Luke*, 204–5.

joyful reception of Jesus, his generosity toward the poor, and his desire to make restitution for past wrongs show repentance at work. Zacchaeus is not merely misunderstood, marginalized by society, or misguided in his vocational pursuits and financial dealings; apart from the Lord Jesus, he is "lost," and the Son of Man seeks, saves, and transforms this sinner into a true "son of Abraham" (vv. 9–10).

Thus, Zacchaeus typifies Jesus's mission to seek and save lost people.[65] This theme of seeking what is lost recalls Jesus's parables of the lost sheep, the lost coin, and the lost son in Luke 15. The shepherd finds his lost sheep, so he rejoices and calls his neighbors to rejoice with him. The woman who finds her lost silver coin responds in the same way. Both parables illustrate the joy in heaven when even one sinner repents (vv. 7, 10). In the third parable, the son who squandered his inheritance realizes that he is lost (v. 17); when he returns, the father calls for celebration because "he was *lost*, and is found" (v. 32).

Significantly, the Son of Man's mission statement in Luke 19:10 also alludes to Ezekiel 34. In this prophecy, the Lord indicts Israel's shepherds for feeding themselves but neglecting their sheep. According to verse 4, they have ruled harshly but have not strengthened the weak, healed the sick, bandaged the injured, brought back the strays, or *sought out the lost* (LXX *to apolōlos ouk ezētēsate*). Thus, the Lord expresses his opposition to these self-serving shepherds while reaffirming his own commitment to rescue his sheep (v. 10).[66] The Lord declares that he will shepherd his people in precisely the ways that their worthless leaders have failed:

> I will seek the lost [LXX *to apolōlos zētēsō*], and I will bring back the strayed, and I will bind up the injured, and I will strengthen the weak, and the fat and the strong I will destroy. I will feed them in justice. . . . I will *rescue* [LXX *sōsō*] my flock; they shall no longer be a prey. (Ezek. 34:16, 22)

He then promises, "I will set up over them one *shepherd*, my servant David" (Ezek. 34:23). This word recalls the Lord's original directive for David to shepherd Israel (2 Sam. 5:2; 7:7), as well as the prophetic hope

65 Ovey, *The Feasts of Repentance*, 31. See Tannehill, *The Narrative Unity of Luke-Acts*, 1:125.

66 Daniel I. Block, *The Book of Ezekiel*, 2 vols., NICOT (Grand Rapids, MI: Eerdmans, 1997–1998), 2:285.

of a future messianic King to rule God's people with wisdom and justice (Jer. 23:5).[67]

How, then, does this Old Testament backdrop inform our understanding of Jesus's mission in Luke 19:10? Elsewhere, Luke's Gospel presents Jesus as the messianic ruler who will sit on David's throne (1:32–33; 2:11). Acts then narrates how the northern kingdom of Samaria receives God's word and is included under the rule of the Lord Jesus, fulfilling the prophetic hopes for restored Davidic rule over Israel (Ezek. 34:23–24; 37:24–25).[68] Thus, some interpreters see Jesus acting as this prophesied Davidic shepherd who cares for God's people.[69] However, Luke 19:10 more precisely alludes to the Lord's promise that *he* would search for and save his lost and scattered people (Ezek. 34:16, 22). Jesus's mission statement signals that he has come to accomplish what God himself resolved to do for his people.[70] Thus, "*Jesus* acts in the place of *God* and realizes what had been announced by the prophets as *God's* salvific action for Israel."[71] Throughout this Gospel, the Pharisees and scribes stridently object to Jesus's fellowship with tax collectors and sinners.[72] By chafing against Christ's mission "to call . . . sinners to repentance" and "to seek and to save the lost" (Luke 5:32; 19:10), these Jewish leaders oppose God's own expressed commitment to his lost people in Ezekiel 34:11–24. Thus, they also take the place of the worthless shepherds in verses 2–10, who neglect the flock and must be removed. Jesus's encounter with Zacchaeus shows that he is the divine Shepherd who sees, seeks, and saves even the most notorious sinners.

Conclusion

Jesus declares that the mission to proclaim forgiveness of sins "to all nations" fulfills what has been "written" long ago in Israel's Scriptures (Luke 24:46–47). Together with verses 48–49, Jesus here anticipates the narra-

---

67　The many parallels with Jer. 23:1–6 suggest that Ezek. 34 alludes to this earlier prophecy, according to Block, *The Book of Ezekiel*, 2:275–76.

68　See Alan J. Thompson, *The Acts of the Risen Lord Jesus: Luke's Account of God's Unfolding Plan*, NSBT 27 (Downers Grove, IL: InterVarsity Press, 2011), 115–16.

69　Nolland, *Luke*, 3:907; and Jipp, *The Messianic Theology of the New Testament*, 94.

70　Jesus's "Good Shepherd" discourse in John 10 similarly draws upon the prophecies in Ezek. 34 and 37. See Andreas J. Köstenberger, "John," in *Commentary on the New Testament Use of the Old Testament*, 462–63.

71　Wolter, *The Gospel according to Luke*, 2:350, emphasis original.

72　See Luke 5:30; 7:39; 15:2; 19:7.

tive of Acts: the exalted Lord pours out the promised Spirit on the day of Pentecost, and his witnesses proclaim repentance and forgiveness "in Jerusalem and in all Judea and Samaria, and to the end of the earth" (Acts 1:8). Jesus sets his face toward Jerusalem in Luke 9:51, and Luke recounts his deliberate journey toward the city where he accomplishes "everything that is written about the Son of Man" by his crucifixion and resurrection (18:31). Jerusalem is the geographic finish line of Luke's Gospel and the starting line for the mission of Jesus's witnesses in Acts. Christ's last words in this Gospel certainly *preview* coming attractions of Acts, but they also *review* the significant emphasis on the good news of God's salvation that Jesus proclaims and also embodies. He is the promised Messiah as well as the Lord of the new exodus. His coming represents good news for "all the people" of Israel, but also salvation for "all flesh" (2:10; 3:6).

This chapter has considered four crucial passages in Luke's Gospel that explain Jesus's identity, mission, and saving work in light of Old Testament prophecy. First, Simeon cradles the Christ child and acclaims him as the embodiment of God's promised salvation, bringing light to the Gentiles and glory to Israel (Luke 2:30–32; cf. Isa. 49:6). Second, a lengthy citation of Isaiah 40:3–5 not only explains John's wilderness ministry but also clarifies the scope of the new exodus salvation that *the Lord* Jesus brings (Luke 3:4–6). Third, Jesus announces that he is the Lord's Spirit-anointed agent sent to preach good news to the poor and liberty to captives (Luke 4:18–19; Isa. 61:1–2). Jesus's rejection in his hometown also aligns him with the Old Testament prophets and anticipates the coming opposition within Israel and the extension of salvation to the Gentiles (Luke 4:24–27). His message of "liberty" (*aphesis*) also anticipates the global proclamation of "forgiveness [*aphesis*] of sins . . . in his name to all nations," according to 24:47. Finally, Jesus explains that he has come "to seek and to save the lost," which alludes to God's own commitment to shepherd his lost and scattered sheep (19:10; Ezek. 34:16, 22). Jesus's meeting with Zacchaeus powerfully illustrates his mission to seek and find even the most lost sinners. Christ's mission to seek and save lost people—including the Gentiles—sets the stage for the narrative of Acts, as Jesus's witnesses proclaim good news in his name and carry out his mission to the end of the earth (Acts 1:8).

5

The Incorruptible Christ

The Apostles' Preaching in Acts

Being therefore a prophet, and knowing that God had sworn with an
oath to him that he would set one of his descendants on his throne,
he foresaw and spoke about the resurrection of the Christ, that
he was not abandoned to Hades, nor did his flesh see corruption.
This Jesus God raised up, and of that we all are witnesses.

ACTS 2:30–32

FEW CHARACTERS IN LITERATURE undergo as dramatic a change as Ebenezer Scrooge. He's the consummate miser: a mean, stingy, lonely man who considers everything—even Christmas—a "humbug." Charles Dickens introduces him this way: "Scrooge! A squeezing, wrenching, grasping, scraping, clutching, covetous, old sinner!"[1] But on Christmas Eve, on the seventh anniversary of the death of his business partner, Jacob Marley, Scrooge receives a terrifying visit from Marley's ghost. Marley warns Scrooge to change his ways to avoid his own miserable fate and tells him to expect three more spirits. First, the Ghost of Christmas Past reveals to Scrooge "shadows of things that have been," including the scene when Belle breaks off her engagement to Scrooge because of his idolatrous pursuit of wealth. Next, the Ghost of Christmas Present transports Scrooge to the humble home

---

1 Charles Dickens, *A Christmas Carol*, repr. ed. (Cambridge, MA: Candlewick, 2006), 8.

of his clerk, Bob Cratchit, who gushes gladness and gratitude during his family's Christmas "feast." Ebenezer then glimpses his jovial nephew, Fred, who proposes a toast to his uncle's health. Finally, the Ghost of Christmas Yet to Come shows Scrooge several sad scenes, finally revealing a neglected gravestone bearing Ebenezer's name. When he awakes in his own bed, he resolves to make amends for his past misdeeds and becomes "as good a friend, as good a master, and as good a man, as the good old city knew."[2] Scrooge requires dramatic external intervention from the visiting spirits to see the emptiness of his pursuit of money and the beauty of others' joy and kindness. This new perspective on himself and others brings about a total transformation of his life.

Christ's apostles undergo a similarly radical change. The Gospels offer a mixed portrait of Jesus's band. They commendably leave everything to follow Christ, yet they consistently lack faith and fail to grasp Jesus's true identity and mission. They are terrified in the storm while Jesus rests peacefully. They worry about lunch right after Christ feeds four thousand people. They misunderstand Jesus's teaching about his coming suffering. They want to call down fire on the Samaritans. They argue about who is the greatest on the very night they share the final Passover meal with Jesus. They sleep in Gethsemane while Jesus struggles in prayer. One of the twelve betrays the King for the going rate of a slave. The others flee when the soldiers come to arrest Jesus. The most brazen disciple denies his Lord before a servant girl and some strangers.[3] Readers might wonder why Jesus chose such a bungling band of disciples.

Yet Acts presents a starkly different picture of Jesus's followers. They preach with courage and clarity. They rejoice when they suffer. They cannot stop speaking about Jesus despite threats from the authorities. They even pray for Samaritans to receive the Spirit. This most unlikely crew turns the world upside down.[4] Their radical transformation does not come after a period of many years, but only days after Jesus ascends to heaven. What causes these disciples to change their doubting, disputing, denying, disappearing ways? It's not visits from Christmas ghosts or personal resolutions,

---

2   Dickens, *A Christmas Carol*, 158.
3   For these examples, see Mark 4:35–41; 8:14–21, 31–33; Luke 9:52–54; 22:24, 45–46; Matt. 26:15, 56, 69–75.
4   For these examples, see Acts 4:13, 18–20; 5:40–42; 8:14–17; 17:6.

but their encounter with the risen Lord Jesus that makes all the difference. He gives them *clarity* to perceive the Bible's teaching about his suffering and resurrection as well as *courage* to proclaim this news by the promised Spirit.

The Courage and Clarity of Christ's Witnesses (Acts 4:11–13)

Acts 4 offers important insight into the remarkable 180-degree turnaround for these disciples. Peter and John's healing miracle and preaching in the temple precincts in chapter 3 provokes stiff opposition from the temple authorities. They arrest the apostles, who are then questioned by the high priest and the Jewish council—the same body that condemned their Lord a few weeks earlier (Acts 4:1–6, 15; cf. Luke 22:66–71). Peter speaks with courage and clarity to this hostile assembly, declaring that Jesus is "the stone that was rejected by you, the builders"; thus, Christ is the only source of salvation (Acts 4:11–12). Luke records the Sanhedrin's reaction in verse 13: "Now when they saw the boldness of Peter and John, and perceived that they were uneducated, common men, they were astonished. And they recognized that they had been with Jesus." Notice two key points in this verse.

First, the apostles preach with *boldness*. The Greek word *parrēsia* is variously translated "boldness" (ESV), "courage" (NIV), and "confidence" (NASB). Outside the Bible, this word expresses a person's freedom to speak frankly.[5] In Acts, the noun *parrēsia* and the related verb *parrēsiazomai* convey the bold, open statement of the truth by Jesus's witnesses even in the face of opposition.[6] This boldness is closely tied to the supernatural empowerment of the Holy Spirit. In Acts 4:8, Peter is "filled with the Holy Spirit" and boldly addresses the Sanhedrin. Likewise, in verse 31, the gathered believers are "filled with the Holy Spirit" and continue speaking God's word "with boldness." The closing verse of Acts describes Paul's bold, unhindered preaching about the kingdom of God and the Lord Jesus even as he is under house arrest in Rome (28:31).

Second, the Jewish leaders perceive that the apostles *have been with Jesus*. Compared to the Jewish elite, these men are "unschooled" and "ordinary" (NIV). These adjectives do not mean that the apostles cannot read and write, but that they lack the extensive, formal biblical training of the scribes.[7] How,

---

5   See *NIDNTTE*, 3:657–58; and LSJ, 1344.

6   For examples and discussion, see Thompson, *The Acts of the Risen Lord Jesus*, 96–99.

7   Eckhard J. Schnabel, *Acts*, ZECNT (Grand Rapids, MI: Zondervan, 2012), 243.

then, do they speak so clearly and confidently? The council concludes that the apostles' schooling derives another source—Jesus himself. It is noteworthy that Peter alludes to Psalm 118:22 when calling Jesus "the cornerstone" (Acts 4:11).[8] Jesus quotes this text at the close of the parable of the wicked tenants in Luke 20:17. He tells this parable immediately after his authority is questioned by the chief priests, scribes, and elders (vv. 1–2)—precisely the group that interrogates Peter and John in Acts 4:5. The apostles make explicit that these Jewish leaders are "the builders" of Psalm 118:22, who have spurned "the stone"—the Davidic king—that God chose as "the cornerstone of the true temple."[9] Following Jesus's own teaching that the Messiah must be "rejected" following the script of Psalm 118:22 (cf. Luke 9:22; 17:25), his apostles appeal to the same psalm in the same way before the same Jewish leaders that rejected their Lord.[10] The Spirit-brought courage and Christ-taught clarity that the disciples demonstrate in Acts 4 is evident throughout Luke's second book, as Jesus's witnesses open the Scriptures to preach about the cross and the empty tomb.

This chapter considers how the apostles proclaim both the Messiah's suffering and his resurrection according to the Scriptures, following the pattern that they learned from Jesus after Emmaus. I have already shown that the apostles reiterate Christ's own explanation of his rejection from Psalm 118:22. Let's now examine three other scriptural supports for the Son's suffering and three biblical proofs for the resurrection in Acts. Jesus's witnesses explain that he is the Lord's anointed against whom the nations rage (Ps. 2:1–2), the cursed one hung on the tree (Deut. 21:23), and the lamb-like servant led to the slaughter (Isa. 53:7–8).[11] Moreover, they

---

8   Jesus's use of Ps. 118:22 in Luke 20:17 is discussed further in chap. 2, pp. 46–48. First Peter 2:7 also cites this psalm; see chap. 7, pp. 193–99.

9   Beale, *The Temple and the Church's Mission*, 216. Beale discusses Jesus's use of Ps. 118 on pp. 183–88.

10   Acts 4:11 uses the Greek verb *exoutheneō* for "reject" instead of *apodokimazō*, the verb used in Luke 20:17 and Ps. 118:22 (117:22 LXX). While these verbs may both be rendered "reject," *exoutheneō* conveys rejection or maltreatment with an attitude of disdain (BDAG, 352), as in Luke 23:11, where Herod and his soldiers treat Jesus with contempt.

11   Due to space constraints, I do not offer a detailed treatment of Peter's appeal to Ps. 69:25 ("May his camp become desolate, and let there be no one to dwell in it") and Ps. 109:8 ("Let another take his office") in Acts 1:20. Peter insists that "the Scripture had to be fulfilled" concerning Judas's betrayal of Jesus (v. 16) and the appointment of another apostle to take his place (vv. 21–26). It is noteworthy that Peter cites Ps. 69 (68 LXX), a Davidic psalm frequently used in the New Testament to explain the righteous suffering of David's greater Son, Jesus (see John 2:17; 15:25;

proclaim that Christ is the holy one, who did not see decay (Ps. 16:8–11). Further, his ascension demonstrates that he is the exalted Lord seated at God's right hand (110:1). Finally, Jesus is the Lord's Son raised to rule on David's throne (2:7).

The Suffering Messiah Fulfills the Scriptures

Odysseus, the namesake of Homer's epic *The Odyssey*, is "the most unlucky man alive."[12] All he wants is to go home to his wife and son in Ithaca, but he suffers for years due to unfortunate circumstances, squabbles between the gods, and bad decisions by his mates. Some sympathetic observers might have similarly dubbed Jesus "the most unlucky man," who suffered a terrible fate because of the Jews' jealousy, Pilate's people-pleasing, and his followers' fickleness. One famous theologian described Jesus laying hold of the wheel of the world to bring history to its conclusion: "It refuses to turn, and He throws himself on it. Then it does turn; and crushes Him."[13] This eloquent, influential perspective on Jesus's death is a work of theological fiction according to the book of Acts. The apostles do not present Jesus as a tragic hero who dies because of bad luck. Rather, they declare that he is "delivered up according to the definite plan and foreknowledge of God" (Acts 2:23) and that he suffers to fulfill "what God foretold by the mouth of all the prophets" (3:18). They do not proclaim the all-important death of Jesus as a stand-alone subject because the story does not conclude at Calvary. They preach Christ *crucified, risen, and reigning in heaven.*

The Lord's Anointed (Acts 4:25–28)

When Peter and John report to the church about the Jewish council's hostile threats, the believers unite in prayer to their sovereign Lord (Acts 4:23–24). They respond to suffering with an exemplary prayer shaped by the Scriptures.[14] They recognize God's awesome power as Creator of heaven and earth

---

19:28; Rom. 11:9–10; 15:3; chap. 7, pp. 185–91. As Ps. 69 typifies the Messiah's afflictions and reproach, it also foreshadows those who oppose and reject him, as Judas does by guiding those who arrested Jesus. See David G. Peterson, *The Acts of the Apostles*, PNTC (Grand Rapids, MI: Eerdmans, 2009), 124–25.

12 Homer, *The Odyssey*, trans. Emily R. Wilson (New York: Norton, 2018), 1.219.

13 Albert Schweitzer, *The Quest of the Historical Jesus: A Critical Study of Its Progress from Reimarus to Wrede* (New York: Macmillan, 1968), 370–71.

14 On Acts 4:24–30 as a model prayer, see Tabb, *Suffering in Ancient Worldview*, 170.

(v. 24), employing the language of Psalm 146:6 (145:6 LXX). Then, in Acts 4:25–28, the church interprets the opposition to Jesus and his followers through the lens of Psalm 2:1–2. The believers do not ask for deliverance from suffering but for courage to continue speaking about Christ amid adversity, and God dramatically answers this request (Acts 4:29–31).

The believers cite Psalm 2:1–2 as the words of the sovereign Lord spoken "through the mouth of our father David, your servant, . . . by the Holy Spirit" (Acts 4:25). By stressing God's speech by the Spirit, the believers express their confidence in the outworking of God's wise and sovereign plan according to his word. By calling David "our father," Christ's followers show that they understand themselves to be God's true people, heirs of God's ancient promises.[15] The quotation in verses 25–26 agrees word for word with Psalm 2:1–2:

> Why did the Gentiles rage,
>> and the peoples plot in vain?
> The kings of the earth set themselves,
>> and the rulers were gathered together,
>> against the Lord and against his Anointed.[16]

Scholars often classify Psalm 2 as a "royal" psalm[17] since it refers to the Lord's anointed king, whom God has installed on Zion (vv. 2, 6). The psalm's opening rhetorical question—"Why do the nations rage and the peoples plot in vain?"—expresses the utter futility and hubris of human rebellion against the sovereign Lord, who sits in heaven and laughs (vv. 1, 4). The Lord's decree in verse 7, "You are my Son," reflects his covenant promise to establish the kingdom of David's offspring, who will be "a son" to God (2 Sam. 7:12–14).[18] While the nations rage in Psalm 2:1, the Lord promises them as an inheritance for his royal Son in verse 8. The psalm promises blessing for all who take refuge in the royal Son while warning the earth's rulers to serve the Lord or else face his wrath (vv. 10–12).

---

15 Witherington, *Acts*, 202.

16 The Greek word *christos*, here rendered "Anointed" in the ESV, is also translated "Christ" (NASB) and "Messiah" (CSB).

17 VanGemeren, *Psalms*, 89; and DeClaissé-Walford, Jacobson, and Tanner, *Psalms*, 65.

18 O. Palmer Robertson, *The Flow of the Psalms: Discovering Their Structure and Theology* (Phillipsburg, NJ: P&R, 2015), 14–15.

Psalm 2 is not only one of the Psalter's two "poetic pillars," along with Psalm 1,[19] it is also one of the most frequently referenced psalms in the New Testament. Luke 3:22 alludes to Psalm 2:7 to affirm Jesus's sonship at his baptism, while Acts and Hebrews cite this verse in connection with Christ's resurrection and heavenly enthronement (Acts 13:33; Heb. 1:5; 5:5; cf. Rom. 1:4).[20] Revelation alludes to Psalm 2:9 to express Christ's regal authority over the nations, authority that his followers share (Rev. 2:27; 12:5; 19:15).[21]

In Acts 4:25–28, the church cites this pillar psalm to explain the united opposition to the Christ and his followers. The Old Testament regularly recounts the nations' proud hostility toward the Lord and his anointed sovereign, and this pattern reaches its climax in Christ's crucifixion. The believers in Acts summarize Jesus's passion narrative using the language of Psalm 2 to stress the correspondence between the biblical text and its fulfillment:[22]

> "Why did *the Gentiles* rage,
>   and *the peoples* plot in vain?
> The kings of the earth set themselves,
>   and the rulers *were gathered together*,
>   against the Lord and against *his Anointed*" —

for truly in this city there *were gathered together* against your holy servant Jesus, *whom you anointed*, both Herod and Pontius Pilate, along with *the Gentiles and the peoples* of Israel, to do whatever your hand and your plan had predestined to take place. (Acts 4:25–28)

It is no surprise that the Gentiles rage against the Lord's anointed one, but ironically, "the peoples of Israel" and the Jewish rulers join this opposition. Yet the believers affirm God's sovereign power and discern his wise plan worked out in this shocking conspiracy against the Messiah. The Gentile

---

19 Robertson, *The Flow of the Psalms*, 13.

20 The citation of Ps. 2:7 in Acts 13:33 is discussed below, pp. 128–33.

21 Cf. Brian J. Tabb, *All Things New: Revelation as Canonical Capstone*, NSBT 48 (London: Apollos, 2019), 92, 203.

22 This is an example of Jewish "pesher" interpretation ("this is that"), according to Richard N. Longenecker, "Acts," in *Luke–Acts*, ed. David E. Garland, EBC 10, rev. ed. (Grand Rapids, MI: Zondervan, 2007), 745.

and Jewish antagonism to Jesus remarkably fulfills the secret purposes of God when seen in the light of Psalm 2:1–2.

The believers see Christ's crucifixion as the clear plan of God as revealed in the Scriptures, and this perspective helps them to make sense of the "threats" they experience from the Jewish leaders (Acts 4:29). The disciples identify themselves as the Lord's "slaves," who are opposed just like God's holy "servant" and now entreat God to act in Jesus's name (vv. 27, 29–30). They recognize that the conspiracy against Christ carries out the script of Psalm 2 and thus fulfills God's secret purposes. The disciples' understanding of Christ's suffering according to the Scriptures gives them confidence to endure adversity and speak God's words with clarity and courage (Acts 4:31).

Cursed on the Tree (Acts 5:30; 10:39)

The cross is commonplace in contemporary Western culture; we see it on church buildings, necklaces, clothing, and bumper stickers. But in the ancient world, crucifixion was considered scandalous, an unmentionable horror. The Roman author Cicero called crucifixion "the most miserable and most painful punishment appropriate to slaves alone."[23] For Jews, a cross connoted not only the most gruesome instrument of execution, but also the curse of their covenant Lord, since the law stated that "a hanged man is cursed by God" (Deut. 21:23).

The apostle Peter twice declares that the leaders in Jerusalem killed Jesus "by hanging him on a tree [*kremasantes epi xylou*]" (Acts 5:30; 10:39). The Greek verb *kremannymi* ("hang") also appears in Luke 23:39 to refer to the criminals suspended on the crosses on Jesus's right and left. Many interpreters have identified Deuteronomy 21:22–23 as the source behind the phrase "hanging on the tree" in Acts 5:30 and 10:39.[24] This law gives direction regarding the proper treatment of a criminal who is executed "on a tree." The criminal's body should receive burial the same day and not

---

23 Cicero, *Against Verres*, in *The Orations of Marcus Tullius Cicero*, trans. C. D. Yonge (London: George Bell & Sons, 1903), 2.5.169. For additional ancient sources referring to crucifixion, see Eckhard J. Schnabel and David W. Chapman, *The Trial and Crucifixion of Jesus: Texts and Commentary* (Peabody, MA: Hendrickson, 2019).

24 See, for example, M. Wilcox, "'Upon the Tree': Deut. 21:22–23 in the New Testament," *JBL* 96 (1977): 90–94; I. Howard Marshall, "Acts," in *Commentary on the New Testament Use of the Old Testament*, 555; and Benjamin R. Wilson, "'Upon a Tree' Again and Again: Redundancy and Deuteronomy 21:23 in Acts," *Neot* 47 (2013): 47–67.

remain on the tree overnight, "for a hanged man is cursed by God." Hanging a body on a tree does not make the person accursed, but expresses the cursed status of one condemned for breaking God's law.[25]

David Chapman argues that the speeches in Acts do not clearly appeal to Deuteronomy 21:23, since "hanging on the tree" was a standard Jewish idiom for bodily suspension in the first century.[26] However, this expression undoubtedly goes back to Deuteronomy 21:23.[27] We should recognize clear allusions to Deuteronomy 21:23 in Acts 5:30 and 10:39 for several reasons. These speeches employ the precise wording found in the Greek translation of Deuteronomy 21:23 (*kremamenos epi xylou*). Additionally, these references to Deuteronomy fit the legal context of Peter's defense before the Jewish council in Acts 5, where he argues that the Jewish leaders condemned Jesus to death yet God overturned their verdict by exalting him. Later in Acts, Paul similarly refers to Jesus's execution on "the tree" and stresses that his opponents unknowingly fulfilled "all that was written of him" (13:29). Moreover, in Galatians 3:13, Paul explicitly cites Deuteronomy 21:23 to support his claim that Christ redeemed his people from the law's curse by becoming a curse for us. Similarly, 1 Peter 2:24 refers to Jesus bearing our sins "on the tree," combining allusions to Isaiah 53:12 and Deuteronomy 21:23.[28]

Why do the witnesses in Acts link Deuteronomy 21:23 with Jesus's crucifixion? They may intend to stress that Christ's resurrection reverses the Jews' wrongful judgment that he was cursed by God as a blasphemer.[29] While this reading accurately expresses the apologetic thrust of Acts 5:30, Peter and the other witnesses in Acts also stress that the Jewish leaders unknowingly carried out God's plan even as they wrongly condemned Jesus to hang on the tree (cf. 2:23; 13:29). The manner of Jesus's death does not invalidate the early church's Christological claims; rather, his crucifixion actually fulfills the biblical testimony concerning the Messiah's suffering.[30] The sermons in

---

25 Peter Craigie, *The Book of Deuteronomy*, NICOT (Grand Rapids, MI: Eerdmans, 1976), 285; and Mary A. Willson, "'Cursed Is Everyone Who Is Hanged on a Tree': Paul's Citation of Deut 21:23 in Gal 3:13," *TrinJ* 36 (2015): 221.

26 David W. Chapman, *Ancient Jewish and Christian Perceptions of Crucifixion* (Grand Rapids, MI: Baker Academic, 2010), 243–44.

27 Wilson, "'Upon a Tree' Again and Again," 47n2.

28 Wilcox, "Upon the Tree," 93.

29 Bock, *Proclamation from Prophecy and Pattern*, 208–9.

30 Wilson, "'Upon a Tree' Again and Again," 57–58.

Acts do not explicitly mention the curse in Deuteronomy 21:23 and do not explain how Jesus bears the law's curse to redeem his people, as Paul does in Galatians 3:13.[31] Nevertheless, the witnesses demonstrate that Christ's death "on a tree" was not simply the result of a wrong verdict about his character and work. Rather, Christ's execution by means of the cursed cross follows the biblical script and thus validates him as the "Savior, to give repentance to Israel and forgiveness of sins" (Acts 5:31).

The Lamb-Like Servant (Acts 8:28–35)

Philip's meeting with the Ethiopian eunuch remarkably illustrates the Lord Jesus's model of biblical exposition and his message about the Messiah's mission to all nations. Acts 8:26–40 includes a number of parallels with Luke 24:13–35; like the Lord Jesus with the two disciples on the road to Emmaus, Philip encounters a pious traveler journeying home, initiates conversation with a question, explains the Scriptures, and vanishes, leaving the disciple filled with joy.[32] The climax of this passage is the citation of Isaiah 53:7–8, from which Philip explains "the good news about Jesus" to the eunuch (Acts 8:35). Jesus fulfills the Scriptures as the Lord's suffering servant who was deprived of justice and led like a lamb to the slaughter.

The final Servant Song in Isaiah features prominently in Luke-Acts and elsewhere in the New Testament.[33] Jesus emphatically cites the last verse of the final Servant Song as a prelude to his passion in Luke 22:37: "And he was numbered with the transgressors" (Isa. 53:12). He also alludes to Isaiah's servant passages when predicting that he will be handed over, spat upon, and scourged (Luke 18:32–33).[34] Peter also alludes to Isaiah 52:13 when he proclaims that God "glorified his servant Jesus" in Acts 3:13. These repeated references to the fourth Servant Song, combined with the lengthy citation of Isaiah 53:7–8 in Acts 8:32–33, signal that Jesus and his followers do not offer simplistic proof texts but are keenly aware of the context and theology of Isaiah's prophecy.

31 See Willson, "Cursed Is Everyone Who Is Hanged on a Tree," 217–40.
32 For these and other parallels, see Keener, *Acts*, 2:1536.
33 For a seminal treatment of Christ's own use of Isa. 53, see R. T. France, "The Servant of the Lord in the Teaching of Jesus," *TynBul* 19 (1968): 26–52. See also Peter Stuhlmacher, "Isaiah 53 in the Gospels and Acts," in *The Suffering Servant: Isaiah 53 in Jewish and Christian Sources*, 147–62.
34 See chap. 2, pp. 50–56; and Mallen, *The Reading and Transformation of Isaiah in Luke-Acts*, 121n80.

Philip meets the Ethiopian official while he is reading "the prophet Isaiah" (Acts 8:28, 30); the direct involvement of the Lord's angel and the Spirit signals that this is no chance encounter in the desert but the deliberate outworking of God's sovereign plan (vv. 26, 29, 39). The Ethiopian does not understand what he reads and so seeks guidance from Philip. Luke then cites the precise passage that perplexes this pious pilgrim:

> Like a sheep he was led to the slaughter
>> and like a lamb before its shearer is silent,
>> so he opens not his mouth.
> In his humiliation justice was denied him.
>> Who can describe his generation?
> For his life is taken away from the earth. (Acts 8:32–33)

This is a verbatim quotation of Isaiah 53:7–8,[35] which focuses specifically on the servant's innocence, shocking disgrace, and unjust suffering and death.[36] These same emphases appear in Luke's account of Christ's arrest, trial, and crucifixion: Jesus does not answer Herod's questions or his opponents' taunts (Luke 23:9, 35–36), he is "innocent" or "righteous" (*dikaios*) yet condemned as a criminal (v. 47; cf. vv. 4, 14–15, 22, 41), and he is "led" from the garden to the high priest, the council, the governor, and then to his death (22:54, 66; 23:1, 26).[37] The verses cited in Acts 8:32–33 do not explicitly refer to vicarious atonement, yet the depiction of the servant "led to the slaughter" may well suggest the image of a sacrificial victim. It seems quite likely that Luke presents this citation as a signpost to the larger context of Isaiah's prophecy, since the eunuch is reflectively reading the scroll of Isaiah, and Luke's wider narrative elsewhere repeatedly draws upon this well-known servant passage.[38]

---

35 The Greek translation of Isa. 53:7–8 that Luke cites "is for the most part sufficiently like" the Hebrew text, according to Marshall, "Acts," 573.

36 The servant's innocence is the key emphasis, according to Robert F. O'Toole, "How Does Luke Portray Jesus as Servant of YHWH," *Bib* 81 (2000): 331.

37 The Greek verbs *agō* and *apagō* occur in these verses and in Luke 23:32, where the two criminals are also "led away."

38 This quotation "should be understood in terms of the Book of Isaiah's redemptive theology," according to David G. Peterson, "Atonement Theology in Luke-Acts: Some Methodological Reflections," in *The New Testament in Its First Century Setting: Essays on Context and Background*

The eunuch's question in Acts 8:34 reveals that he is stumped by the servant's identity in Isaiah's prophecy: "About whom . . . does the prophet say this, about himself or about someone else?"[39] Philip then explains to him the gospel about Jesus "beginning with this Scripture" (v. 35), which parallels Jesus's exposition "beginning with Moses and all the Prophets" for the disciples on the Emmaus road (Luke 24:27). The narrator makes clear that Philip interprets Isaiah 53 Christologically but does not need to elaborate further, since Christian readers may fill in the details given how Jesus and the apostles elsewhere expound the prophecy of Isaiah.[40]

Luke refers to the traveler from Ethiopia as "the eunuch" five times in Acts 8:27–39. Given the law's restriction on eunuchs entering the assembly of God's people (Deut. 23:1), this official who "had come to Jerusalem to worship" (Acts 8:27) would have been unable to enter the temple beyond the outer court.[41] Yet the Ethiopian who studies the prophet Isaiah and seeks answers from Philip responds eagerly to the good news about Jesus, receives baptism, and goes on his way rejoicing. Luke's narrative deliberately recalls Isaiah 56:3–8, where the Lord promises to give eunuchs "an everlasting name that shall not be cut off" (v. 5), to make foreigners rejoice in his house of prayer that will be "for all peoples" (v. 7), and to gather the outcasts (v. 8).[42] Other prophecies express hope for worshippers "beyond the rivers of Cush," which is another name for Ethiopia (Isa. 18:1, 7; Zeph. 3:10).[43] The servant's suffering and vindication in Isaiah 53 opens the way for even foreigners to be God's servants and for eunuchs to receive a glorious heritage in Isaiah 56. Thus, Acts 8:26–40 signals that the suffering of Jesus fulfills God's script and offers

---

in Honour of B. W. Winter on His 65th Birthday, ed. Peter J. Williams et al. (Grand Rapids, MI: Eerdmans, 2004), 70.

39 Ironically, some scholars downplay the significance of the servant's identity. For example, John Goldingay identifies the prophet as the Lord's servant but claims that the passage's theology is not affected "if it was written about him by someone else, or if it is his vision of some other unidentified person being attacked and vindicated." *The Theology of the Book of Isaiah* (Downers Grove, IL: InterVarsity Press, 2014), 70.

40 Stuhlmacher, "Isaiah 53 in the Gospels and Acts," 157.

41 Keener, *Acts*, 2:1567; and Schnabel, *Acts*, 425.

42 Thompson, *The Acts of the Risen Lord Jesus*, 116–17.

43 The LXX translators render "Cush" as "Ethiopia" in these texts and elsewhere. The "Ethiopian" official in Acts 8:27 comes from the ancient kingdom of Nubia, south of Egypt. See the extended discussion by Keener, *Acts*, 2:1550–65.

good news not only for Israel but also for foreigners and outcasts such as the Ethiopian eunuch.

We have seen several examples in Acts where Jesus's disciples illustrate their Lord's teaching "that the Christ should suffer" according to the Scriptures (Luke 24:46). The apostles boldly proclaim that Jesus is the rejected stone of Psalm 118:22, following Christ's own application of this passage (Acts 4:11; Luke 20:17). The gathered church responds to threats by recognizing that the Jewish and Gentile conspiracy against the messianic King remarkably accomplished God's purposes according to Psalm 2:1–2 (Acts 4:25–28). Peter explains that Jesus's scandalous death "on a tree" (Deut. 21:23) does not invalidate his messianic claims but confirms him as the promised "Savior, to give repentance to Israel and forgiveness of sins" (Acts 5:30–31). Likewise, Philip tells the good news about Jesus beginning with Isaiah's prophecy of the Lord's servant who was unjustly slaughtered (Acts 8:32–35; Isa. 53:7–8). But Jesus not only suffered according to the Scriptures; he also rose to life on the third day (Luke 24:46).

The Risen Lord Fulfills the Scriptures

On January 26, 2020, in Calabasas, California, a helicopter crash claimed the lives of nine passengers, including the legendary basketball player Kobe Bryant (age forty-one) and his daughter (age thirteen).[44] The news sent shockwaves throughout the sports and entertainment worlds, as friends, fans, and fellow athletes expressed their admiration for the superstar and their dismay and disbelief at his untimely death. One athlete commented, "I'm shocked and sad. . . . I thought guys like him lived forever."[45] Lebron James of the Los Angeles Lakers vowed to continue Bryant's legacy and offered a prayer wish to the departed player on social media: "Please give me the strength from the heavens above and watch over me."[46] These tributes to Bryant reflected the anger and angst people have when dealing with death's dark shadow, as well as their hope that death cannot really be the end of the story.

The public response to Bryant's unexpected death reminds us of the sadness and shock of Christ's followers after their Lord was brutally executed

44 Chris Chavez, "Kobe Bryant, Daughter Die in California Helicopter Crash," *Sports Illustrated*, January 28, 2020, http://www.si.com/.

45 Al Iannazzone, "Super Bowl LIV: Chiefs' Tyreek Hill, 49ers' Richard Sherman Express Shock over Kobe Bryant's Tragic Death," *Newsday*, January 28, 2020, http://www.newsday.com/.

46 LeBron James, @kingjames, Instagram post, January 27, 2020, http://www.instagram.com/.

on a hill outside Jerusalem. There were no public vigils to commemorate Jesus's legacy. The apostles did not give interviews to share their fondest memories about him. It was *over*. All their hopes and dreams had been suffocated on the cross and buried in Joseph's tomb. The downcast disciples journeying to Emmaus fittingly expressed the feelings of the faithful: "*We had hoped* that he was the one to redeem Israel" (Luke 24:21). Jesus's lifeless corpse killed the expectations of his disciples.[47] We need to appreciate how devastating Jesus's death was in order to grasp the gladness and glory of the great reversal of resurrection Sunday, when Christ presented himself *alive* to his disciples (Luke 24:39–40; Acts 1:3). The risen Lord then revealed to them how the biblical puzzle fit together, how his suffering and resurrection fulfilled what was written long ago.

Before his ascension into heaven, the risen Lord gives his disciples a new *identity* as his witnesses and promises that they will receive new *power* by the Holy Spirit (Luke 24:48–49; Acts 1:8). This sets the stage for the day of Pentecost, when the gathered disciples are "all filled with the Holy Spirit" and begin to speak in other tongues (Acts 2:4). Peter's foundational sermon in verses 14–36 offers an authoritative interpretation of this remarkable event, explaining that "this is what was uttered through the prophet Joel" (v. 16).[48] While we might expect Peter to offer an extended discussion of the Holy Spirit, he immediately moves from the Joel quotation to proclaim that God raised Jesus after his death (vv. 22–24). Peter bears witness to Christ's resurrection while appealing to Psalm 16:8–11 and Psalm 110:1 (Acts 2:25–35). He concludes that Jesus is the promised Messiah and risen Lord (v. 36). As the exalted Lord, Christ himself has done what God promised by pouring out God's Spirit (v. 33; cf. Joel 2:28), has ushered in the long-awaited "last days" (Acts 2:17; cf. Isa. 2:2), and offers salvation to all who call on his name (Acts 2:21; cf. Joel 2:32).

The book of Acts offers "not simply a few isolated comments . . . but a sustained emphasis" on Christ's resurrection.[49] Thus, this section of the chapter focuses on the foundational biblical arguments for the resurrection

---

47 These three sentences are adapted from Brian Tabb, "The Unexpected God: How He Meets Us in Disappointment," Desiring God, May 8, 2017, http://www.desiringgod.org/. Used with permission.

48 Peter's citation of Joel 2:28–32 (3:1–5 LXX) receives further discussion in chap. 6, pp. 141–47.

49 Crowe, *The Hope of Israel*, 21.

by Peter in his Pentecost speech (Acts 2:14–41) and by Paul in his Antioch sermon (Acts 13:16–41).

The Incorruptible Christ (Acts 2:24–32)

Both Peter and Paul appeal to Psalm 16 as prophetic proof of Jesus's resurrection in Acts 2:24–32 and 13:35. Peter proclaims that the miraculous events of Pentecost fulfill Joel's prophecy that God would pour out his Spirit in the "last days" (2:16–21). The apostle demonstrates that Jesus—the one that his hearers crucified—is the promised Christ and exalted Lord (v. 36), who has poured out the Holy Spirit and now offers salvation for all who call on his name. Peter's sermon in Acts 2 makes clear that the risen Lord has made good on his promise to send the Spirit (Acts 2:33; cf. Luke 24:49; Acts 1:4–5). We also see Peter's *identity* as a "witness" that he received from Christ (Acts 2:32; cf. Luke 24:48; Acts 1:8), as well as his new *interpretation* of the Scriptures that he learned from Christ (Acts 2:15–35; cf. Luke 24:44–47).

Peter supports his assertion that death could not keep hold of Jesus by appealing to what "David says concerning him" (Acts 2:24–25).[50] In verses 25–28, the apostle cites an extended portion of Psalm 16:8–11, a prayer of confidence and trust in the Lord through life and death.[51] The apostle then explains why this psalm offers a biblical rationale for Christ's resurrection. Let's follow Peter's biblical-theological logic in Acts 2:24–32.

Peter insists that he speaks as a witness of Christ's resurrection (Acts 2:32). He did not come to his conclusions about Psalm 16 by careful, independent investigation of the Scriptures. Rather, he went to Jesus's empty tomb (Luke 24:12), saw and touched the risen Lord's hands and feet (24:39–40; cf. Acts 1:3), and learned from Christ himself how he fulfilled the Law, Prophets, and Psalms (Luke 24:44–47). Peter speaks about the resurrection not merely as an informed exegete of the Scriptures but as an eyewitness of Christ's glory.

Further, Peter presupposes that David wrote Psalm 16 and that God spoke by the psalmist's prophetic pen. We typically think of David as the giant slayer, the great king of Israel, and the man after God's heart, but not as a prophet. While the Old Testament nowhere explicitly refers to David as a prophet, 2 Samuel 23:1–2 offers clues to support Peter's claim. This text calls

---

50 Ps. 16 in English and Hebrew Bibles corresponds to Ps. 15 LXX. Peter's quotation precisely follows the Greek translation of this psalm.

51 See VanGemeren, *Psalms*, 185–86.

David God's "anointed" (*christos*) and "the sweet psalmist of Israel," and it records David's "oracle" that opens with the bold claim "The Spirit of the LORD speaks by me." Jesus and his followers affirm the divine inspiration of the Psalms (Mark 12:36; Acts 4:25), and early Jewish authors refer to David's prophetic activity.[52] Thus, Peter concludes that David was a prophet who wrote God's words. He also reminds his hearers that the great David "died and was buried," and points to his well-known tomb nearby.[53] This royal grave proves Peter's point that David's body decayed even though he wrote confidently that the holy one would not see corruption (Ps. 16:10), and thus David's prophetic words must have implications beyond his own life.

Peter also reads Psalm 16 in light of God's covenant promise to David (2 Sam. 7:12–16). The apostle states that David wrote this psalm "knowing that God had sworn with an oath to him that he would set one of his descendants on his throne" (Acts 2:30). Peter here alludes to Psalm 132:11, where the psalmist reflects on the enduring validity of the Davidic covenant and declares that "the LORD swore to David a sure oath from which he will not turn back." At the outset of Luke's Gospel, the angel promised that the Lord would give to Jesus "the throne of his father David" and that he would reign forever (Luke 1:32–33). On Pentecost, Peter does not anticipate Jesus's future kingdom but announces the *present* reign of Christ, who has exercised his authority by sending the Holy Spirit to his people (Acts 2:33).[54]

Thus, the apostle concludes that David in Psalm 16 "foresaw and spoke about the resurrection of the Christ" (Acts 2:31). Peter's conclusion about Psalm 16 is unambiguous, though his hermeneutical approach to this psalm prompts questions. Does the apostle read Psalm 16 as a predictive prophecy that concerns the future Messiah's glory? Or does Psalm 16 refer first to its human author, David, whose description of his own confidence before God presents a pattern—a type—that indirectly predicts the resurrection of the incorruptible Christ? Does the first person "I" throughout the psalm refer

---

52 For example, Josephus comments on 1 Samuel 16:14, "The Deity abandoned Saul and passed over to David, who, when the divine spirit had removed to him, began to prophesy." *Jewish Antiquities*, 6.166. For additional references, see Joseph A. Fitzmyer, "David, 'Being Therefore a Prophet' (Acts 2:30)," *CBQ* 34 (1972): 332–39.

53 Josephus recounts that after Hyrcanus stole silver from David's sepulcher and Herod the Great secretly removed gold furniture and other treasures, the king built an expensive white stone monument at the tomb's entrance. *Jewish Antiquities*, 16.179–83.

54 Darrell L. Bock, *Acts*, BECNT (Grand Rapids, MI: Baker, 2007), 128.

to David himself, or does he write from the perspective of the Messiah or directly address the Messiah in the psalm? Peter's use of Psalm 16 raises challenging and important issues that require our careful attention. We'll consider several versions of the predictive prophecy view of Psalm 16 and then turn to the typological interpretation.

Many interpreters reason that Peter evidently treats Psalm 16 as a predictive prophecy of the Messiah. They argue that in this text David not only speaks *about* Christ, he speaks "prophetically in the voice of the messiah."[55] So when we read the first-person language in Psalm 16—"*I* bless the LORD . . . *I* have set the LORD . . . *I* shall not be shaken . . . *my* heart is glad . . . you will not abandon *my* soul to Sheol"—we should understand that the Messiah, David's promised descendant, is the one speaking about his own confidence that God will preserve him through death. This reading makes good sense of Peter's characterization of David as a "prophet" who "foresaw" the resurrection. However, it stretches the limits of Peter's introductory comment in Acts 2:25, "David says *concerning him* [Greek, *eis auton*]," to say that David speaks *as the Christ*. Apart from clear signals or controls within the biblical text, readers may wonder how to tell when "I" refers to the stated speaker and when it shifts to the Messiah's voice.

David Moessner offers an alternative proposal for understanding Psalm 16 as a messianic prophecy. He reasons that "the LORD" (Greek, *kyrios*) whom David sees in verse 8 and addresses as "you" throughout the psalm is not God but the Messiah.[56] In this reading, David expresses his solidarity with the Christ, whose incorruptible life beyond suffering and presence with David offer him unshakable resurrection hope. This interpretation makes good sense of the repeated Greek verb *prooraō* (Acts 2:25, "I saw"; cf. v. 31, "foresaw") and the reference to the Messiah as the *kyrios* at God's "right hand" in Psalm 110:1, which Peter cites in Acts 2:34. However, Moessner's thesis hangs on the Greek translation of Psalm 16:8, "I saw the

---

55 Strauss, *The Davidic Messiah in Luke-Acts*, 137. See Marshall, "Acts," 538; and Kenneth Duncan Litwak, *Echoes of Scripture in Luke-Acts: Telling the History of God's People Intertextually*, JSNTSup 282 (London: T&T Clark, 2005), 177. God's "holy one" refers to David, "yet not David as a mere person but David as the recipient and conveyor of God's ancient but ever-renewed promise," according to Walter C. Kaiser Jr., *The Uses of the Old Testament in the New* (Chicago: Moody, 1985), 34.

56 David P. Moessner, "Two Lords 'at the Right Hand'? The Psalms and an Intertextual Reading of Peter's Pentecost Speech (Acts 2:14–36)," in *Literary Studies in Luke-Acts: Essays in Honor of Joseph B. Tyson*, ed. Richard P. Thompson and Thomas E. Phillips (Macon, GA: Mercer University Press, 1998), 225–27.

Lord [*proōrōmēn ton kyrion*] ahead of me always" (AT). The Hebrew text is formally translated as "I have set the LORD always before me." Moessner reasons that "the LORD" in Psalm 16:8 and "my Lord" in Psalm 110:1 both refer to the Messiah.[57] However, it is important to note that Psalm 110:1 includes *two* Lords: "*The* LORD says to *my Lord*." In English translations, "the LORD" reflects God's covenant name (Yahweh), while "my Lord" renders a different Hebrew term (Adonai). The Septuagint translators use the same title, *kyrios*, for both Yahweh and Adonai. Peter and many if not most of his Jewish hearers in Jerusalem speak Hebrew and recognize this important distinction. Moreover, Moessner reads the two lines of Psalm 16:10 as distinct references to David's own future ("you will not abandon my soul to Sheol") and that of the Messiah ("or let your holy one see corruption").[58] It is far more likely that both lines refer to the same person (David) since they appear in Hebrew poetic parallelism.[59]

A third possibility is to interpret the apostle's application of Psalm 16 in Acts 2 as typology.[60] In chapter 1, I define "typology" as the study of the Old Testament people, events, or institutions (types) that correspond to and prophetically prefigure a later and greater fulfillment (antitype) within biblical history.[61] Genuine typology displays four characteristics: (1) historical correspondence between earlier and later events, people, places, etc.; (2) escalation from type to antitype such that the fulfillment is much better and greater; (3) biblical warrant that the text presents a model or pattern for something later; and (4) the progression of the covenants through the biblical story.[62] Are these factors observable in the use of Psalm 16 in Acts 2? There is clear warrant for Peter to appeal to David, the great king and psalmist, as an example, since Jesus himself did so (e.g., Luke

---

57 Ps. 110 in English Bibles corresponds to Ps. 109 LXX.

58 Moessner, "Two Lords 'at the Right Hand'?" 226.

59 For a similar point, see Marshall, "Acts," 538–39.

60 See, for example, Leonhard Goppelt, *Typos: The Typological Interpretation of the Old Testament in the New*, trans. Donald H. Madvig (Grand Rapids, MI: Eerdmans, 1982), 122–23; and Martin Rese, "Die Funktion der alttestamentliche Zitate und Anspielungen in den Reden der Apostelgeschickte," in *Les Actes des Apôtres: Traditions, Rédaction, Théologie*, ed. Jacob Kremer, BETL 48 (Leuven: Leuven University Press, 1979), 76.

61 Adapted from Gentry and Wellum, *Kingdom*, 39. For similar assessments of typology, see Beale, *Handbook on the New Testament Use of the Old Testament*, 13–25; and Mitchell L. Chase, *40 Questions about Typology and Allegory* (Grand Rapids, MI: Kregel, 2020), 35–39.

62 Summarizing Peter J. Gentry, *How to Read and Understand the Biblical Prophets* (Wheaton, IL: Crossway, 2017), 90.

6:3–4; 20:42, 44). There is also certainly correspondence and escalation between David and Jesus, whom the Gospels call "Son of David" (e.g., Matt. 1:1; Luke 18:38–39) and identify as the promised King in David's line (Luke 1:31–33). Moreover, the mention of God's oath in Acts 2:30 highlights the fulfillment of the Davidic covenant in Christ's reign.

While the use of Psalm 16:8–11 in Acts 2:25–31 reflects these essential features of typology, there are two related challenges to concluding that Peter employs this psalm typologically. First, some question whether it is fitting "to use the term 'typological' of a statement that was not true of the 'type' himself."[63] Second, the apostle appears to emphasize God's covenant *promise* to David more than the *pattern* of David's life (cf. Paul in Acts 13:23). Indeed, the text highlights a significant contrast between David, who died and experienced corruption, and Christ, who died yet was raised to life. But there is also significant continuity between David and his greater Son, who both remained confident in God to protect and preserve their lives in the face of death.[64] Moreover, Peter states that David himself speaks *eis auton*, "concerning" or "unto" Christ, but not *as* Christ (2:25). The repeated first-person "I" throughout Psalm 16 refers first to David himself, as he expresses his own trust in the Lord as refuge, whose presence with him offers unshakable confidence now and joy forever.

Consider how the Old Testament presents David's experience using the same language of faith reflected in Psalm 16. David prays, "*Preserve* me, O God" (Ps. 16:1), and in 1 Samuel 30:23 he reminds his men, "He has *preserved* us." David declares, "In you *I take refuge*" (Ps. 16:1). Likewise, in 2 Samuel 22, David extols God as "my rock, in whom *I take refuge*" (v. 3) when he recounts how God rescued him from all his foes and from Saul's hand (v. 1). This is not simply David's individual experience; rather, he explains later in the song that God "is a shield for *all those who take refuge in him*" (v. 31). Further, David's confidence that "you will not abandon my soul to *Sheol*" (Ps. 16:10) finds expression in the same song of salvation: when "the cords of *Sheol* entangled me," the Lord "heard my voice" (2 Sam. 22:6–7). Moreover, another psalm of David expresses the same conviction that the faithful God "will not *abandon* his faithful ones" (Ps. 37:28 CSB). These examples illustrate that the expressions of trust in God and confidence

---

63 Marshall, "Acts," 538.
64 Monique Cuany, "The Divine Necessity of the Resurrection: A Re-Assessment of the Use of Psalm 16 in Acts 2," *NTS* 66 (2020): 400–404.

in his character and commitment to his people recorded in Psalm 16 are typical of the life of David, who offers a pattern for God's people to follow in the face of adversity. Christ is the supreme example of this pattern, as he is preserved through death and raised to unending life.[65] Yet Peter also insists that Israel's sweet psalmist and beloved king penned this psalm with God's covenant promises etched in his mind (Acts 2:30; cf. 2 Sam. 7:12–16; Ps. 132:11). The glorious hope that the Lord would build David an enduring house informed how David expressed his experience of faith and expectations for the future. Moreover, the resurrection of David's greater Son secures the hope of unending joy and life beyond death for David and all who take refuge in his Lord.

Having looked in depth at Peter's typological use of Psalm 16:8–11, let's now briefly consider Paul's citation of the same psalm in his synagogue sermon in Antioch. Paul declares the good news that God has fulfilled his ancient promises by raising Jesus from the dead (Acts 13:32–33). He cites three supporting Old Testament passages in verses 33–35: Psalm 2:7, Isaiah 55:3, and finally Psalm 16:10.[66] Paul then explains how these texts—particularly Psalm 16—attest to Jesus's resurrection: "For David, after he had served the purpose of God in his own generation, fell asleep and was laid with his fathers and saw corruption, but he whom God raised up did not see corruption" (Acts 13:36–37). Paul employs similar reasoning to Peter's in Acts 2, focusing specifically on the contrast between David's decay in death and Christ's incorruptible resurrection life.[67] The resurrection validates that Christ is God's true "Son" (13:33), and he reigns forever as the king in David's line and as the promised "Savior" of God's people (vv. 23, 34, 38).

The Seated Lord (Acts 2:34–35)

Peter orients his Pentecost sermon around three biblical citations: he quotes Joel 2:28–32 to explain the outpouring of the Spirit, then appeals to Psalm 16:8–11 as proof for Christ's resurrection, and concludes with David's words in Psalm 110:1. Let's examine the apostle's citation of Psalm 110:1 in Acts 2:34–35, which explains *where* Jesus is and also *who* he is as the exalted Lord seated at God's right hand.

---

65 Bock, *Acts*, 138.

66 Paul's citation of Ps. 2:7 is considered further below, pp. 128–33.

67 Bock, *Proclamation from Prophecy and Pattern*, 255.

To understand Peter's use of Psalm 110 on the day of Pentecost, recall Jesus's own citation of this same text in Luke 20:41–44. There the Lord poses a riddle: How can the Messiah be David's "son" if David himself calls him "Lord" in Psalm 110? Jesus does not explicitly predict his resurrection and ascension in Luke 20:41–44 and does not directly answer this provocative question. How can David refer to his messianic Son as "Lord"? Peter's answer is that Jesus is both Lord and Christ (Acts 2:36), who has been raised from death and exalted to reign on heaven's throne.

Consider the apostle's argument in Acts 2:33–36. Peter dramatically declares that Jesus has "poured out" the Holy Spirit after ascending to God's right hand and receiving the promised Spirit from the Father (v. 33). Jesus is thus responsible for the dramatic events of Pentecost that Peter's audience is "seeing and hearing." The crucified, risen, and exalted Christ has poured out the Spirit—the very thing God himself promised to do in Joel 2:28–29. Thus, Jesus "fulfills an explicitly divine role";[68] he is the "Lord of the Spirit."[69] Next, Peter supports this remarkable Christological claim by explaining that David "did not ascend into the heavens"; rather, he says in Psalm 110:1,

> The Lord said to my Lord,
> "Sit at my right hand,
> until I make your enemies your footstool." (Acts 2:34–35)

Peter does not elaborate on this Old Testament quotation, but the point is clear for those who recall Jesus's appeal to Psalm 110:1 in Luke 20: God commands David's "Lord"—not David himself—to sit at his side. The key phrase "sit at my right hand" reiterates the previous verse's claim about Jesus's present location: "exalted at the right hand of God."[70] The reference to God's right hand also connects this Davidic psalm to the earlier citation of Psalm 16:8 ("he is at my right hand").[71] Finally, after explaining Jesus's

---

68 Keener, *Acts*, 1:957. Within Luke's two volumes, the Greek verb *ekcheō* ("pour out") occurs only in Acts 2:17–18 (citing Joel 2:28–29) and v. 33.

69 Turner, *Power from on High*, 303.

70 "Jesus' *bodily* but now *non-earthly* location" means that "a comprehensive reordering of space has occurred," according to Matthew Sleeman, *Geography and the Ascension Narrative in Acts*, SNTSMS 146 (Cambridge: Cambridge University Press, 2009), 101–2, emphasis original.

71 This connection between Pss. 16:8 and 110:1 illustrates the exegetical principle of *gezerah shawah*, an argument from an analogy, according to Schnabel, *Acts*, 149n94.

location (at God's right hand) and his divine activity (pouring out the end-time Spirit to fulfill prophecy), the apostle infers ("therefore") that "God has made him both Lord and Christ, this Jesus whom you crucified" (Acts 2:36).

Earlier in this speech, Peter appeals to God's sworn promise to set David's descendant on his throne (Acts 2:30; 2 Sam. 7:12–16; Ps. 132:11). The events of Pentecost and David's oracle in Psalm 110:1 together prove that David's Son is indeed seated on his throne as the exalted Lord of heaven. This biblical proof for Jesus's identity as "Lord" brings Peter's argument back to his quotation of Joel's prophecy: the crucified and risen Son of David is the exalted Lord who has poured out the end-time Spirit, and everyone who calls on the name of the Lord Jesus shall be saved (Acts 2:17, 21). Thus, "In Acts the lordship of Christ means that Jesus is exalted to the right hand of God, fulfilling Psalm 110. . . . The outpouring of the Spirit indicates that Jesus is the living, ascended king who reigns over all nations."[72]

The Lord's Son (Acts 13:33)

Paul's longest recorded sermon in Acts comes in Pisidian Antioch, after the Holy Spirit directs the church in Syrian Antioch to set apart Barnabas and Paul for a new work (Acts 13:2–3).[73] The missionaries attend the local synagogue, and Paul offers a "word of encouragement" following the Scripture readings (13:14–15).[74] Paul's sermon unfolds in three parts, signaled by direct appeals to his hearers: "Men of Israel and you who fear God" (v. 16); "brothers, sons of the family of Abraham, and those among you who fear God" (v. 26); and "brothers" (v. 38).[75] He rehearses God's dealings with Israel, proclaims that Jesus is the promised Savior descended from David, and urges his hearers to respond rightly to this

---

72 Crowe, *The Hope of Israel*, 28.

73 Acts 13 begins what is often called Paul's first of three missionary journeys. However, Eckhard Schnabel identifies fifteen phases of Paul's missionary activity, beginning in Damascus and Arabia nearly fifteen years before the Spirit's call in Acts 13:1–4. Eckhard J. Schnabel, *Paul the Missionary: Realities, Strategies and Methods* (Downers Grove, IL: IVP Academic, 2008), 58–74.

74 The context signals that this "word of encouragement" (*logos paraklēseōs*) or "message of exhortation" (NET) refers to "a homily based on the interpretation of Scripture," according to Withering-ton, *Acts*, 406n190. Paul similarly refers to the reading of Scripture and "exhortation" in 1 Tim. 4:13, and the author of Hebrews describes his work as a "word of exhortation" (Heb. 13:22).

75 For a similar analysis of the sermon's structure and a survey of other views, see John Eifion Morgan-Wynne, *Paul's Pisidian Antioch Speech (Acts 13)* (Cambridge: James Clarke, 2014), 62–68, 210–11.

message of salvation lest they perish in unbelief as the prophet warned
(vv. 40–41, citing Hab. 1:5).

Some scholars have proposed specific passages from "the Law and the
Prophets" (Acts 13:15) that may have been read before Paul's synagogue
sermon, such as Deuteronomy 4:25–46 and 2 Samuel 7:6–16.[76] His biblical
theological summary in Acts 13:16–23 strikingly parallels 2 Samuel 7, as
illustrated by Table 5.1.[77] Paul's speech also includes notable similarities with
Peter's Pentecost message in Acts 2, particularly his exposition of Psalm 16
as a scriptural proof for Christ's resurrection.[78]

Theme	Acts 13	2 Samuel 7	Biblical Book
Choice of the patriarchs	v. 17	–	Genesis
Exodus from Egypt	v. 17	v. 6	Exodus
Wilderness wanderings	v. 18	–	Numbers
Inheritance of the land	v. 19	v. 10	Joshua
Raising up judges	v. 20	v. 11	Judges
Choice of David	v. 22	v. 8	1 Samuel
Promise to raise up David's offspring	v. 23	v. 12	2 Samuel
Promise of a father-son relationship	v. 33	v. 14	2 Samuel
Promise of sure blessings/kingdom	v. 34	vv. 15–16	2 Samuel
David's death	v. 36	v. 12	2 Samuel

Table 5.1. Parallels between Acts 13 and 2 Samuel 7

Paul rehearses God's choice of the patriarchs, Israel's exodus from Egypt,
the people's wilderness wanderings, the conquest of Canaan and inheritance
of the land, the rule of the judges until Samuel, the people's request for a king
and Saul's reign and removal, and finally the installation of David as king

---

76 These texts are suggested by Schnabel, *Acts*, 574.
77 This table draws on Strauss, *The Davidic Messiah in Luke-Acts*, 154–55; and Marcel Dumais,
   Le langage de l'évangélisation: L'annonce missionnaire en milieu juif (Actes 13,16–41) (Montréal:
   Bellarmin, 1976), 90–95; cf. Morgan-Wynne, *Paul's Pisidian Antioch Speech*, 77–78.
78 See, for example, Keener, *Acts*, 2:2052.

(Acts 13:17–22).[79] He then moves from David to Jesus, the promised Savior from David's stock (v. 23). Paul proclaims "the message of this salvation" to Abraham's family (v. 26) and explains that the Jews in Jerusalem unwittingly "fulfilled" the prophets' words by condemning the Christ and "carried out all that was written of him" (vv. 27, 29).[80] However, God has fulfilled his promise to the patriarchs "by raising Jesus" from the dead (vv. 32–33). The missionary then cites three Scripture passages—Psalm 2:7, Isaiah 55:3, and Psalm 16:10—to support his claim that Christ's resurrection fulfills God's ancient promises (Acts 13:33–35). Let's focus attention on Paul's appeal to "the second Psalm" (v. 33).

Psalm 2 is a royal psalm focused on the Lord's cosmic purposes for his anointed. Though the nations of earth rage against Israel's king (vv. 1–2), the God who sits in the heavens has set him on Zion (vv. 4–6). The psalmist recounts a divine decree in verses 7–9 concerning "the Davidic king and the establishment of God's kingdom on earth."[81] O. Palmer Robertson explains that "the Lord's covenant with David provides the essential theological framework for understanding the Psalms,"[82] and this emphasis is front and center in Psalm 2:7: "The LORD said to me, 'You are my Son; today I have begotten you.'" The "decree" in verse 7 refers to God's foundational promise regarding David's descendent: "I will be to him a father, and he shall be to me a son" (2 Sam. 7:14).[83] By employing the sonship language of the Davidic covenant, Psalm 2 addresses not merely David's own reign but especially that of his messianic heir, whose throne God promised to establish forever.

I have already considered the early church's appeal to Psalm 2:1–2 to explain the concerted hostility toward Christ and his followers (Acts 4:25–28).[84] The heavenly declarations "You are my . . . Son" and "This is my

---

79 "Paul's sermon singles out the fulfilment of the covenant with David as the climax of the story of Israel," according to Chris Bruno, Jared Compton, and Kevin McFadden, *Biblical Theology according to the Apostles: How the Earliest Christians Told the Story of Israel*, NSBT 52 (London: Apollos, 2020), 81.

80 "The tree" in Acts 13:29 likely alludes to Deut. 21:23; see the discussion above, pp. 114–16, and Wilson, "'Upon a Tree' Again and Again," 60–64.

81 VanGemeren, *Psalms*, 95.

82 Robertson, *The Flow of the Psalms*, 14.

83 Various commentators note this allusion, including Longman, *Psalms*, 1:62. Hebrews 1:5 quotes Ps. 2:7 alongside 2 Sam. 7:14, and an anthology of biblical quotations from Qumran cites 2 Sam. 7:10–14 alongside a number of biblical texts, including Ps. 2:1 (4Q174 lines 1–19).

84 See above, pp. 111–14.

Son" at Jesus's baptism and transfiguration also probably allude to Psalm 2:7 (Luke 3:22; 9:35).[85] Paul then proclaims that God has raised Jesus, "as also it is written in the second Psalm, 'You are my Son, today I have begotten you'" (Acts 13:33).[86]

Paul quotes Psalm 2:7 LXX as clear biblical proof for Christ's resurrection. Yet scholars do not agree about when Jesus is "raised up" and "begotten" as God's Son. They variously explain Acts 13:33 as a reference to (1) Christ's birth;[87] (2) his baptism, when he is anointed with the Spirit;[88] (3) his entire life, death, and resurrection;[89] or (4) his resurrection, which is closely linked to his exaltation to God's right hand in Acts 2:33–36.[90]

This final view is most likely: God has fulfilled the promise of Psalm 2:7 by raising Jesus from the dead. Christ's resurrection is "the logical key" to Paul's entire speech in Antioch[91] and is the explicit focus of his argument in Acts 13:30–37. It is likely that "by raising Jesus" (*anastēsas Iēsoun*) in verse 33 is equivalent to the clear references to resurrection in the immediate context: "God *raised* [*ēgeiren*] him from the dead" (v. 30); "he *raised* [*anestēsen*] him from the dead, no more to return to corruption" (v. 34); and "he whom God *raised up* [*ēgeiren*] did not see corruption" (v. 37). It does not follow that "Jesus was *made* the Messiah at his resurrection."[92] Before Jesus is even conceived in Mary's womb, the angel identifies him as "the Son of the Most High" and "the Son of God" (Luke 1:32, 35). The resurrection does not mark the beginning of Christ's sonship; rather, it powerfully proves that he

85 The allusion to Ps. 2:7 at Luke 9:35 is discussed in chap. 3, pp. 71–72. Ps. 2:7 is also cited in Heb. 1:5 and 5:5, and Paul likely alludes to this verse in Rom. 1:4.

86 Codex Bezae (D) expands Paul's citation in Acts 13:33 to include Ps. 2:8 as well ("Ask of me, and I will make the nations your heritage, and the ends of the earth your possession").

87 Schnabel, *Acts*, 581. John Calvin similarly explains Acts 13:33: Jesus "was appointed of God . . . that he might fulfil the office of the Messiah, as the Scripture teacheth everywhere that kings and prophets are raised up." *Commentary upon the Acts of the Apostles*, trans. Henry Beveridge, repr. ed. (Bellingham, WA: Logos Bible Software, 2010), 1:533.

88 F. F. Bruce, *The Book of the Acts*, rev. ed., NICNT (Grand Rapids, MI: Eerdmans, 1988), 260. He clarifies that "Jesus entered into no *new* relation of sonship to his heavenly Father" at his baptism, thus distancing his view from Arianism (p. 260, emphasis original).

89 Strauss, *The Davidic Messiah in Luke-Acts*, 164.

90 Peterson, *The Acts of the Apostles*, 392. See Robert F. O'Toole, "Christ's Resurrection in Acts 13,13–52," *Bib* 60 (1979): 366; and Morgan-Wynne, *Paul's Pisidian Antioch Speech*, 146.

91 Crowe, *The Hope of Israel*, 58.

92 Richard I. Pervo, *Acts: A Commentary*, Hermeneia (Minneapolis: Fortress, 2009), 339, emphasis added.

is God's Son (see Rom. 1:4) and also signals "a new era of the eternal Son's messianic sonship."[93] In this respect, "today I have begotten you" parallels Paul's reference to Christ as "the firstborn from the dead" (Col. 1:18) and indicates that his resurrection serves as the beginning of the new creation in the last days. The risen Son has begun to reign at God's right hand (Acts 2:30, 33–35), and he offers "salvation" and "forgiveness of sins" for all who call on his name (13:26, 38; cf. 2:21, 38). While Paul appeals here to Psalm 2:7 to argue for Jesus's resurrection, it is noteworthy that in Psalm 2:8 the Lord promises his royal Son "the nations" and "the ends of the earth" as his heritage and possession. Paul employs this very language in Acts 13:47 in his citation of Isaiah 49:6 as support for his mission to the Gentiles.[94]

Paul offers two further scriptural proofs for Christ's resurrection in Acts 13:34–35:

> And as for the fact that he raised him from the dead, no more to return to corruption, he has spoken in this way,
>
> "I will give you the holy and sure blessings of David."
>
> Therefore he says also in another psalm,
>
> "You will not let your Holy One see corruption."

Paul cites portions of Isaiah 55:3 and Psalm 16:10 (15:10 LXX) in these verses. His exposition of Psalm 16 closely parallels Peter's argument in Acts 2:24–32: while David was laid to rest and saw corruption, his greater Son, Jesus, did not see corruption because God raised him from the dead (13:36–37).[95] Let's briefly address this quotation of Isaiah 55:3, which reflects an awareness of the context of Isaiah's prophecy.[96]

In Isaiah 55:1–3, the Lord offers a sweeping invitation to "come" and "hear, that your soul may live." Paul's appeal to the "blessings of David"

93 Crowe, *The Hope of Israel*, 61. See G. K. Beale, *A New Testament Biblical Theology: The Unfolding of the Old Testament in the New* (Grand Rapids, MI: Baker Academic, 2011), 499.
94 The use of Isa. 49:6 in Acts 13:47 is discussed at length in chap. 6, pp. 149–55.
95 See above, pp. 121–26.
96 Keener, *Acts*, 2:2072.

(Acts 13:34) explains the "everlasting covenant" that God promises to make with his people in Isaiah 55:3 (cf. 61:8). These "blessings of David" from 55:3 recall the Lord's promise to make David a sure house and establish the kingdom of his messianic descendant (2 Sam. 7:12–16), and Paul stresses that God has fulfilled this covenant promise through Jesus, his risen Son (Acts 13:23, 32–33). Thus, these "holy and sure blessings" (Acts 13:34) refer to the benefits that flow from the heavenly reign of David's greater Son, the risen Lord Jesus.[97] The resurrection of David's descendent confirms God's covenant commitment to establish his throne forever (2 Sam. 7:16).[98] It is also noteworthy that immediately after highlighting the "blessings of David," Isaiah identifies David as "witness" and "leader" for the peoples (55:4). Within Isaiah, this recalls the mission of the Lord's servant in 49:6 (cf. 42:6), which also serves as the scriptural foundation for the mission of Jesus's witnesses in Acts 1:8 and the missionaries' turn to the Gentiles in Acts 13:46–47.[99]

Thus, Paul stresses in Acts 13 that God has raised Jesus from the dead and thereby fulfilled his ancient promise to raise up David's offspring. Paul announces that Jesus is Israel's long-awaited Savior from David's line (v. 23), and his resurrection confirms his identity as David's heir and God's "Son," who reigns forever, according to the testimony of Psalm 2:7, Isaiah 55:3, and Psalm 16:10.

Conclusion

In Acts, Christ's witnesses preach about their Lord's suffering and resurrection with Spirit-brought courage and Christ-taught clarity. As Christ opened their minds to understand the Scriptures, so these witnesses demonstrate that the Messiah was crucified and raised just as God planned (Acts 2:23; 3:18; 13:29). They expound the Scriptures to show that Christ is the Lord's anointed against whom the Gentiles and Israel conspired (Ps. 2:1), he is the cursed one hung on the tree (Deut. 21:23), and he is the lamb-like servant who was slaughtered (Isa. 53:7–8). The witnesses also testify to the radical

---

97 See Crowe, *The Hope of Israel*, 54–55.
98 See Bock, *Proclamation from Prophecy and Pattern*, 254.
99 It was natural for early Christians to read Isa. 55:3–4 "as a statement about the Messiah and his universal salvific mission," according to Jacques Dupont, *The Salvation of the Gentiles: Essays on the Acts of the Apostles*, trans. John R. Keating (New York: Paulist, 1979), 145–46.

reversal brought about by the resurrection, which validated Jesus as the incorruptible Christ in David's line (Ps. 16:8–11), God's Son (2:7), and the exalted Lord enthroned in heaven (110:1). This Jesus is the promised Lord and Messiah, who has sent the Holy Spirit to his people, who has set in motion the time of the last days, and who offers salvation and forgiveness for all who turn to him (Joel 2:28–32).

Acts demonstrates that the resurrection of Jesus is the great fulcrum of holy Scripture and of human history. Without the resurrection, there is no church to gather, no news to proclaim, no mission to carry out, and no firm hope for the future beyond vague sentimentality about "a better place." Peter, Andrew, and the Zebedees would have gone back to fishing. Jesus of Nazareth would be a footnote in the history books, which would remember him perhaps as a powerful yet controversial teacher, a martyr for truth whose life was cut tragically short. But everything changed because Christ rose from the dead on the third day according to the Scriptures. And before the risen Lord ascended to take his seat on heaven's throne, he commissioned his followers for a mission—*his* mission—"to the ends of the earth." To this mission we now turn.

6

To the End of the Earth

The Apostles' Mission in Acts

But you will receive power when the Holy Spirit has come
upon you, and you will be my witnesses in Jerusalem and
in all Judea and Samaria, and to the end of the earth.

ACTS 1:8

IT FELT SURREAL TO WEAR latex gloves and a face mask the first time I went into our local supermarket during the COVID-19 pandemic. Yet the rapid spread of the deadly virus made such drastic measures necessary. In January 2020, the world learned about a "novel coronavirus" that had infected thousands of people in China. But only two months later, this epidemic in a single country had become a global pandemic that had infected millions of people.[1] Church buildings remained closed on Easter Sunday. The NCAA basketball tournament was shelved. Schools at all levels, from preschool to postgraduate studies, were forced to shift to online and distance learning options. In my state, the governor's executive orders halted all public gatherings, closed all businesses deemed "nonessential," and mandated the oxymoronic practice of "social distancing." In a matter of weeks, this microscopic coronavirus spread across the globe, infecting people of every ethnic group, age bracket, and socioeconomic status—including the UK

---

1 See further Brian J. Tabb, "Theological Reflections on the Pandemic," *Themelios* 45 (2020): 1–7.

prime minister and the US president. Various government restrictions and community precautions aimed to slow the spread of this disease, yet this rogue virus continued its relentless advance to every corner of the earth.

The book of Acts recounts the rapid spread of the gospel in Jerusalem, in Judea and Samaria, and to the nations. All sorts of people, from Sadducees to silversmiths, attempt to stop or slow this movement, but those who oppose Christ and his people are only fighting against God and kicking against the goads (Acts 5:39; 26:14). The gospel goes viral, and it turns the world upside down (17:6). Luke's Gospel presents Christ's mission to seek the lost and bring salvation to all peoples as the fulfillment of Old Testament hopes, and Luke's sequel shows how Jesus empowers his witnesses to proclaim good news in his name and carry out his mission "to the end of the earth."

Witnesses of the Risen Lord (Acts 1:8)

I have argued that Jesus's "last words" in the Gospel of Luke serve as a crucial lens for seeing how the Messiah and his mission fit in the biblical story. Luke's Gospel concludes with Jesus's ascension and the disciples' return to Jerusalem, so we might expect the sequel to begin with the disciples waiting in Jerusalem for the Spirit. Instead, Acts opens with the risen Lord teaching his disciples about God's kingdom and giving them final commands until he is "taken up" into heaven (Acts 1:2–3).[2] The Lord's last words before his ascension come in response to the disciples' question in verse 6: "Lord, will you at this time restore the kingdom to Israel?" They evidently are reasoning that the resurrection of the Davidic Messiah and his promise that they will soon receive the Spirit are sure signs that God is about to consummate his plans for end-time restoration, including the reestablishment of Israel's sovereignty. But Jesus does not give the response they expect in verses 7–8.[3] He does not rebuke his followers for expecting restoration. Rather, he redirects their focus from *when* this restoration will take place (v. 7) to *how* God's purposes will be fulfilled: by the Spirit-empowered mission of Christ's witnesses within Israel and to distant lands (v. 8).

---

2   For an extensive list of parallels between Luke 24 and Acts 1, see Keener, *Acts*, 1:648.

3   For similar assessments of the relationship of the disciples' question (Acts 1:6) and Jesus's response (vv. 7–8), see Pao, *Acts and the Isaianic New Exodus*, 95; Peterson, *The Acts of the Apostles*, 108–9; and Thompson, *The Acts of the Risen Lord Jesus*, 105.

Acts 1:8 records Jesus's final words before his ascension in verse 9: "But you will receive power when the Holy Spirit has come upon you, and you will be my witnesses in Jerusalem and in all Judea and Samaria, and to the end of the earth." The Lord's promise establishes the trajectory for the book's storyline: the Holy Spirit comes on the day of Pentecost (2:1–4), empowering Jesus's followers to bear witness to their risen Lord in Jerusalem (chaps. 2–7), Samaria and Judea (chaps. 8–12), and to the very limits of the known world (chaps. 13–28). Summary statements in Acts highlight the progress of this mission: the word advances "in Jerusalem" (6:7), the church is built up "throughout all Judea and Galilee and Samaria" (9:31), and the word increases and prevails as Gentiles turn to the Lord in Antioch and beyond (12:24; 19:20). Thus, we could say that Acts 1:8 summarizes Jesus's plan for the church's mission after his ascension.

Acts 1:8 not only outlines the unfolding narrative of the gospel's advance in Acts; Jesus's programmatic promise also contains three allusions to Isaiah that signal the biblical-theological significance of the mission of Jesus's witnesses. First, Jesus's promise that the Holy Spirit will come upon his disciples recalls the promise of Isaiah 32:15 LXX: "until the Spirit from on high comes upon you" (AT). Notably, while Acts 1:8 does not include Isaiah's phrase "from on high," Luke 24:49 speaks of the Spirit's coming in precisely these terms: "And behold, I am sending the promise of my Father upon you. But stay in the city until you are clothed with power *from on high*." This parallel with Isaiah 32:15 in Jesus's last words in Luke serves as confirmation that Acts 1:8 draws upon Isaiah's prophecy.[4] In Isaiah 32, the prophet announces coming judgment on God's unrepentant people, which will leave Judah "forsaken" and "deserted" (v. 14). Then the outpouring of God's Spirit will turn the wilderness into a fruitful field and usher in justice, righteousness, peace, and lasting security (vv. 15–18). The Spirit's coming marks the dawn of the new age of salvation, turning the forsaken land into a place of fruitfulness and faithfulness. Also, the transformation of the wilderness in Isaiah 32 anticipates further prophecies of end-time salvation in the book of Isaiah. For example, "the wilderness and the dry land shall

---

4   Pao, *Acts and the Isaianic New Exodus*, 92. See also Max Turner, "The 'Spirit of Prophecy' as the Power of Israel's Restoration and Witness," in *Witness to the Gospel*, 345.

be glad" when God's glory is revealed (35:1–2). The Lord describes this coming salvation as a new creation: "Behold, I am doing a new thing. . . . I will make a way in the wilderness" (43:19). Further, he promises to comfort Zion, making "her wilderness like Eden" (51:3). Thus, the Spirit's coming marks the beginning fulfillment of Isaiah's prophecies of a new exodus, when the Lord will make a way in the wilderness and reveal his glorious salvation (40:3–5).[5]

Second, Jesus calls his disciples "my witnesses," which closely parallels the Lord's refrain, "You are my witnesses," in Isaiah 43:10, 12 and 44:8. These verses feature an extended "courtroom motif," in which the Lord summons Israel and the nations to supply evidence to prove or challenge his claim to be the only true God.[6] The Lord contrasts his divine power to create, save, and reveal the future with the impotence of the idols of the nations. Ironically, he calls to the witness stand "the people who are blind, yet have eyes, who are deaf, yet have ears!" (43:8). This is God's "chosen" servant Israel; they have trusted in false gods and now resemble those blind and deaf idols (42:1, 17–20).[7] The Lord's "witnesses" have received God's word and beheld his saving power, yet they need the Lord to save them and overcome their blindness and deafness (29:18; 35:5). Thus, Isaiah anticipates that "the people of God will become witnesses to the salvation of God when the new age arrives."[8]

Luke 24 helps us see the importance of this Old Testament background for Acts 1:8. The Lord Jesus presents himself alive to his disciples and opens their minds to grasp God's word (Luke 24:36–45).[9] He then summarizes the Scriptures' central message and declares, "You are witnesses of these things" (v. 48). Thus, the disciples serve as Christ's witnesses only after he reveals himself to them and gives them the spiritual capacity to understand the Scriptures. Peter explains that he and the other apostles serve as "witnesses" to Christ's resurrection[10] as they proclaim salvation in his name alone (Acts 4:12). Later, Paul recounts how Jesus revealed himself on the Damascus road and commissioned him as "a servant and witness"

5   I discuss the use of Isa. 40:3–5 in Luke 3:4–6 in chap. 4, pp. 90–94.

6   House, *Isaiah*, 2:343.

7   See Beale, *We Become What We Worship*, 41–51 (and throughout the book).

8   Pao, *Acts and the Isaianic New Exodus*, 93.

9   This reversal is discussed further in chap. 1, pp. 25–26.

10   See Acts 1:22; 2:32; 3:15; 5:32; 10:39–42.

(26:16). Paul's own blindness and recovery of sight after his encounter with the risen Lord strikingly illustrates his mission "to open their eyes" (26:18; cf. 9:17–18).[11] The twelve apostles certainly have a unique role as eyewitnesses of the resurrection (1:22),[12] but the mission of Jesus's witnesses is neither restricted to nor exhausted by the apostles.[13] Acts explicitly refers to Paul and Stephen as witnesses (22:15, 20), and presents other believers speaking the word boldly (e.g., 4:31; 18:24–28). Moreover, while the apostles remain in Jerusalem, Philip brings the gospel to Samaria (8:1, 4–7), other scattered believers evangelize Gentiles (11:19–21), and Paul and Barnabas explicitly express their own calling to bring the message of salvation "to the end of the earth" (13:46–47).

The third Old Testament allusion in Acts 1:8 comes in the closing line: "to the end of the earth." This phrase occurs four times in the Septuagint of Isaiah, and here it alludes to the Lord's commission to his servant in Isaiah 49:6: "I will make you as a light for the nations, that my salvation may reach *to the end of the earth*."[14] This prophecy is applied to Jesus in Luke 2:32 and to the call of Paul and Barnabas to turn to the Gentiles (Acts 13:47).[15]

Scholars have variously identified "the end of the earth" in Acts 1:8 as Rome, Spain, and Ethiopia.[16] Alternatively, David Pao explains that "the end of the earth" in Isaiah 49:6 and in Acts is an "ethnic" or "theopolitical" reference to "the Gentiles" rather than a geographic location.[17] This interpretation fits well with the narrative of Acts, which stresses the significance of the Gentiles receiving the message of salvation and the promised Holy Spirit, and being included within God's people. Likewise, Isaiah 49:6 closely links salvation reaching "the end of the earth" with the "nations" or "Gentiles" receiving light. However, when the Greek

---

11 Saul's blindness in Acts 9:8 could also recall "the blindness of Israel, the Lord's servant-witness" (Isa. 42:16–17), as argued by Johnson, "Jesus against the Idols," 350–51.

12 Acts employs "witness" as a technical term for the activity of the twelve apostles and Paul, according to Peter G. Bolt, "Mission and Witness," in *Witness to the Gospel*, 191–93.

13 Mallen, *The Reading and Transformation of Isaiah in Luke-Acts*, 192–93.

14 "To the end of the earth" (*heōs eschatou tēs gēs*) also occurs in Isa. 8:9; 48:20; 62:11 LXX, as well as in the pseudepigraphal text Psalms of Solomon 1:4.

15 For discussion of Luke 2:32, see chap. 4, pp. 86–89. Acts 13:47 is considered later in this chapter, pp. 149–55.

16 For a summary of these and other interpretations, see Pao, *Acts and the Isaianic New Exodus*, 93; Schnabel, *Early Christian Mission*, 1:372–73; and Keener, *Acts*, 1:704–8.

17 Pao, *Acts and the Isaianic New Exodus*, 94–95.

preposition *heōs* ("to") is followed by a location in the genitive case, this construction expresses a geographical limit: believers "traveled *as far as* Phoenicia and Cyprus and Antioch" (Acts 11:19), the church "sent Barnabas *to* Antioch" (11:22), soldiers go "*as far as* Caesarea" (23:23), and Paul says he persecuted believers "even *to* foreign cities" (26:11).[18] This usage suggests that "*to* [*heōs*] the end of the earth" conveys movement as far as a geographical limit, which makes sense of the specific locations mentioned earlier in Acts 1:8: Jerusalem, Judea, and Samaria. Eckhard Schnabel argues plausibly that the phrase "designates the farthest regions of the earth" and thus "describes the geographical scope of the missionary assignment of the disciples."[19]

The use of Isaiah 49:6 in Acts 1:8 also signals that the witnesses' mission to the farthest reaches of the earth is an outworking of the promised new exodus that not only involves restoring Israel but also extending God's salvation to the Gentiles. Jesus's reference to "all Judea and Samaria" recalls the prophetic hopes that the divided northern and southern kingdoms would one day be reunited under a Davidic king.[20] As the Lord promised to regather the people of Israel who had been scattered to foreign lands, so also the message of salvation would extend to "all flesh" (Isa. 40:5) in remote and distant places. Acts narrates how Paul and his companions travel as far as Rome, in accord with the Lord's directives (19:21; 23:11; 28:14). Paul's preaching in Rome does not exhaust the disciples' mission to "the end of the earth"—Paul himself longs to reach Spain after visiting Rome (Rom. 15:24, 28)—yet the journey to Rome is representative of the global mission of Jesus's witnesses.[21] Their mission starts in Jerusalem, expands into the nearby regions of Judea and Samaria, and ultimately extends beyond geographic and ethnic barriers, such that it is truly a "world mission."[22]

---

18 BDAG lists five definitions for *heōs* and includes the usage in Acts 1:8 under category 3: "marker of limit reached, *as far as, to*" (p. 423).

19 Schnabel, *Early Christian Mission*, 1:373, 375.

20 Thompson, *The Acts of the Risen Lord Jesus*, 106.

21 Keener, *Acts*, 1:703, 707; and C. K. Barrett, *The Acts of the Apostles*, 2 vols., ICC (London: T&T Clark, 1994–1998), 80. The word's advance to Rome in Acts 28 guarantees its spread to the whole world, according to Daniel Marguerat, *Les Actes des Apôtres*, 2 vols., CNT 5A–B (Genève: Labor et Fides, 2007–2015), 1:42.

22 Schnabel, *Acts*, 80.

Thus, the allusions to Isaiah in Acts 1:8 signal that the mission of Jesus's followers fulfills Old Testament prophecy. Luke explains that his Gospel deals with "all that Jesus *began* to do and teach" (1:1); the word "began" suggests that Luke's sequel narrates the *ongoing* work of the risen and ascended Lord.[23] Jesus is the Lord's promised servant who is himself true "Israel" and who acts to restore Israel and bring God's salvation to the nations (Isa. 49:3, 5–6).[24] Acts 1:8 makes clear that the risen Lord exercises this servant vocation *through* the work of his Spirit-empowered followers, who act as *his* witnesses and carry out *his* mission unto the farthest reaches of the world.

The Power for Mission in the Last Days (Joel 2:28–32)

Steve Rogers is a scrawny asthmatic from Brooklyn who desperately wants to be a soldier like his late father, who was killed in World War I shortly before Steve's birth.[25] Rogers tries to enlist but is repeatedly rejected for military service due to his poor health. Dr. Abraham Erskine overhears Rogers's conversation with his friend, James "Bucky" Barnes, and approves his enlistment. Dr. Erskine selects Rogers for a special program in the Strategic Scientific Reserve. Rogers is injected with a secret serum and exposed to vita rays, and this experimental treatment transforms him from a ninety-pound weakling into a tall, muscular super soldier. Rogers is initially assigned to tour as "Captain America" to promote the war effort, but when he hears that Barnes's regiment is missing in action, Rogers attempts a daring solo rescue operation. He infiltrates the compound of the Nazi Hydra division, frees four hundred American prisoners of war, and confronts Hydra's dangerous leader, Johann Schmidt. From the outset of the story, Rogers is brave and selfless, but he lacks the requisite strength and stamina to serve his country. Dr. Erskine's super-soldier serum gives Rogers a new power to carry out his glorious mission to rescue his comrades and save the world from Schmidt's sinister scheme. Like Rogers, Jesus's followers need empowerment to carry out the mission for which they are called.

John the Baptist prepares the way for the Lord Jesus, who "will baptize you with the Holy Spirit and fire" (Luke 3:16); this prophecy "casts its

---

23 Thompson, *The Acts of the Risen Lord Jesus*, 48.

24 See Thompson, *The Acts of the Risen Lord Jesus*, 118.

25 Joe Johnston, dir., *Captain America: The First Avenger* (Burbank, CA: Marvel Studios, 2011).

shadow" across Luke's two volumes.[26] Before his ascension, the risen Lord promises that his followers will soon be "clothed with power from on high" and "baptized with the Holy Spirit" (Luke 24:49; Acts 1:5). This promise is fulfilled in dramatic fashion on the day of Pentecost, as tongues of fire rest on the disciples and they are "filled with the Holy Spirit" (Acts 2:3–4). Luke records the initial responses from those Jews "from every nation under heaven" gathered in Jerusalem, who marvel that these Galilean disciples proclaim God's mighty acts "in our own tongues" (vv. 5–13). The apostle Peter then interprets and explains this amazing and controversial event, concluding that Jesus is both Lord and Christ, and calling his hearers to repent and be baptized in Jesus's name (vv. 14–41). The coming of the Holy Spirit is a massively significant development in the biblical storyline. It fulfills ancient prophecy and offers proof that "the last days" have begun (vv. 16–21). The Spirit's arrival also confirms Peter's claims that Jesus has overcome death, ascended to heaven, and poured out the Spirit (as God promised in Joel 2:28). There are various important biblical-theological implications of Pentecost, but here I focus particularly on the crucial role of the Spirit in empowering Jesus's witnesses to carry out his mission to the nations.[27]

Peter explains that the disciples' unusual behavior and miraculous speech in other languages "is what was uttered through the prophet Joel" (Acts 2:16). The short book of Joel repeatedly stresses the coming day of the Lord, which will be a time of judgment on Israel (Joel 1:2–2:11) and on the nations (3:2). This day will also mean salvation for the "survivors . . . whom the LORD calls" (2:32). The prophet summons the people of Israel to wholeheartedly "return" to the Lord their God (vv. 12–13) and then explains how the Lord's own jealousy and pity (v. 18) move him to restore his people and judge those nations that have scattered Israel (2:19–3:21). The apostle cites Joel 2:28–32, where the Lord promises to pour out his Spirit "on all flesh" and save "everyone who calls on the name of the LORD."[28]

---

26 Bock, *A Theology of Luke and Acts*, 216.

27 For additional discussion of the Holy Spirit in Acts, see Turner, "Spirit of Prophecy," 327–48; Peterson, *The Acts of the Apostles*, 59–64; Thompson, *The Acts of the Risen Lord Jesus*, 125–43; and Bock, *A Theology of Luke and Acts*, 211–26.

28 Peter's quotation follows Joel 3:1–5 LXX (2:28–32 in English versions) with minor variations, which are discussed in Marshall, "Acts," 534; and Steven E. Runge, "Joel 2.28–32A in

Joel 2:28 emphasizes both "the fullness of the Spirit . . . and the democ-ratization of the Spirit."[29] The Old Testament recounts the Spirit's influence on some individuals, including prophets, select kings, and craftsmen for the tabernacle, but Joel's prophecy describes a new era in which all God's people will experience the power and presence of the Spirit. Joel recalls Moses's words in Numbers 11:29—"Would that all the LORD's people were prophets, that the LORD would put his Spirit on them!"—transforming Moses's hope "into a formal prophecy."[30]

Commentators typically explain that "all flesh" in Joel 2:28 refers to Judah[31] or all Israel.[32] There are at least three reasons for this interpretation: (1) verse 27 describes the Lord "in the midst of Israel"; (2) the remainder of verse 28 specifies the Spirit's effects on "your" sons, daughters, old men, and young men; and (3) some scholars argue that Joel interprets the similar prophecy in Ezekiel 39:29, where the Lord promises to "pour out my Spirit upon the house of Israel." However, elsewhere in the Old Testament the phrase "all flesh" consistently refers to all humanity. Isaiah 40:5 stresses that "all flesh" shall see the Lord's glory revealed, and the Septuagint specifies that "all flesh will see God's salvation." Luke's Gospel cites Isaiah's foundational new exodus prophecy to signal that the Lord Jesus brings salvation for "all flesh," not only for ethnic Israel.[33] By appealing to Joel 2:28 on the day of Pentecost, Peter similarly stresses that the Lord Jesus has poured out the Spirit on "all flesh" in the last days.

Acts 2.17–21: The Discourse and Text-Critical Implications of Variation from the LXX," in *Early Christian Literature and Intertextuality, Vol. 2: Exegetical Studies*, ed. Craig A. Evans and Zacharias H. Daniel, LNTS 392 (London: T&T Clark, 2009), 103–13.

29 Stuart, *Hosea–Jonah*, 260.

30 Beale, *The Temple and the Church's Mission*, 210. On the use of Num. 11:1–12:8 in Joel 2:28–29, see Raymond B. Dillard, "Joel," in *The Minor Prophets: An Exegetical and Expository Commentary*, ed. Thomas E. McComiskey (Grand Rapids, MI: Baker Academic, 1992), 1:294–95.

31 Leslie C. Allen, *The Books of Joel, Obadiah, Jonah and Micah*, NICOT (Grand Rapids, MI: Eerdmans, 1976), 98; and James L. Crenshaw, *Joel*, AB 24C (New York: Doubleday, 1995), 165.

32 Hans Walter Wolff, *Joel and Amos: A Commentary on the Books of the Prophets Joel and Amos*, ed. S. Dean McBride Jr., trans. Waldemar Janzen, S. Dean McBride Jr., and C. A. Muenchow, Hermeneia (Philadelphia: Fortress, 1977), 67; Duane A. Garrett, *Hosea, Joel*, NAC 19A (Nashville: Broadman & Holman, 1997), 369; Tchavdar S. Hadjiev, *Joel and Amos: An Introduction and Commentary*, TOTC 25 (Downers Grove, IL: InterVarsity Press, 2020), 46; and Dillard, "Joel," 295, though he acknowledges, "Paul understands that Joel spoke better than he knew."

33 For discussion of the quotation of Isa. 40:3–5 in Luke 3:4–6, see chap. 4, pp. 90–94.

Peter's quotation of "the prophet Joel" (Acts 2:16) opens with the phrase "in the last days" (v. 17)—strikingly, these words do not come from Joel but from Isaiah 2:2 LXX:

> For *in the last days*
>   the mountain of the Lord shall be manifest,
> and the house of God shall be on the tops of the mountains
>   and shall be raised above the hills,
> and all the nations shall come to it. (NETS)

It is a common practice for New Testament authors (and their Jewish contemporaries) to combine similar Old Testament passages.[34] James Crenshaw suggests that the Hebrew syntax of Joel 2:28 (3:1 MT) recalls Isaiah 2:2;[35] the reference to Mount Zion in Joel 2:32 also parallels Isaiah 2:2–4. Peter's combination of Isaiah 2:2 and Joel 2:28–32 is exegetically significant for at least two reasons. First, he links the outpouring of the Spirit as prophesied by Joel with the initial fulfillment of Isaiah's prophecy that the nations would flow to the end-time temple of God.[36] Additionally, Isaiah 2:3 prophesies that God's word will go out "from Jerusalem" in the last days, which the outpouring of the Spirit makes possible. According to Pao, Isaiah 2:3 offers "a one sentence summary statement of the journey of the word in Acts" from Jerusalem to the nations.[37]

It may appear that Peter's sermon abruptly shifts from explaining the outpouring of the Spirit (Acts 2:15–21) to proclaiming the death and resurrection of Jesus (vv. 22–36), but in fact the latter is integrally related to the former. Peter concludes his quotation of Joel by declaring that "everyone who calls upon the name of *the Lord* shall be saved" (v. 21). The apostle then explains that Jesus is "both *Lord* and Christ" (v. 36). Moreover, the risen and ascended

---

34 See, for example, Jesus's composite citation of Isa. 61:1–2 and 58:6 in Luke 4:18–19 and James's appeal to "the prophets" in Acts 15:16–18. For extensive treatment of these "composite citations," see Sean A. Adams and Seth M. Ehorn, eds., *Composite Citations in Antiquity, Volume Two: New Testament Uses*, LNTS 593 (London: Bloomsbury T&T Clark, 2018).

35 Crenshaw, *Joel*, 164.

36 Beale, *The Temple and the Church's Mission*, 209.

37 Pao, *Acts and the Isaianic New Exodus*, 159. For a complementary emphasis on restoration for the nations in the last days, see Chris Blumhofer, "Luke's Alteration of Joel 3.1–5 in Acts 2.17–21," *NTS* 62 (2016): 505–6.

Lord Jesus has poured out the promised Spirit (v. 32)—the very thing that God announced that he would do in Joel 2:28. In Acts 10:45, the Holy Spirit is "poured out even on the Gentiles," recalling the foundational Spirit outpouring in Jerusalem and demonstrating that Jesus truly "is *Lord* of all" (v. 36).

The coming of the Holy Spirit is the watershed event in the book of Acts, fulfilling Old Testament prophecy and also the risen Lord's promise that his followers would be "clothed with power from on high" (Luke 24:49; cf. Acts 1:8). This event clarifies *how* Jesus continues to work after his ascension: he pours out the Holy Spirit to empower his witnesses to speak about their risen Lord.[38] On the day of Pentecost, the Spirit-filled disciples "speak in other tongues" about "the mighty works of God" (2:4, 11), and Peter proclaims that Jesus is Lord and Messiah (v. 36). In 4:8–12, Peter is "filled with the Holy Spirit" and boldly declares to the Jewish council that there is salvation in Jesus's name alone. Joel's prophecy stresses the outpouring of the Spirit on "all flesh," on men and women, young and old, and even servants, leading them to prophesy, see visions, dream dreams, and call on the Lord's name for salvation (Acts 2:17–21). Acts regularly highlights how Peter, Paul, and other Spirit-filled leaders bear witness to Christ, yet 4:29–31 presents a larger gathering of believers who pray for God's help, are "filled with the Holy Spirit," and continue "to speak the word of God with boldness." Similarly, Luke explains that Philip and other believers scattered by persecution preach the word in Samaria, Antioch, and elsewhere, while the apostles remain in Jerusalem (8:1, 4–5; 11:19–20).[39]

The "devout men from every nation under heaven" who gather in Jerusalem on the day of Pentecost (Acts 2:5) may be "missiologically and eschatologically representative" of "all nations" that must hear preaching about forgiveness in Jesus's name (Luke 24:47).[40] While these representatives from the nations are "Jews and proselytes" (Acts 2:11), this scene anticipates the church's mission to all nations. The fifteen places named in verses 9–11 illustrate "every nation" in verse 5. This list probably recalls the nations that "spread abroad on the earth after the flood" (Gen. 10:32).[41] Acts

38 Max Turner summarizes the scholarly consensus: "For Luke, the Spirit is largely the 'Spirit of prophecy'; in Acts especially as an 'empowering for witness.'" "Spirit of Prophecy," 330.

39 These examples undermine Turner's claim that Luke "nowhere explicitly states that the rank-and-file of the church . . . actively spread the word." "Spirit of Prophecy," 340.

40 Keener, *Acts*, 1:835.

41 The Hebrew text of Gen. 10 lists seventy nations, while the Septuagint records seventy-two.

includes representative samples of nations to the east, north, south, and west of Jerusalem, including examples of the descendants of Noah's three sons.[42] This allusion to the Table of Nations is anticipated in Luke 10:1, when Jesus sends out seventy-two (or seventy) disciples.[43] These witnesses may "represent the nations of the world to be evangelized," recalling the list in Genesis 10.[44] While God directs Noah's sons to "be fruitful and multiply and fill the earth" (Gen. 9:1), their descendants instead unite at Babel to make a name for themselves and avoid being dispersed (11:4). The Lord then confuses their language and disperses the people (11:9), thus overcoming their resistance to "fill the earth" as God had commanded (9:1, 7; cf. 1:28).[45]

The allusions to Genesis 10–11 indicate that the coming of the Spirit at Pentecost marks a reversal of Babel. At Babel, the Lord comes down to "confuse" the people's language so that they cannot "understand" each other (Gen. 11:7). But in Acts 2:6, the gathered multitude is "bewildered" because they each are "hearing" the disciples "speak in his own language." G. K. Beale explains the biblical-theological significance of this development:

> Babel's sin of uniting and consequent judgment of confused languages and of people being scattered throughout the earth is reversed at Pentecost: God causes representatives from the same scattered nations to unite in Jerusalem in order that they might receive the blessing of understanding different languages as if all these languages were one.[46]

Thus, on the day of Pentecost, the risen Lord pours out God's Spirit on "all flesh," fulfilling the prophecies of Joel and John the Baptist (Acts 2:17, 33;

---

42 The list in Acts 2:9–11 updates the names of the nations in Gen. 10, as Josephus does in *Jewish Antiquities*, 1.122–47. Japheth's descendants include residents of Asia, as well as Medes and Cappadocians (Gen. 10:2–5; and *Jewish Antiquities*, 1.122–28); Egypt, Libya, and Judea are among Ham's ancestors (Gen. 10:6–20; and *Jewish Antiquities*, 1.130–39); and Elam is the first son of Shem (Gen. 10:21–31; and *Jewish Antiquities*, 1.143–47). For an overview of the nations in Acts 2:9–11, see Keener, *Acts*, 844–51.

43 There is strong manuscript evidence for "seventy" and "seventy-two" in Luke 10:1, perhaps reflecting the difference between the Hebrew and Greek versions of Gen. 10. See Bovon, *Luke 2*, 26; and Bruce M. Metzger, *A Textual Commentary on the Greek New Testament*, 2nd ed. (Stuttgart: Deutsche Bibelgesellschaft, 1994), 126–27.

44 Beale, *The Temple and the Church's Mission*, 201.

45 Beale, *The Temple and the Church's Mission*, 201–2.

46 Beale, *The Temple and the Church's Mission*, 202; see Keener, *Acts*, 1:842–44.

cf. Joel 2:28; Luke 3:16). We have seen that the coming of the Spirit signals the dawn of the promised "last days," when God would save his people, the nations would flock to Zion, and God's word would go forth from Jerusalem (Isa. 2:2–3). Acts emphasizes that the Holy Spirit empowers Jesus's witnesses to carry out his mission (1:8). The Spirit's coming also brings about a redemptive-historical reversal of the nations' plight since Babel, as the multitude "from every nation" hears the disciples speak intelligibly in various languages. This scene previews the global scope of the mission for which Jesus has called and empowered his witnesses.

Blessing for Every Family of the Earth (Acts 3:25–26)

The opening verse of the New Testament identifies Jesus as "the son of Abraham" (Matt. 1:1), and the Lord's promises to the patriarch feature prominently in Luke and Acts. Mary and Zechariah stress God's commitment to keep his covenant oath to Abraham (Luke 1:55, 73), while John the Baptist declares that God can raise up children for Abraham from stones (3:8). Jesus teaches that Abraham and the patriarchs will welcome people from east, west, north, and south into the kingdom of God, while others will surprisingly be cast out (13:28–29). He also highlights the Abrahamic heritage of two outsiders—a disabled woman and a notorious tax collector (13:16; 19:9), and he cites the Lord's self-description as the patriarchs' God (20:37).[47] Peter similarly refers to the Lord as "the God of Abraham, the God of Isaac, and the God of Jacob, the God of our fathers" (Acts 3:13).

The apostle returns to God's covenant with Abraham in Acts 3:25–26:

> You are the sons of the prophets and of the covenant that God made with your fathers, saying to Abraham, "And in your offspring shall all the families of the earth be blessed." God, having raised up his servant, sent him to you first, to bless you by turning every one of you from your wickedness.

Peter quotes God's foundational promise to Abraham in Genesis 12:3 ("in you all the families of the earth shall be blessed"), which is restated in 22:18, after God tests Abraham ("in your offspring shall all the nations of the

---

47 See chap. 3, pp. 62–66.

earth be blessed").[48] Peter's point here is that Jesus is Abraham's promised descendent in whom all peoples will be blessed by God.[49]

In Genesis 12:2–3, God promises to bless Abraham and "all the families of the earth" in him. This promise of blessing signals a shift in the narrative of Genesis, as Stephen Dempster explains: "Against the dark background of the Table of Nations and the fiasco of Babel, the blessing of Abraham is clearly an answer to the fundamental problem of the human condition. . . . Terah's son Abram will be the agent of blessing for the world."[50]

We have seen that Acts 2:5–11 alludes to Genesis 10–11 to indicate that the coming of the Spirit at Pentecost marks a reversal of Babel while anticipating the global mission of Jesus's followers. In Acts 3, Peter appeals to the ancient covenant promises and saving work of the God of Abraham, Isaac, and Jacob. God has "glorified his servant Jesus" (3:13; cf. Isa. 52:13) and thus accomplished what he foretold by the prophets (Acts 3:18). The apostle calls his Jewish hearers to repent of their sins and listen to Jesus, the promised prophet like Moses (vv. 19, 22). He calls them "the sons of the prophets and of the covenant that God made with your fathers" (v. 25) to stress that they are heirs to the ancient promises that God has fulfilled though Jesus.[51]

Some interpreters argue that Abraham's "offspring" (*sperma*) in Acts 3:25 refers collectively to the people of Israel,[52] but the logic of Peter's sermon implies that Christ is the "offspring" promised in Genesis. The grammar of Genesis 22:17–18 suggests that Abraham's "offspring" denotes an individual descendant through whom Abraham's blessing would flow to the world.[53] Acts 3:26 fittingly applies this promise to Christ, whom Peter calls God's "servant," just as he does in verse 13, to recall Isaiah's prophecies of

---

48 This promise is also restated with minor variations in Gen. 18:18; 26:4; 28:14; cf. Gal. 3:8. For a detailed treatment of the source of Peter's quotation, see James A. Meek, *The Gentile Mission in Old Testament Citations in Acts: Text, Hermeneutic, and Purpose*, LNTS 385 (London: T&T Clark, 2008), 114–16.

49 Marshall, "Acts," 549. For a survey of interpretations, see Barrett, *Acts*, 212–13.

50 Stephen G. Dempster, *Dominion and Dynasty: A Biblical Theology of the Hebrew Bible*, NSBT 15 (Downers Grove, IL: InterVarsity Press, 2003), 77.

51 See Peterson, *The Acts of the Apostles*, 87–88.

52 Jacob Jervell, *Die Apostelgeschichte*, KEK 17 (Göttingen: Vandenhoeck & Ruprecht, 1998), 170.

53 Jason S. DeRouchie and Jason C. Meyer, "Christ or Family as the 'Seed' of Promise? An Evaluation of N. T. Wright on Galatians 3:16," *SBJT* 14.3 (2010): 39–40.

the Lord's servant.[54] Thus, the Lord Jesus fulfills the hopes of the Law and the Prophets as the promised descendant of Abraham and the glorified suffering servant.[55] Peter argues that God sent Jesus "to you first, to bless you," signaling both the Jews' redemptive-historical privilege as heirs of the covenant and also their inclusion among "all the families of the earth" to be blessed in Abraham's offspring (vv. 25–26). "First" in verse 26 anticipates the missionaries' logic in 13:46–47, as they speak the word "first" to Jews and then turn to the Gentiles to carry out the servant's mission to the end of the earth (Isa. 49:6).

Thus, Peter's sermon in Acts 3 reflects on the necessary suffering and exaltation of Jesus, the Lord's righteous servant, who is "sent" first to Israel while also being the agent of blessing for the nations as the Lord's servant and Abraham's promised son. While later passages in Acts offer more explicit biblical rationale for the mission to the Gentiles, Peter anchors the hope for the nations in God's foundational promise to the patriarch, which Jesus has fulfilled.

Turning to the Gentiles (Acts 13:46–47)

The risen Lord declares that the mission of his witnesses will extend "to the end of the earth" (Acts 1:8), fulfilling the servant prophecy of Isaiah 49:6. The book of Acts then narrates *how* Jesus's followers carry out this mission in accord with his programmatic promise in Jerusalem (chaps. 2–7), Samaria and Judea (chaps. 8–12), and beyond (chaps. 13–28). Strikingly, the Lord charges the most unlikely witness to bring the gospel "to the end of the earth"—Saul of Tarsus, the church's most zealous opponent.[56] While on a mission to detain and destroy the disciples of Jesus, Saul encounters the risen Lord (9:1–5), who then identifies this persecutor as "a chosen instrument of mine to carry my name before the Gentiles and kings and the children of Israel" (v. 15). Saul immediately begins to proclaim Christ and experience persecution in Damascus and Jerusalem following his dramatic conversion (vv. 19–30). He later ministers with Barnabas in Syrian Antioch before bringing aid to Jerusalem (11:25–30). The Holy Spirit directs the church in

---

54 Beers, *The Followers of Jesus*, 134–35.

55 Bock, *Proclamation from Prophecy and Pattern*, 196–97.

56 For extended discussion of Saul's conversion and call in Acts, see Tabb, *Suffering in Ancient Worldview*, 121–54.

Antioch to "set apart" Barnabas and Saul for a new work to which God has called them (13:2). The missionaries travel to Cyprus (vv. 4–12)[57] and then to Pisidian Antioch, where Paul preaches in the synagogue (vv. 14–41). On the following Sabbath, a large crowd assembles to hear the word of the Lord, but "the Jews" contradict and oppose Paul out of jealousy (vv. 44–45).[58]

This opposition prompts a bold response from the missionaries: "It was necessary that the word of God be spoken first to you. Since you thrust it aside and judge yourselves unworthy of eternal life, behold, we are turning to the Gentiles" (Acts 13:46). Then they cite Isaiah 49:6 as a biblical rationale for their Gentile outreach:

For so the Lord has commanded us, saying,

"I have made you a light for the Gentiles,
    that you may bring salvation to the ends of the earth." (Acts 13:47)

Isaiah 49:6 is a well-known prophecy concerning the Lord's servant.[59] In Isaiah 42:1, the Lord introduces "my servant, whom I uphold, my chosen, in whom my soul delights." This verse recalls an earlier description of Israel as "my servant . . . whom I have chosen," whom the Lord promises to strengthen, help, and uphold with his right hand (41:8–10). The Lord declares concerning his servant,

I will give you as a covenant for the people,
    a light for the nations,
to open the eyes that are blind,
    to bring out the prisoners from the dungeon. (42:6–7)

Yet God also calls his servant "blind" and "deaf" (v. 19). Though Israel received the glorious divine law, the people did not obey it and were

---

57 According to Acts 4:36, Barnabas is a native of Cyprus.

58 Since "many Jews" followed Paul and Barnabas, according to Acts 13:43, "the Jews" who revile them in verse 45 cannot refer to all the Jews in Antioch. Their "jealousy" recalls the description of the high priest and Sadducees who arrest the apostles (5:17–18), suggesting that the opposition in 13:45 comes from the unbelieving Jewish leaders and those whom they incite against the missionaries (v. 50).

59 I discuss the use of Isa. 49:6 in Acts 1:8 above, pp. 136–41.

plundered by their enemies as an expression of God's anger over their sin (vv. 21–25).

Andrew Abernethy argues that Isaiah 42:1–9 does not refer to an individual messiah but to the nation as God's servant, as in 41:8.[60] He explains, "Strategically positioned in exile, scattered among the nations, God's servant, Israel, is to carry forth God's mission of bringing justice and spiritual transformation throughout the world."[61] Because Israel fails to carry out this task due to its spiritual blindness, the Lord promises to "use an individual servant to achieve atonement for and effect spiritual change in Israel and all nations (49:1–13; 50:4–9; 52:13–53:12)."[62] There are two primary weaknesses with this collective interpretation of the servant in Isaiah 42:1. First, the Lord declares that he has put his Spirit upon this servant (v. 1), which recalls the description of the Spirit resting upon the Davidic Messiah (11:2) and anticipates the Lord's agent anointed to proclaim good news (61:1). Elsewhere Isaiah recalls how the Israelites grieved the Holy Spirit and how the divine Spirit was in their midst in "the days of old" (63:10–11), but the prophet speaks of a future time of salvation when the Lord will pour out the Spirit upon his people (32:15; 44:3; 59:21). The servant's anointing by the Spirit to bring about justice thus suggests an individual agent. Moreover, the Lord appoints his servant "as a covenant for the people" and "a light for the nations" in 42:6, using similar language in 49:6. Abernethy suggests that "covenant for the people" in 42:6 denotes "how Israel is to enable the nations to experience God's salvation."[63] However, the singular "the people" more naturally refers to Israel, in contrast with the plural "nations."[64] This suggests that in both 42:1–9 and in 49:1–6, the Lord's servant is an individual who acts on behalf of Israel and the nations.

The servant says, "Listen to me, O coastlands" (Isa. 49:1). This rare first-person speech recalls 48:16: "And now the Lord GOD has sent me, and his

---

60 Abernethy, *The Book of Isaiah and God's Kingdom*, 138. See Matthew S. Harmon, *The Servant of the Lord and His Servant People: Tracing a Biblical Theme through the Canon*, NSBT 54 (Downers Grove, IL: InterVarsity Press, 2021), 115–16; and John Goldingay and David Payne, *Isaiah 40–55: A Critical and Exegetical Commentary*, 2 vols., ICC (London: T&T Clark, 2006), 1:212. Isa. 42:1 LXX supports this view by specifying, "Jacob is my servant . . . Israel is my chosen."

61 Abernethy, *The Book of Isaiah and God's Kingdom*, 141.

62 Abernethy, *The Book of Isaiah and God's Kingdom*, 138.

63 Abernethy, *The Book of Isaiah and God's Kingdom*, 195n47.

64 House, *Isaiah*, 323; and Oswalt, *The Book of Isaiah*, 2:117–18.

Spirit." The phrase "and now" further links 48:16 and 49:5, suggesting that both texts refer to the Lord's servant.[65] The servant recounts his divine call from the womb and the Lord's decree, "You are my servant, Israel, in whom I will be glorified" (49:1, 3). He then confesses that he has "labored in vain" (v. 4).

Isaiah 49:1–6 is variously interpreted.[66] Some scholars read verses 1–4 as referring to the nation of Israel, while verses 5–6 are referring to an individual servant (the speaker from 48:16–22).[67] However, the use of the first person in 49:1–4 continues in verse 5 and suggests the same referent: "the LORD called *me* from the womb" (v. 1) closely parallels "he who formed *me* from the womb to be his servant" (v. 5). Further, the declaration that "my God has become my strength" (v. 5) naturally follows from verse 4, "I have spent my strength." Others identify the servant throughout verses 1–6 as the prophet, who embodies Israel and shares the Lord's light with the Gentiles.[68] Alternatively, others explain that while the Lord's servant bears Israel's name and takes up Israel's mission in verses 1–4, this servant is still an individual agent with a mission to reach Israel.[69] In this reading, the servant's lament concerning his spent strength and futility (v. 4) points forward to the servant's humility and suffering in the final two Servant Songs.[70] The servant's total commitment to speak God's word (50:4–5) brings about resistance and suffering (50:6).[71]

Thus, I understand the Lord's servant in Isaiah 49:1–6 to be an individual agent who is chosen and prepared by God for a mission to restore Israel and bring light to the nations, extending God's salvation "to the end of the earth." Verses 7–12 further explain the servant's mission to Israel and the nations: he will be despised yet vindicated (v. 7) and will be "a covenant to the people" in the day of salvation (v. 8), bringing light

---

65 House, *Isaiah*, 419–20. The individual servant of Isa. 49:1–6 "step[s] forward" in 48:16, according to Christopher R. Seitz, "The Book of Isaiah 40–66," in *The New Interpreter's Bible, Volume VI*, ed. Leander E. Keck (Nashville: Abingdon, 2001), 429.

66 For additional views beyond those surveyed here, see House, *Isaiah*, 429–31.

67 House, *Isaiah*, 428, 431.

68 Goldingay, *The Message of Isaiah 40–55*, 368–74. Goldingay refers to this prophet as "Second Isaiah," distinct from Isaiah the son of Amoz (p. 370).

69 Abernethy, *The Book of Isaiah and God's Kingdom*, 147.

70 In the Septuagint, "my pain" in Isa. 49:4 anticipates the servant's "pain" in 53:4, 11.

71 See Abernethy, *The Book of Isaiah and God's Kingdom*, 148.

to those in darkness and freedom for prisoners (v. 9), shepherding God's people (v. 10), and gathering God's people from distant lands (vv. 11–12).[72]

The Lord identifies this agent as "my servant, Israel" (Isa. 49:3), which recalls repeated references to God's people as his servant in chapters 41–48. Yet Israel is a blind and deaf servant (42:19), prone to fear (44:2), and in need of redemption (48:20). The faithful individual servant who is introduced in 42:1 and speaks in 48:16 and 49:1–6 is identified as "Israel" (49:3) by the principle of corporate solidarity—the one who represents the many. "He will be for Israel, and the world, what Israel could not be."[73] Strikingly, after Isaiah 53:11 describes the righteous individual *servant* who will "make many to be accounted righteous" and bear their sins, Isaiah 54–66 refers ten times to the Lord's *servants* (plural).[74] "As a result of the servant's mission, a community of 'servants' . . . will arise to take up Israel's mission of bringing God's justice to the world."[75] This group of servants will include not only "offspring from Judah" (65:9), but also "foreigners who join themselves to the LORD" (56:6).

Having discussed the context of Isaiah 49:6 at length, let's now consider its quotation in Acts 13:47. Paul and Barnabas introduce this citation of Isaiah's prophecy by saying, "For so the Lord has commanded us." The conjunction "for" indicates that their appeal to Isaiah provides a rationale for why they are turning to the Gentiles in response to Jewish opposition (v. 46).

Moreover, interpreters debate whether "the Lord" (*kyrios*) who commands Paul and Barnabas in verse 47 refers to God or Jesus,[76] though in some sense both are true. In Isaiah 49:6, the prophet records the Lord's commission to his servant. Luke 2:32 rightly identifies Jesus as the Lord's servant who will be a light to the nations as Isaiah prophesied. The risen Lord Jesus then commissions his witnesses to go "to the end of the earth" (Acts 1:8) and later reveals himself to Paul and summons this ardent adversary to be his chosen servant sent to the Gentiles (9:15;

---

72 See House, *Isaiah*, 431.

73 Oswalt, *The Book of Isaiah*, 2:291. See Motyer, *Isaiah*, 351; and Beale, *A New Testament Biblical Theology*, 656–57.

74 "Servants" occurs in Isa. 54:17; 56:6; 63:17; 65:9, 13–15; 66:14.

75 Abernethy, *The Book of Isaiah and God's Kingdom*, 156.

76 *Kyrios* in Acts 13:47 refers to God, according to Jervell, *Apostelgeschichte*, 364. *Kyrios* refers to Jesus, according to Pao, *Acts and the Isaianic New Exodus*, 101.

26:16–18). Thus, Isaiah's prophecy is *God's* scriptural word, which *the Lord Jesus* fulfills and then applies to his followers as they carry out his mission as the servant.

Therefore, Isaiah 49:6 offers biblical grounding for Paul and Barnabas's mission to the Gentiles through the principle of corporate solidarity. This principle is at work within the book of Isaiah itself. The Lord identifies Israel and his righteous agent as "my servant," and his individual servant bears Israel's name, will restore the scattered nation, and will accomplish the mission to the nations that Israel fails to fulfill due to its spiritual blindness. Further, this righteous servant will make many righteous and will create a community of servants who love the Lord and enjoy his favor (53:11; 56:6). Simeon identifies Jesus as "a light for revelation to the Gentiles" (Luke 2:32), which indicates that "foundationally, he is the one in whom Isaiah's prediction is fulfilled."[77] Jesus himself declares at the beginning and end of his ministry that he fulfills the servant prophecies of Isaiah 61:1–2 (Luke 4:17–21) and Isaiah 53:12 (Luke 22:37). Carl Holladay reasons that "Luke presents Paul and Barnabas as the replacement of 'Israel, the servant of the Lord'" in Isaiah 49.[78] However, by moving directly from Israel to the missionaries, this analysis misses two crucial biblical-theological steps. First, in Isaiah, the righteous individual servant fulfills Israel's mission and accomplishes the nation's restoration. Second, Jesus fulfills Isaiah's servant prophecy and then commissions his servants to share in his mission. Paul later explains the Scriptures' teaching "that the Christ must suffer and that, by being the first to rise from the dead, he would proclaim light both to our people and to the Gentiles" (Acts 26:23). He also recounts his own commission to the Gentiles "to open their eyes, so that they may turn from darkness to light" (v. 18), which reflects the servant's mission to be "a light for the nations" and "open the eyes that are blind" (Isa. 42:6–7). Thus, Christ is the Lord's servant "Israel," and his witnesses share in his mission to the nations.[79]

---

77 Peterson, *The Acts of the Apostles*, 398.

78 Carl R. Holladay, *Acts: A Commentary*, NTL (Louisville: Westminister John Knox, 2016), 281–82.

79 See Beale, *A New Testament Biblical Theology*, 684. Harmon reasons, "Christ the servant dwells in Paul to fulfil the mission of the servant to be a light to the nations," interpreting Acts 13:46–47 in light of Paul's words in Gal. 1:15–16 and 2:20. *The Servant of the Lord and His Servant People*, 193.

On several occasions in Acts, intense persecution serves as a catalyst for gospel advance in Jerusalem, Judea and Samaria, and beyond (1:8).[80] Following Stephen's death, "a great persecution" scatters the Jerusalem church throughout Judea and Samaria (8:1). Ironically, this scattering serves as a vehicle for spreading the good news beyond Jerusalem to Samaria, Phoenicia, Cyprus, and Antioch, where the believers evangelize Gentiles (8:4–25; 11:19–21). Similarly in Acts 13:46, Paul and Barnabas boldly declare that they "are turning to the Gentiles" in response to Jewish opposition to their message. The Lord Jesus designates Paul as his chosen representative to the Gentiles in Acts 9:15, but it is the Jews' antagonism in Antioch that spurs the missionaries' outreach to Gentiles. Luke contrasts the Jews' jealousy and rejection of their message (13:45, 50) with the Gentiles' joy and reception of the word of the Lord (vv. 48, 52) and the word's spread "throughout the whole region" (v. 49). Of course, this is not the first instance of outreach to Gentiles in Acts—the Spirit is poured out on the Gentiles in Acts 10:44–45. Additionally, the missionaries' declaration in 13:46 does not end their ministry among Jews. Paul reasons with the Jews in the synagogues at Iconium, Thessalonica, Berea, Athens, Corinth, and Ephesus.[81] He also addresses his fellow Jews in Jerusalem (21:40–22:21) and seeks an audience with the Jews in Rome (28:17). Following the missionaries' statement of turning to the Gentiles in Antioch, Paul makes similar declarations in Corinth (18:6) and Rome (28:28). Even at the close of the book, Paul welcomes "all" who come to him to hear about the Lord Jesus (28:30).

While Jewish opposition to the word of God is a catalyst for the mission of Jesus's witnesses beyond Jerusalem in Acts, the citation of Isaiah 49:6 signals that the missionaries do not "call an audible" or turn to the Gentiles as an afterthought.[82] Isaiah provides the underlying biblical-theological warrant for the outreach to the Gentiles.[83] Luke makes clear that this expanding mission of Jesus's followers fulfills not only the Lord's promise in Acts 1:8 but also the prophecy of the servant's mission that stands behind Jesus's words.

---

80 See Brian J. Tabb, "Salvation, Spreading, and Suffering: God's Unfolding Plan in Luke-Acts," *JETS* 58 (2015): 51–54.

81 Acts 14:1; 17:1, 10, 17; 18:4, 19; 19:8.

82 Peterson, *The Acts of the Apostles*, 398.

83 See Beers, *The Followers of Jesus*, 163; and Meek, *The Gentile Mission in Old Testament Citations in Acts*, 45.

The Gentiles Seek the Lord (Acts 15:15–17)

The mission to the Gentiles is a central focus throughout Acts. The risen Lord explains that "all the nations" must receive the message of forgiveness of sins in his name (Luke 24:47), and he promises to empower his followers to carry out this global mission (Acts 1:8). Peter witnesses the Spirit poured out "even on the Gentiles" (10:45), believers from Cyprus and Cyrene evangelize the Hellenists in Antioch (11:20), and Paul and Barnabas announce that they are turning to the Gentiles in obedience to the Lord's command (13:46–47). Many Gentiles repent and believe the gospel, turn to the Lord, and are baptized in Jesus's name (10:48; 11:21; 13:48). But their favorable response to the message of salvation raises pressing theological and practical questions for the infant church about how these Gentile converts should relate to the Old Testament law and to Jewish believers. These questions come to the fore in Acts 15, as teachers from Judea insist that Gentile believers must be circumcised according to the law in order to be saved (v. 1). Paul and Barnabas vigorously debate with them in Antioch and then journey to Jerusalem to meet with the apostles and elders (v. 2). The missionaries recount God's work among the Gentiles, while believers from the Pharisees insist that these Gentile converts must be circumcised and keep the law (vv. 4–5). The apostles and elders consider the testimony of Peter, Barnabas and Paul, and the Scriptures (vv. 6–18), and they conclude that they "should not trouble those of the Gentiles who turn to God" (v. 19).

James offers the decisive argument from Scripture to bring resolution to the Jerusalem Council.[84] He explains that "the words of the prophets agree" with Peter's testimony that God has visited the Gentiles to take from them "a people for his name" (Acts 15:14–15), applying a well-known description of Israel to Gentile believers.[85] James then cites Amos 9:11–12:

> After this I will return,
> and I will rebuild the tent of David that has fallen;
> I will rebuild its ruins,

---

84 Richard Bauckham, "James and the Gentiles (Acts 15.13–21)," in *History, Literature, and Society in the Book of Acts*, 154.

85 See, for example, Ex. 19:5; Deut. 7:6; 14:2; and Beale, *A New Testament Biblical Theology*, 685–86.

and I will restore it,

that the remnant of mankind may seek the Lord,

and all the Gentiles who are called by my name,

says the Lord, who makes these things known from of old.

(Acts 15:16–18)

The prophecy of Amos "delivers a resounding message from God to Israel regarding judgment coming against the northern kingdom for its sin."[86] Amos declares that "the LORD roars from Zion" (1:2); while he will surely punish the nations for their transgressions (1:3–2:3), he reserves the most severe words for iniquitous Israel, who will be judged for her sexual immorality, idolatry, and injustice (2:6–6:14). The prophet receives a series of visions of Israel's coming destruction (7:1–9:10), concluding with the Lord's warnings that he will "shake the house of Israel among the nations" and "all the sinners of my people shall die by the sword" (9:9–10). Yet the Lord will not completely destroy Israel, even though she is a "sinful kingdom" (v. 8). After Amos's relentless focus on Israel's sin and punishment, the book closes with a glorious prophecy of Israel's salvation on the other side of judgment (vv. 11–15).[87] The Lord will "raise up" David's fallen booth with implications for the nations (vv. 11–12), and he will reverse the earlier disasters against his people by restoring their fortunes (vv. 13–15).[88]

James's quotation in Acts 15:16–18 does not closely match either the Hebrew or Septuagint versions of Amos 9:11–12, so it's necessary to wander into the tall grass of textual comparison in order to grasp the theological and missiological implications of this pivotal passage. Table 6.1 presents the agreements (underlined) and differences (bold) between the wording of Amos 9:11–12 and Acts 15:16–18.[89]

---

86 Michael G. McKelvey, "Amos," in *Daniel–Malachi*, ESVEC 7 (Wheaton, IL: Crossway, 2018), 303.

87 "In Amos, salvation comes through judgment by and for the glory of God," writes James M. Hamilton, *God's Glory in Salvation through Judgment: A Biblical Theology* (Wheaton, IL: Crossway, 2010), 245.

88 The judgments in Amos 8:9–13 "are reversed and rectified" in 9:11–15, according to Francis I. Andersen and David Noel Freedman, *Amos: A New Translation with Introduction and Commentary*, AB 24A (New Haven: Yale University Press, 1989), 887.

89 This table uses the ESV for Amos 9:11–12 Hebrew and Acts 15:16–18, and my own translation of Amos 9:11–12 LXX.

Amos 9:11–12 Hebrew	Amos 9:11–12 LXX	Acts 15:16–18
"In that day I will raise up <u>the booth of David</u> <u>that is fallen</u> and repair its breaches, and raise up <u>its ruins</u> and rebuild it as in the days of old, that they may possess the remnant of Edom and <u>all the nations who</u> <u>are called by my name,"</u> <u>declares the LORD who</u> <u>does</u> this.	"On that day I will raise up <u>the tent of David</u> <u>that has fallen</u> and <u>I will</u> <u>rebuild</u> its fallen places and raise up <u>its ruins,</u> and rebuild it as the days of old, <u>that the remnant</u> <u>of mankind may seek,</u> <u>and all the Gentiles who</u> <u>are called by my name,"</u> <u>says the Lord, who does</u> <u>these things.</u>	**"After this I will return, and I will rebuild** <u>the</u> <u>tent of David that has</u> <u>fallen;</u> <u>I will rebuild its</u> <u>ruins,</u> **and I will restore it,** <u>that the remnant of</u> <u>mankind may seek</u> **the Lord,** <u>and all the Gentiles</u> <u>who are called by my</u> <u>name,</u> <u>says the Lord,</u> who makes these things **known from of old."**

Table 6.1. The Use of Amos 9 in Acts 15

The Greek translation of Amos 9:11 closely follows the Hebrew text, but there are striking differences in verse 12: the Hebrew text is formally rendered, "that they may possess the remnant of Edom," while the Septuagint reads, "that the remnant of mankind may seek."[90] While "possess" and "seek" have quite different connotations, in Hebrew the verbs look very similar: *yrš* ("possess") and *drš* ("seek"). Similarly, "Edom" and "mankind" use the same three consonants in Hebrew (*'dm*) and differ only in vowel pointing, which Jewish scribes added centuries after the New Testament period. A third difference in Amos 9:12 is the function of "the remnant" in the sentence—it is the object of the verb in Hebrew but the subject in the LXX. Some scholars conclude that the Greek translator misread the Hebrew text of Amos,[91] though it is more likely that this translator offered a theologically motivated reading that reflects the influence of other prophecies, such as Zechariah 8:22.[92] Further, some suggest that "mankind" is a fitting interpretation of the Hebrew for "Edom" in Amos 9:12, since it occurs alongside "all the nations."[93] The Edomites were the descendants of Esau (Gen. 36:1), who

---

90   For detailed discussion, see W. Edward Glenny, *Finding Meaning in the Text: Translation Technique and Theology in the Septuagint of Amos*, VTSup 126 (Leiden: Brill, 2009), 217–28.

91   Anthony Gelston, "Some Hebrew Misreadings in the Septuagint of Amos," *VT* 52 (2002): 498–99.

92   See Glenny, *Finding Meaning in the Text*, 225–26.

93   Jeffrey Niehaus, "Amos," in *The Minor Prophets: An Exegetical and Expository Commentary*, 1:491.

settled in territory south of Israel and Judah. In Amos 1:11–12, the Lord declares that he will punish Edom for transgressions against "his brother" (Israel), so the promise that Israel would "possess the remnant of Edom" (9:12) signals a reversal in Israel's relationship to her hostile neighbors and a fulfillment of Balaam's prophecy in Numbers 24:17–19.[94] The decision to render "Edom" as "mankind" reflects an interpretation from the lesser to the greater—if even the Edomites will be among those called by God's name, then by extension all the nations will be able to seek the Lord.[95]

Acts 15:16–18 is closer to the Greek translation of Amos 9:11–12 than to the Hebrew original—especially verse 12—though James's quotation diverges from Amos LXX in several ways.[96] James refers to the agreement of "the words of the *prophets*" in Acts 15:15, which suggests that he reads Amos 9:11–12 together with other biblical prophecies.[97] "After this" (*meta tauta*) may recall Hosea 3:5 LXX: "And *after these things* [*meta tauta*], the children of Israel shall return and seek the LORD their God and David their king." Additionally, "I will return" may allude to God's promises to return to his people in Jeremiah 12:15 or Zechariah 8:3. "I will restore" (*anorthōsō*) in Acts 15:16 also deviates from Amos 9:11 LXX ("raise up"). This difference may signal a reference to God's promise to "restore" (*anorthōsō*) David's throne forever (2 Sam. 7:13; 1 Chron. 17:12 LXX). "Seek the Lord" reflects the influence of Zechariah 8:22: "Many peoples and strong nations shall come *to seek the LORD of hosts* in Jerusalem." Finally, the phrase "known from of old" in Acts 15:18 may allude to Isaiah 45:21 LXX: "that they might *know* together who made these things *from the beginning* that are to be heard."[98] While Amos 9:11–12 is the central text cited in Acts 15:16–18, these other Old Testament passages strike complementary notes, creating a prophetic

---

94 Beale, *The Temple and the Church's Mission*, 242–43.

95 Edward W. Glenny, "The Septuagint and Apostolic Hermeneutics: Amos 9 in Acts 15," *BBR* 22 (2012): 9. This reflects the common Jewish interpretive method *qal wahomer*, "light and heavy."

96 See the bold type in Table 6.1 above.

97 See Glenny, "The Septuagint and Apostolic Hermeneutics," 11–14; and Bauckham, "James and the Gentiles," 162–65. Alternatively, Aaron W. White questions these proposed biblical allusions as "too numerous and too complex," arguing that the literary context of Acts is the primary reason for variances between James's quotation and Amos 9:11–12. "Revisiting the 'Creative' Use of Amos in Acts and What It Tells Us About Luke," *BTB* 46.2 (2016): 199.

98 Marshall, "Acts," 591. Bauckham suggests that Acts 15:18 draws upon the Hebrew text of Isa. 45:21. "James and the Gentiles," 165.

symphony[99] of support for God's work among the Gentiles in the last days.

There are two primary interpretations of God's promise to "rebuild the tent of David" (Acts 15:16).[100] First, David's tent may refer to the restored temple of the messianic era.[101] The Greek word *skēnē* ("tent") regularly refers to the Old Testament "tabernacle" (Ex. 25:9), and Acts 7:43–44 references Israel's "tent of witness" and the "tent of Moloch."[102] Richard Bauckham reasons that the repeated Greek verb *anoikodomeō* connotes restoring a building, and notes that Jewish interpreters expected God himself to build the eschatological temple when the Davidic Messiah would come to rule over God's people, according to Ezekiel 37:24–28.[103] Alternatively, the promise cited in Acts 15:16 may denote the restoration of David's dynasty through Jesus's resurrection and heavenly reign.[104] This interpretation fits well with Luke's emphasis that Jesus is the promised Savior and ruler from the house of David (Luke 1:32–33, 69; Acts 13:22–23). Edward Glenny counters Bauckham's claim that "rebuild" must refer to temple construction, observing that "rebuild" (*anoikodomeō*) and "restore" (*anorthoō*) in Acts 15:16 recall God's covenant promises to build David an enduring house.[105] For example, God declares of David's son, "He shall *build* [*oikodomēsei*] me a house for my name, and I will *restore* [*anorthōsō*] his throne forever" (2 Sam. 7:13 NETS). As the Lord and Messiah, Jesus has poured out God's Spirit from heaven and saves everyone who calls on his name (Acts 2:21, 33, 36).

Thus, God has fulfilled his ancient promise to "rebuild" and "restore" the decrepit Davidic dynasty by raising Jesus from the dead and exalting him to heaven's throne. Amos 9:11–12, in concert with other prophecies, explains the missional purpose[106] for which Davidic rule is restored: that all nations

---

99 Note the Greek word *symphōneō* in Acts 15:15, translated "agree" in the ESV.

100 For a survey of additional views, see Glenny, "The Septuagint and Apostolic Hermeneutics," 16–18.

101 Bauckham, "James and the Gentiles," 158.

102 White argues that "the tent of David" (Acts 15:16) deliberately contrasts with these two man-made "tents" in Stephen's speech. "Revisiting the 'Creative' Use of Amos in Acts," 203.

103 Bauckham, "James and the Gentiles," 157–59. See Beale, *The Temple and the Church's Mission*, 243–44.

104 Glenny, "The Septuagint and Apostolic Hermeneutics," 18; following Strauss, *The Davidic Messiah in Luke-Acts*, 190.

105 Glenny, "The Septuagint and Apostolic Hermeneutics," 19–20.

106 The conjunction *hopōs* ("that") in Acts 15:17 and Amos 9:12 LXX indicates purpose.

might seek the Lord. The apostles and elders in Jerusalem recognize that the Gentiles' response to the apostolic gospel and their reception of the Holy Spirit confirm that God has included Gentiles *as Gentiles* among his people "called" by his name through their faith in the exalted Lord Jesus.

The Gentiles Will Listen (Acts 28:25–28)

Acts opens with Jesus's promise that his Spirit-empowered followers will bear witness "to the end of the earth" (1:8), and the book concludes with Paul boldly preaching about the Lord Jesus in Rome (28:31), which serves as a provisional fulfillment of the global mission of Jesus and his followers. Paul resolves to "see Rome" after his journey to Jerusalem (19:21), and Luke recounts that Paul reaches his goal: "And so we came to Rome" (28:14). But this is no matter-of-fact summary of a well-planned trip. Paul is attacked and arrested in Jerusalem (21:27–36), sits in prison for several years (24:27), and finally asserts his right to make his case before Caesar (25:11–12). The missionary prisoner's sea voyage to Rome is far from smooth sailing—he and his companions experience delays, a violent storm, near starvation, and a shipwreck (27:1–44), and Paul even survives a deadly snakebite (28:3–6). But Paul receives "help . . . from God" (26:22) and reaches Rome to fulfill the Lord's purpose (23:11), showing that "nothing can hinder the gospel."[107]

Luke does not record details of Paul's hearing before Caesar, but instead focuses on Paul's two meetings with the Jews in Rome. Paul explains to local Jewish leaders that he comes to Rome in chains because of "the hope of Israel," and they invite him to share his views (Acts 28:17–22). Then a large number of Jews gather at Paul's lodging to hear him preach about the kingdom of God and Jesus (v. 23). This teaching convinces some of these Jews, while others do not believe him (v. 24), so they depart in disagreement after one final word from Paul:

The Holy Spirit was right in saying to your fathers through Isaiah the prophet:

"Go to this people, and say,
'You will indeed hear but never understand,

---

107 Jervell, *Apostelgeschichte*, 616, my translation.

and you will indeed see but never perceive.'
For this people's heart has grown dull,
and with their ears they can barely hear,
and their eyes they have closed;
lest they should see with their eyes
and hear with their ears
and understand with their heart
and turn, and I would heal them."

Therefore let it be known to you that this salvation of God has been sent to the Gentiles; they will listen. (vv. 25–28)

Paul fittingly concludes his day-long exposition of the Law and Prophets with an appeal to Isaiah's prophetic commission (Isa. 6:9–10 LXX). Let's consider three facets of this quotation of Isaiah at the close of Acts. First, Paul presents himself as a prophet like Isaiah who has been sent to a spiritually obtuse people. Second, Paul's reference to Isaiah 6 recalls Jesus's allusion to the same passage in Luke 8:10. Third, Israel's inability to "hear" God's word offers biblical justification to send the message of salvation to the Gentiles, who will "listen."

While New Testament authors frequently reference Isaiah 6:9–10, only Acts 28:26 includes the initial command to Isaiah: "Go to this people, and say." By citing Isaiah's own commission to go and speak to Israel, Paul aligns himself with the prophet's mandate.[108] Indeed, Jesus uses the same command ("go") when sending Paul to the Gentiles (22:21). Paul's encounter with the risen Lord and his commission to bear his name parallels the calls of Old Testament prophets such as Isaiah, who "saw the Lord" (Isa. 6:1) and received a prophetic commission to speak God's word (vv. 9–13).[109] Throughout Acts, Paul heralds God's message before a stubborn people and faces opposition and persecution, just as the Lord Jesus promised in Acts 9:15–16.[110]

---

108 Daniel Marguerat, *The First Christian Historian: Writing the 'Acts of the Apostles,'* trans. Richard Bauckham, SNTSMS 121 (Cambridge: Cambridge University Press, 2002), 225.

109 For other examples, see Craig A. Evans, "Prophet, Paul as," in *Dictionary of Paul and His Letters*, ed. Gerald F. Hawthorne, Ralph P. Martin, and Daniel G. Reid (Downers Grove, IL: InterVarsity Press, 1993), 761–62.

110 For discussion of the relationship between Paul's mission and suffering in Acts 9:15–16, see Tabb, *Suffering in Ancient Worldview*, 145–49.

Paul's appeal to Isaiah 6:9–10 also parallels Luke 8:10, where Jesus alludes to Isaiah's commission to explain why his ministry is met with rejection.[111] Isaiah's charge to go and speak the word to a spiritually blind and deaf people serves as a typological preview of the greater ministry of Jesus, who proclaims the mysteries of God's kingdom and is himself the one about whom Isaiah prophesied (Luke 4:21; 22:37; Acts 8:32–35). The Roman Jews' divided response to Paul's preaching about Jesus in Acts 28:23–25 continues this pattern of opposition to Jesus's message and person in Luke's Gospel.

Because Israel is unable to "hear" God's word, Paul reasons that God has sent the message of salvation to the Gentiles, who will "listen" (Acts 28:28).[112] This recalls the scene in Pisidian Antioch, when Paul and his coworkers turn to the Gentiles in response to Jewish opposition and in obedience to God's command (13:46–47; 18:6; cf. 9:15; 22:21). Within the book of Isaiah, the Lord indicts his recalcitrant people who have become deaf and blind like the idols they revere (Isa. 6), then later announces comfort and hope in his coming salvation (Isa. 40). Surprisingly, Luke's two volumes reverse Isaiah's order of judgment-salvation by concluding with a strong word of judgment from Isaiah 6:9–10.[113] Luke's Gospel opens with the expectation that all will "see" God's salvation (Luke 3:6; Isa. 40:5), yet in the final scene of Acts the Jews who disbelieve Paul's preaching "see but never perceive" (Acts 28:26; Isa. 6:9). Robert Tannehill concludes that Luke-Acts thus narrates "a tragic story" of Israel's rejection of salvation.[114] However, it is more accurate to observe in Acts 28 "an unresolved tension between the promise intended for Israel and the historical turning that signifies its refusal."[115]

Significantly, the distinctive phrase "this salvation of God" (*touto to sōtērion tou theou*) in Acts 28:28 alludes to Isaiah 40:5, part of the new exodus prophecy, a verse that is prominently cited in Luke 3:6: "All flesh shall see the salvation of God [*to sōtērion tou theou*]." The rare word *sōtērion* ("salvation") also occurs in Luke 2:30, when Simeon takes the Christ child in his arms and exclaims, "My eyes have seen *your salvation*." Simeon prophesies that this salvation is for "all peoples," bringing light to the Gentiles

---

111 See chap. 2, pp. 44–46.
112 See Keener, *Acts*, 4:3748, 3756.
113 Pao, *Acts and the Isaianic New Exodus*, 108.
114 Robert C. Tannehill, "Israel in Luke-Acts: A Tragic Story," *JBL* 104 (1985): 85.
115 Marguerat, *The First Christian Historian*, 226.

and glory for Israel (Luke 2:31–32; cf. Isa. 49:6).[116] Thus, Acts 28:28 stresses that the prophetic hopes of salvation for all peoples are being fulfilled as the gospel message is sent to the Gentiles, who will listen. Many of Paul's fellow Jews reject and oppose his preaching in every city (cf. 20:23), yet their spiritual stubbornness does not thwart the progress of God's word but actually serves as a catalyst for the mission to the nations (cf. Rom. 11:11).[117]

Paul welcomes "all" who come to him to hear his message in Acts 28:30–31, which doubtless includes not only Gentiles (v. 28) but also the Jews who were "convinced" by Paul's exposition (v. 24).[118] Luke does not explain what happens to Paul at the end of two years (v. 30), but concludes the book by stressing the bold, unhindered proclamation of the kingdom of God and the Lord Jesus in the heart of the Gentile world. The book's intentionally open-ended conclusion thus presents the continued advance of the gospel—regardless of Paul's fate—and serves as an invitation to readers of Acts to participate in Christ's mission "to the end of the earth."[119]

Conclusion

We've seen that the mission of Jesus's followers to all nations fulfills Old Testament prophecy, just as Jesus explained in Luke 24:47–49. The risen Lord continues his work in the book of Acts (1:1), and his programmatic promise in 1:8 previews the storyline of Luke's sequel, which narrates the advance of the gospel message in Jerusalem, Judea and Samaria, and "to the end of the earth." Significantly, this mission plan that Jesus sets forth also includes an outworking of Isaiah's prophecies that the Lord would pour out his Spirit (Isa. 32:15), call his people as witnesses (43:10), and commission his servant to bring salvation "to the end of the earth" (49:6). Jesus is not absent or uninvolved in the story after his ascension into heaven (Acts 1:9–11);[120] rather, he reigns as "Lord of all" (10:36), pours out the promised Spirit in

---

116 I discuss Simeon's allusions to Isaiah in Luke 2:30–32 in chap. 4, pp. 86–89.

117 Jerry L. Ray reflects on this "irony of reversal" in *Narrative Irony in Luke-Acts: The Paradoxical Interaction of Prophetic Fulfillment and Jewish Rejection* (Lewiston, NY: Mellen, 1996), 160.

118 A few later Greek manuscripts make this reading explicit by inserting "both Jews and Greeks" at the end of Acts 28:30.

119 See Brian Rosner, "The Progress of the Word," in *Witness to the Gospel*, 232.

120 Arie W. Zwiep argues that Acts presents an "absentee christology," in which the Lord Jesus is inactive in the world, in *The Ascension of the Messiah in Lukan Christology*, NovTSup 87 (Leiden: Brill, 1997), 182. This view is decisively answered by Sleeman, *Geography and the Ascension Narrative in Acts*, 15–17.

the last days, and saves everyone who calls on his name (Acts 2:16–21; Joel 2:28–32; Isa 2:2). Christ is the promised descendent of Abraham, through whom God's blessing reaches all families of the earth, beginning with Israel (Acts 3:25–26; Gen. 12:3; 22:18). Jesus's exaltation to heaven's throne leads to the restoration of Israel and the inclusion of Gentiles as full members of God's people, in harmony with the prophets' words (Acts 15:16–18; Amos 9:11–12). Paul and Barnabas appeal to the Lord's command in Isaiah 49:6 as the biblical rationale for their outreach to Gentiles (Acts 13:46–47). Jesus is the Lord's servant who would be "a light to the Gentiles," and Paul and Barnabas take on and carry out Christ's mission to the nations. While Paul reasons with his fellow Jews in every city, his message frequently falls on deaf ears and dull hearts, following the pattern of Isaiah and the Lord Jesus (Isa. 6:9–10; Luke 8:10). The Jews' resistance to Paul's preaching does not hinder the spread of God's word, but actually serves as a catalyst for God's message of salvation to reach the Gentiles, just as God promised (Acts 28:28; cf. Luke 3:6; Isa. 40:5).

7

The Hope of the Nations

New Testament Soundings on the Messiah and His Mission

*For I tell you that Christ became a servant to the circumcised to
show God's truthfulness, in order to confirm the promises given
to the patriarchs, and in order that the Gentiles might glorify
God for his mercy. As it is written, "Therefore I will praise you
among the Gentiles, and sing to your name." And again it is
said, "Rejoice, O Gentiles, with his people." And again, "Praise
the Lord, all you Gentiles, and let all the peoples extol him."
And again Isaiah says, "The root of Jesse will come, even he
who arises to rule the Gentiles; in him will the Gentiles hope."*

ROMANS 15:8–12

BEING A PROPHET IN ANCIENT ISRAEL was a dangerous and lonely calling. Elijah knew well the occupational hazards and solitude of this vocation.
He saw his people abandon their covenant with the true God, and he was
forced into hiding as Israel's leaders sought to kill him. The Lord sustained
him through a drought and dramatically answered his prayers on Mount
Carmel, but Jezebel's violent threats forced him to flee for his life and even
led him to despair (1 Kings 19:1–4). Elijah then met the Lord in a cave and
recounted his prophetic predicament: "For the people of Israel have forsaken
your covenant, thrown down your altars, and killed your prophets with the

sword, and I, even I only, am left, and they seek my life, to take it away" (v. 14). But while Elijah assumed that he was all alone, God had preserved a remnant of seven thousand followers in Israel and had identified Elijah's successor (vv. 16, 18). What seemed like a prophetic solo act was actually a choir of faithful worshippers.

This book's first six chapters examined how Jesus and his first followers offer a biblical case for the Messiah and his mission in Luke's Gospel and Acts. This chapter considers representative passages from four other New Testament books—Matthew, John, Romans, and 1 Peter. I seek to show that Luke does not sing a canonical solo but joins a chorus of other biblical voices that emphasize the centrality of Christ's suffering, resurrection, and global mission according to the Scriptures. First, I turn to Matthew 8:17 and 12:17–21, which present Jesus fulfilling Isaiah's servant prophecies through his healings and his teaching about true justice. Next, I examine the Gospel of John, which repeatedly describes Jesus as "sent" by his Father. John 12:37–41 cites two passages from Isaiah to explain the apparent failure of Jesus's mission among his people, and 20:19–23 recounts how the risen Lord commissions and empowers his followers for mission. Third, in Romans 15, Paul cites the Law, Prophets, and Psalms to demonstrate that the risen Lord has extended God's saving mercy to the Gentiles. The apostle also views his own missionary work among the unreached as the outworking of Isaiah 52:15. Finally, Peter cites a cluster of Old Testament texts to explain the identity and mission of Christ, the chosen cornerstone, and his priestly people, who are called to proclaim Christ's excellencies (1 Pet. 2:4–10).

The Servant Who Fulfills Scripture (Matthew)

Matthew's Gospel opens by identifying Jesus Christ as "the son of David, the son of Abraham" (1:1). Thus, he is the prophesied heir to David's throne, the wise king whose reign never ends. He is also the great patriarch's descendent, in whom the nations will be blessed, the one "who establishes the new people of God."[1] The Gospel's closing verses powerfully tie these and other themes together, as the risen Lord declares his supreme authority

---

1   Patrick Schreiner, *Matthew, Disciple and Scribe: The First Gospel and Its Portrait of Jesus* (Grand Rapids, MI: Baker Academic, 2019), 176.

and enduring presence with his people and commissions them to "make disciples of all nations" (28:18–20).[2]

Matthew's Scripture-soaked portrait of Jesus stresses that he has come "to fulfill" the Scriptures, from his virgin birth (1:22–23) to his betrayal and death (26:54; 27:9–10). The evangelist shows how Jesus fulfills various Old Testament prophecies and patterns as the righteous messianic King, the Lord's servant, and "the true Israel," who recapitulates the nation's history and reverses the people's sinfulness.[3] Isaiah is particularly prominent in Matthew's account, which explicitly names "Isaiah" six times and directly cites this prophetic book eight times in all.[4] Here I focus attention on the biblical quotations in Matthew 8:17 and 12:17–21, where Jesus fulfills Isaiah's prophecies of the Lord's servant.

The Servant Who Bears Sins and Sicknesses (Matt. 8:17)

Matthew summarizes Jesus's early ministry of word and deed in 4:23 and 9:35: he was "teaching in their synagogues and proclaiming the gospel of the kingdom and healing every disease and every affliction." The Sermon on the Mount illustrates Jesus's authoritative teaching (Matt. 5–7). Next, 8:1–16 offers three examples of Jesus's healing ministry (a leper, a centurion's servant, and Peter's mother-in-law) and concludes with a report of Christ casting out demonic spirits and healing "all who were sick" (v. 16). Matthew then explains Jesus's actions by citing Scripture: "This was to fulfill what was spoken by the prophet Isaiah: 'He took our illnesses and bore our diseases'" (v. 17). This quotation closely reflects the extant Hebrew text of Isaiah 53:4, which describes the Lord's servant bearing "our infirmities" and carrying "our diseases" (NRSV). In contrast, Isaiah 53:4 LXX states that the servant "bears our sins and suffers pain for us" (NETS).

---

2 "When Jesus commands the disciples to go out into the nations, he instructs them as the king, the new Moses, the new Abraham, and the new Israel," according to Schreiner, *Matthew, Disciple and Scribe*, 242.

3 Following Brandon D. Crowe, "Fulfillment in Matthew as Eschatological Reversal," *WTJ* 75 (2013): 123–24.

4 (1) Matt. 1:22–23 (Isa. 7:14); (2) Matt. 3:3 (Isa. 40:3); (3) Matt. 4:14–16 (Isa. 9:1–2); (4) Matt. 8:17 (Isa. 53:4); (5) Matt. 12:17–21 (Isa. 42:1–4); (6) Matt. 13:13–15 (Isa. 6:9–10); (7) Matt. 15:7–9 (Isa. 29:13); (8) Matt. 21:13 (Isa. 56:7). For an overview of these citations and the allusion to Isaiah in Matt. 24:29, see Richard Beaton, "Isaiah in Matthew's Gospel," in *Isaiah in the New Testament*, ed. M. J. J. Menken and Steve Moyise (London: T&T Clark, 2005), 63–78.

Isaiah 52:13–53:12 vividly depicts the vicarious suffering and divine vindication of the Lord's "servant." The passage opens and concludes with God's perspective on his servant (52:13–15; 53:11–12),[5] which frames the confession of Isaiah in solidarity with the people ("we") in 53:1–11. The precise identity of the "we" group is ambiguous; it could be referring specifically to believing Israel[6] or more broadly to "all persons who recognize that their sin has caused the Servant to suffer."[7] The community describes the servant's undesirable physical appearance and their own lack of esteem for him (53:2–3). However, the people acknowledge that this servant has suffered in their stead: the "man of sorrows . . . acquainted with sickness" (v. 3) has "borne *our* sicknesses and carried *our* sorrows" (v. 4).[8] The Hebrew verbs *nś'* ("borne") and *sbl* ("carried") "convey the bearing of a load for someone else."[9] Verses 11–12 employ these same terms to show that the servant who has carried others' sicknesses and sorrows also "*shall bear* their iniquities" and "*bore* the sin of many." This servant bears sicknesses and sins according to divine design: "It was the will of the LORD to crush him; he has made him sick" (v. 10 ESV mg.). He does not merely suffer in solidarity with the people[10] but suffers to bring others peace and healing, and to make many righteous (vv. 5, 11). Thus, the Lord's servant "takes the 'place' of others,"[11] bearing the community's sicknesses, sorrows, and sins according to the divine script.

The apostles and their associates frequently reference this passage to explain how Jesus's rejection and resurrection fulfill the Scriptures, following Christ's own interpretation of Isaiah's servant prophecy.[12] Some interpreters read Matthew 8:17 as a citation of a few words from Scripture "without any

---

5   Janowski, "He Bore Our Sins," 61.

6   See Brevard S. Childs, *Isaiah: A Commentary*, OTL (Louisville: Westminster John Knox, 2001), 413.

7   Oswalt, *The Book of Isaiah*, 2:410n4. Other "we" confessions in the Old Testament prophets include Jer. 3:22–25; Daniel 9:5–15; Hos. 6:1–3.

8   Here I prefer the translation "sickness" for the Hebrew *ḥŏli* in Isa. 53:3–4, following the ESV marginal note, CSB, and Luther Bibel ("Krankheit").

9   House, *Isaiah*, 2:494.

10 As argued by Goldingay, *The Message of Isaiah 40–55*, 501, who compares the servant with Jeremiah.

11 Janowski, "He Bore Our Sins," 53–54.

12 See the discussion of Luke 22:37 and Acts 8:32–33 in chap. 2, pp. 50–56, and in chap. 5, pp. 116–19.

regard for their context,"[13] while others suggest that this quotation misses "the true sense of the OT text."[14] But Matthew repeatedly references the prophecy of Isaiah and may allude to the final Servant Song when depicting Jesus's silence before his accusers (Matt. 27:12; cf. Isa. 53:7), his burial by "a rich man" (Matt. 27:57; cf. Isa. 53:9), and his mission "to serve, and to give his life as a ransom for many" (Matt. 20:28; cf. 26:28; Isa. 53:10–12). Thus, it is essential to interpret Matthew's citation of Isaiah 53:4 in light of the whole Servant Song.[15]

In what sense does Jesus "fulfill" Isaiah's words in Matthew 8:17? The Greek conjunction *hopōs* ("so that," CSB) indicates that Jesus "healed all who were sick" (v. 16) for the purpose of fulfilling prophecy (v. 17).[16] While it is clear that Isaiah 53:4 offers biblical support for Jesus's healing ministry, interpreters debate whether Matthew 8:17 focuses exclusively on Jesus's messianic healings or includes a reference to his redemptive suffering. Some scholars claim that the evangelist offers an "atomistic" reading of Isaiah that contains no reference to the servant's vicarious suffering.[17] Others suggest that Christ's healing ministry serves as "a type" of his redemptive suffering.[18] While the first lines of Isaiah 53:4 refer to the servant bearing the sicknesses of others, the context of Isaiah 53, along with the close biblical link between sin and sickness, suggests that "the way he bears the sickness of others is through his suffering and death."[19] In Matthew's Gospel, the angel announces that Jesus "will save his people from their sins" (1:21), and Christ himself declares that he pours out his blood "for many for the forgiveness of sins"

---

13 Ulrich Luz, *Matthew 8–20: A Commentary*, trans. James E. Crouch, Hermeneia (Minneapolis: Fortress, 2001), 14.

14 W. D. Davies and Dale C. Allison, *A Critical and Exegetical Commentary on the Gospel according to Saint Matthew*, 3 vols., ICC (Edinburgh: T&T Clark, 1988–1997), 2:38.

15 D. A. Carson, "Matthew," in *Matthew-Mark*, ed. Tremper Longman III and David E. Garland, EBC 9, rev. ed. (Grand Rapids, MI: Zondervan, 2010), 243.

16 The evangelist uses the same fulfillment formula (*hopōs plērōthē to rhēthen*) in Matt. 2:23; 13:35.

17 Lidija Novakovic, "Matthew's Atomistic Use of Scripture: Messianic Interpretation of Isaiah 53.4 in Matthew 8.17," in *Biblical Interpretation in Early Christian Gospels: The Gospel of Matthew*, ed. Thomas R. Hatina (London: T&T Clark, 2008), 148. She suggests that Matt. 8:17 reflects Ezekiel's prophecy of the Davidic king who would shepherd God's weak, sick, and injured people (Ezek. 34:4, 23). For a similar assessment, see Matthias Konradt, *Israel, Church, and the Gentiles in the Gospel of Matthew*, trans. Kathleen Ess (Waco, TX: Baylor University Press, 2014), 44.

18 Davies and Allison, *Matthew*, 2:38.

19 Carson, "Matthew," 243; cf. Richard Beaton, *Isaiah's Christ in Matthew's Gospel*, SNTSMS 123 (Cambridge: Cambridge University Press, 2002), 116.

(26:28). Jesus also explains that "those who are sick" need a physician, and so he calls "sinners" (9:12–13). Thus, Matthew identifies Jesus as the Lord's servant, who heals many *and* suffers and dies for the sins of others.[20]

Matthew 11:2–6 further links Jesus's powerful deeds to the Old Testament expectation for the Messiah:

> Now when John heard in prison about the deeds of the Christ, he sent word by his disciples and said to him, "Are you the one who is to come, or shall we look for another?" And Jesus answered them, "Go and tell John what you hear and see: the blind receive their sight and the lame walk, lepers are cleansed and the deaf hear, and the dead are raised up, and the poor have good news preached to them. And blessed is the one who is not offended by me."

Christ's references to his healing ministry and proclamation of good news recall at least two restoration prophecies. Isaiah 35:5–6 presents healings of the blind, lame, deaf, and mute as indications that God has come to save his people (v. 4). Additionally, Isaiah 61:1 depicts the Lord's Spirit-anointed agent proclaiming good news and liberty to the poor and oppressed.[21] Thus, Jesus's healings signify that he is "the one who is to come," and that the age of future salvation has dawned.

The Servant Who Brings Justice to the Gentiles (Matt. 12:17–21)

Matthew again highlights that Jesus "fulfills" Isaiah's servant prophecy in chapter 12, amid a series of confrontations between Jesus and the Pharisees (joined by the Jewish scribes in v. 38) over the Sabbath, Jesus's signs, and the source of his power. Christ responds to his opponents' malicious questions and slanderous accusations by asserting that he is "greater than the temple" (12:6) and is "lord of the Sabbath" (v. 8), and that he exorcises demons "by the Spirit of God" (v. 28). After Jesus heals a man's withered hand in the synagogue and the Pharisees plot to destroy him, he withdraws from that

---

20 Christ's "mission of healing fulfills the character of the mission of the servant, who at the ultimate cost of his own life would reveal God's concern for a broken humanity," according to Craig S. Keener, *The Gospel of Matthew: A Socio-Rhetorical Commentary* (Grand Rapids, MI: Eerdmans, 2009), 273.

21 I discuss Isa. 61 at length in chap. 4, pp. 94–101.

place (vv. 9–15). He continues to heal "many" people who follow him, but directs them "not to make him known" (vv. 15–16).

Christ's retreat from conflict and his order for secrecy prompt Matthew's extended citation of prophecy (Isa. 42:1–4):[22]

This was to fulfill what was spoken by the prophet Isaiah:

> "Behold, my servant whom I have chosen,
>> my beloved with whom my soul is well pleased.
> I will put my Spirit upon him,
>> and he will proclaim justice to the Gentiles.
> He will not quarrel or cry aloud,
>> nor will anyone hear his voice in the streets;
> a bruised reed he will not break,
>> and a smoldering wick he will not quench,
> until he brings justice to victory;
>> and in his name the Gentiles will hope." (Matt. 12:17–21)

Let's briefly consider the context of this passage from Isaiah and then explore how Jesus fulfills this prophecy.

Isaiah 41 offers an extended contrast between the true Lord, who alone knows the future, and the worthless, impotent "gods" of the nations (vv. 1–7, 21–29). As God calls the nations to account, he also reassures his chosen "servant" Israel (vv. 8–9), whom he promises to help and redeem (vv. 10, 14). The opening line of Isaiah 42:1—"Behold my servant, whom I uphold"—recalls God's earlier description of Abraham's descendants (41:8).[23] This leads many interpreters to conclude that this passage presents Israel's mission to bring justice to the nations (42:1, 3), which God's chosen people do not fulfill because they are spiritually deaf and blind (vv. 18–20).[24] However, several details in vv. 1–9 suggest that this unnamed servant is an

---

22 See France, *Matthew*, 470. Some scholars argue that Matthew cites a version of Isa. 42:1–4 LXX. More likely, the evangelist draws on the original Hebrew text of Isaiah with minor variations to suit the emphases of this Gospel. Cf. Davies and Allison, *Matthew*, 2:323; Carson, "Matthew," 330.

23 Isa. 42:1 LXX reads, "*Jacob* is my servant . . . *Israel* is my chosen," making the link to 41:8 explicit.

24 Abernethy, *The Book of Isaiah and God's Kingdom*, 138–42; cf. Goldingay and Payne, *Isaiah 40–55*, 212.

individual, who acts on behalf of Israel as well as the nations.[25] First, the Lord gives his servant "as a covenant for the people, a light for the nations" (v. 6). While some commentators interpret "people" as a general reference to humanity, synonymous with "nations,"[26] this verse more likely expresses a dual mission to Israel and to the nations, as in Isaiah 49:6, 8.[27] Second, the Lord declares, "I have put my Spirit upon him" (42:1), recalling the earlier promise that God's Spirit shall rest on the Davidic Messiah (11:2). Moreover, this Spirit-endowed ruler shall execute true justice and righteousness (11:3–5), just as the servant brings "justice to the nations" (42:1; cf. v. 4). Andrew Abernethy argues that the servant Israel and the Davidic ruler are distinct agents, yet "share a common 'royal' mission under King YHWH."[28] However, the parallels to Isaiah 11:1–9 suggest that the Lord's servant in 42:1–9 is a "messianic figure,"[29] God's Spirit-empowered agent with a mission to Israel as well as the nations.

The lengthy fulfillment quotation in Matthew 12 may appear out of place in the context of Jesus's healings and controversies with the Pharisees. But upon closer inspection, we see that Isaiah 42:1–4 brings together a number of key emphases in this Gospel and remarkably captures the tenor of Christ's whole ministry as "the unobtrusive servant of the Lord," who acts with compassion while avoiding quarrels.[30] Jesus fulfills what Isaiah wrote as the Spirit-anointed servant of God who proclaims justice, ministers in meekness, and brings hope to the nations. Let's examine these emphases in turn.

Isaiah's prophecy that God's servant will be endowed by *God's Spirit* (Matt. 12:18) recalls the account of Christ's baptism: the divine Spirit descends like a dove and rests on Jesus, and a heavenly voice says, "This is my beloved Son [*ho huios mou ho agapētos*], with whom I am well pleased [*eudokēsa*]" (3:16–17).[31] Matthew 12:18 expands on the wording of Isaiah 42:1 to identify the Lord's servant as "my beloved [*ho agapētos mou*] with whom my soul is well pleased [*eudokēsen*]," creating a strong verbal tie to Christ's baptism, as well as his transfiguration (Matt. 17:5). The early

---

25 Cf. Oswalt, *The Book of Isaiah*, 2:108; and House, *Isaiah*, 2:314.

26 Childs, *Isaiah*, 326; and Goldingay and Payne, *Isaiah 40–55*, 1:227.

27 House, *Isaiah*, 323. See my earlier discussion of Isa. 42 and 49 in chap. 6, pp. 149–55.

28 Abernethy, *The Book of Isaiah and God's Kingdom*, 140.

29 Oswalt, *The Book of Isaiah*, 2:110.

30 Davies and Allison, *Matthew*, 2:324.

31 See Beale, *A New Testament Biblical Theology*, 568.

chapters of Matthew stress that Jesus is conceived, anointed, and led by the Holy Spirit (1:20; 3:16 4:1), and John the Baptist announces that Christ will baptize with the Spirit and fire (3:11). The quotation of Isaiah's servant prophecy in Matthew 12:17–21 also prepares for Jesus's controversy with the Pharisees concerning the source of his power in verses 22–32. After Jesus heals a demon-oppressed man who is blind and mute, the Pharisees slanderously charge that he casts out demons by the prince of demons (vv. 22–24). Jesus responds, "But if it is by the Spirit of God that I cast out demons, then the kingdom of God has come upon you" (v. 28). Thus, Christ is God's Spirit-anointed servant, whose healings and exorcisms signal the inbreaking of God's kingdom.

Jesus fulfills Isaiah's servant prophecy by proclaiming and enacting *justice*. The repetition of "justice" (*krisis*) in Matthew 12:18 and 20 expresses a pronounced emphasis in Isaiah 42:1–4.[32] This Old Testament citation also anticipates Jesus's scathing critique of the scribes and Pharisees: "For you tithe mint and dill and cumin, and have neglected the weightier matters of the law: *justice* and mercy and faithfulness" (Matt. 23:23). These Jewish leaders "preach, but do not practice. They tie up heavy burdens, hard to bear, and lay them on people's shoulders" (vv. 3–4). Alternatively, Jesus invites those who are heavy laden to come to him to find true rest and an easy yoke (11:28–30).[33] The controversy over whether it is "lawful" to heal on the Sabbath powerfully contrasts the unjust judgments of the Pharisees with Christ's true justice in Matthew 12:9–13. While the Pharisees view healing as out-of-bounds on the Sabbath day, Jesus explains that "it is lawful to do good on the Sabbath," and then heals and restores a man with a withered hand (vv. 12–13). As "lord of the Sabbath" (v. 8), Jesus gives life and promotes the law's concern for true justice, which challenges and infuriates his opponents. Thus, Matthew's Gospel links the arrival of God's justice to "the compassionate deeds and message of Jesus," the Spirit-anointed servant and messianic "son of David."[34]

---

32 Goldingay notes the threefold reference to justice in Isa. 42:1–4 in *The Message of Isaiah 40–55*, 153.

33 See Richard Beaton, "Messiah and Justice: A Key to Matthew's Use of Isaiah 42.1–4?," *JSNT* 22 (1999): 18–19.

34 Beaton, *Isaiah's Christ in Matthew's Gospel*, 156. Jesus shows compassion and heals as the "son of David" in Matt. 9:27–29; 12:22–23; 15:22–28; 20:30–34; 21:14–15. Cf. Konradt, *Israel, Church, and the Gentiles in the Gospel of Matthew*, 39–48.

Further, Jesus fulfills Isaiah's prophecy through his ministry of *meekness*. When the Pharisees seek to destroy him, Jesus withdraws and continues to heal people out of the limelight (Matt. 12:14–16). He is "the unobtrusive servant of the Lord," who "does not wrangle or quarrel or continue useless strife. He seeks to avoid self-advertisement and to quiet the enthusiasm that his healings inevitably create."[35] Christ describes himself as "gentle and lowly in heart" (11:29); he sees and responds to the needs of harassed, helpless people—bruised reeds and smoldering wicks—with compassionate concern and powerful healing (9:36; 12:13, 15, 22; 14:14; 15:32).

Finally, as the Lord's servant, Jesus offers hope for the *Gentiles*, mentioned twice in the quotation of Isaiah 42:1–4. Matthew 12 lacks explicit examples of Jesus ministering to Gentiles, though the "many" who follow him and receive healing in 12:15 may include Gentiles from Galilee, Tyre, and Sidon, based on the parallel passage in Mark 3:7–8. Jesus and his disciples primarily minister "to the lost sheep of the house of Israel" (Matt. 10:6; 15:24), yet this focus on Israel does not exclude Gentiles who come to King Jesus in faith.[36] In fact, the title "son of Abraham" in 1:1 suggests that Christ is the promised Israelite in whom the nations will be blessed. Matthew explains that Jesus travels to Galilee and Capernaum to fulfill Isaiah's prophecy that even "Galilee of the Gentiles" will see the light of salvation (4:12–16; cf. Isa. 9:1–2).[37] He commends the faith of a Gentile centurion and explains that "many will come from east and west" to feast with Israel's patriarchs in the kingdom (Matt. 8:10–11). Moreover, when a Canaanite woman entreats the Son of David for help, he initially states that his mission concerns only Israel (15:24). Yet Jesus eventually commends this Gentile's persistent faith and heals her daughter (v. 28), showing that his mercy extends to all who trust in Israel's messianic shepherd. Finally, in Matthew's closing scene, the risen Lord commands his followers to "make disciples of all nations" (28:19), signaling the way that the Gentiles' hopes will be realized.[38]

---

35 Davies and Allison, *Matthew*, 2:324.

36 See Schreiner, *Matthew, Disciple and Scribe*, 117. The description of Israel as "lost sheep" probably alludes to Ezek. 34:11–16 and Jer. 50:6–7. Cf. Hays, *Echoes of Scripture in the Gospels*, 128–29.

37 Matthew's citation of Isa. 9:1–2 prefigures the proclamation of salvation to the Gentiles, according to Hays, *Echoes of Scripture in the Gospels*, 176–78.

38 For extensive discussion of the Great Commission, see Schreiner, *Matthew, Disciple and Scribe*, 183–90.

Thus, Jesus "fulfills" Isaiah's prophecies concerning the mission of the Lord's servant by offering *healing* for the physically and spiritually sick as well as *hope* for the Gentiles. Christ's mighty works demonstrate he is "the one who is to come" (Matt. 11:3), whose ministry inaugurates the blessings associated with end-time salvation (Isa. 35:4–6). As the Lord's servant, Jesus not only bears people's sicknesses but also saves them from their sins through his suffering and death (Matt. 8:17; Isa. 53:4; cf. Matt. 1:21; 20:28). Matthew's lengthy quotation of Isaiah 42:1–4 highlights Jesus as God's Spirit-anointed agent who proclaims true justice in contrast to the Pharisees' unjust judgments, who ministers with lowliness without seeking the limelight, and who offers hope to the Gentiles (Matt. 12:17–21).

The Suffering and Glory of the Sent Son (John)

He's a chip off the old block; the apple doesn't fall far from the tree; like father, like son. These proverbial sayings capture the truth that sons often resemble their fathers in their mannerisms, behaviors, and actions. In contemporary Western society, it is very rare for a son to pursue the same career path as his father (although I did become a professor like my father). But in the ancient world, nearly all sons followed their fathers vocationally.[39] They did not go off to the university to pursue vocational training, but learned the family business by serving in the fields or the shops with their fathers. James and John, the sons of Zebedee, are fishermen like their father (Matt. 4:21). Likewise, Jesus is called "the carpenter's son" (13:55), presumably because he learned the trade of his adoptive father, Joseph. But Jesus himself claims that he uniquely knows *God* as his Father and carries out his Father's business: "for whatever the Father does, that the Son does likewise" (John 5:19).

The Gospel of John repeatedly refers to Jesus as God's *Son*, who is "sent" into the world to bring salvation and speak God's words (3:16, 34). Christ insists that he does his Father's will and accomplishes his work (4:34; 5:30).[40]

---

39 See D. A. Carson, *Jesus the Son of God: A Christological Title Often Overlooked, Sometimes Misunderstood, and Currently Disputed* (Wheaton, IL: Crossway, 2012), 19–20.

40 John's Gospel frequently employs two Greek verbs for sending: *pempō* (e.g., 4:34) and *apostellō* (e.g., 17:18). For a careful discussion of these terms, see Andreas J. Köstenberger, *The Missions of Jesus and the Disciples according to the Fourth Gospel: With Implications for the Fourth Gospel's Purpose and the Mission of the Contemporary Church* (Grand Rapids, MI: Eerdmans, 1998), 97–106.

As the sent Son, Christ faithfully fulfills his mission in vital relationship with his Father (7:29; 8:29), representing the one who sent him (12:44–45) and seeking his glory (7:18).[41] In fact, Jesus matter-of-factly explains to Philip a stunning truth: "Whoever has seen me has seen the Father" (14:9). John summons readers to "believe that Jesus is the Christ, the Son of God," and so have life (20:31).

Jesus is the sent one *par excellence*, and his unique mission is central and preeminent in the Fourth Gospel. At the same time, the risen Lord commissions his followers to continue his mission with the Spirit's help (John 20:21–22; cf. 17:18). This section focuses on two key passages related to the mission of Christ and his people. First, I consider John 12:37–41, where the evangelist quotes two passages from Isaiah to explain the apparent failure of Jesus's mission among his people. Second, I reflect on Jesus's commissioning of his disciples in John 20:21–22.

Rejection and Revelation of Divine Glory (John 12:37–41)

John 12:37–41 serves as a pivotal hinge in the Gospel's structure. This passage concludes John's extended presentation of "the Signs of the Messiah" (1:19–12:50) and introduces "the Book of Glory" (chaps. 13–20), the narrative of Jesus's death and resurrection—the reality to which the messianic signs point.[42] Earlier in John 12, a large crowd hails Jesus as "the King of Israel" (v. 13) as he approaches Jerusalem. Yet the crowd's question in verse 34—"Who is this Son of Man?"—shows that they do not grasp Christ's identity or mission.

John cites two passages from Isaiah to explain the people's stunning refusal to believe in Christ despite his "many signs" (12:37).[43] First, their unbelief fulfills Isaiah 53:1: "Lord, who has believed what he heard from us, and to whom has the arm of the Lord been revealed?" (John 12:38).

---

41 For complementary emphases, see Köstenberger, *The Missions of Jesus and the Disciples*, 107–11.

42 See Craig A. Evans, "On the Quotation Formulas in the Fourth Gospel," *BZ* 26 (1982): 82–83. The "Book of Signs" and "Book of Glory" are standard divisions among scholars. Cf. Andrew T. Lincoln, *The Gospel according to Saint John*, BNTC 4 (Peabody, MA: Hendrickson, 2005), 4–5; and Marianne Meye Thompson, *John: A Commentary*, NTL (Louisville: Westminister John Knox, 2015), 16–17. For an alternative proposal for the book's structure, see J. Ramsey Michaels, *The Gospel of John*, NICNT (Grand Rapids, MI: Eerdmans, 2010), 36.

43 This section expands on Brian J. Tabb, "Johannine Fulfillment of Scripture: Continuity and Escalation," *BBR* 21 (2011): 501–3.

Second, their response to Jesus reflects God's "judicial hardening,"[44] as expressed in Isaiah 6:10:

> He has blinded their eyes
> and hardened their heart,
> lest they see with their eyes,
> and understand with their heart, and turn,
> and I would heal them. (John 12:40)[45]

Jesus and the apostles frequently appeal to Isaiah 6—the prophet's commission to speak God's word to people who refuse to listen—and to Isaiah 53, the climactic prophecy of the Lord's suffering servant.[46] John 12:37–41 explicitly links these two familiar passages and also refers three times to Isaiah by name, which suggests the evangelist's familiarity with the wider context of the book of Isaiah.[47]

There are a number of parallels linking Isaiah's vision of divine glory and prophetic commissioning (Isa. 6) to the book's final servant passage (52:13–53:12).[48] For example, Isaiah presents both "the Lord" (6:1) and the "servant" (52:13) as "high and lifted up," then highlights the people's unbelief (6:9–10; 53:1).[49] Additionally, while Israel sees and hears yet does not understand the prophetic word in 6:9–10, in 52:15 the nations "see" and "understand" what they have not previously "heard" concerning the Lord's servant.

The suffering, glory, and mission of the Son all converge in John 12. Jesus's own people reject him even though they have seen many signs that

---

44 D. A. Carson, *The Gospel according to John*, PNTC (Grand Rapids, MI: Eerdmans, 1991), 448; cf. Köstenberger, "John," 477.

45 John's quotation of Isa. 53:1 agrees precisely with the LXX, while John 12:40 does not precisely follow the known versions of Isa. 6:10. For discussion, see Craig A. Evans, *To See and Not Perceive: Isaiah 6.9–10 in Early Jewish and Christian Interpretation*, JSOTSup 64 (Sheffield: JSOT Press, 1989), 129–32; M. J. J. Menken, *Old Testament Quotations in the Fourth Gospel: Studies in Textual Form* (Kampen: Kok Pharos, 1996), 99–122; and Daniel J. Brendsel, *Isaiah Saw His Glory: The Use of Isaiah 52–53 in John 12*, BZNW 208 (Berlin: de Gruyter, 2014), 83–88.

46 I discuss the use of Isa. 6 in Luke 8:10 and Acts 28:25–27 in chaps. 2 and 6, pp. 44–46, 161–64. Isa. 53 is considered earlier in this chapter, pp. 168–72, and in chaps. 2 and 5, pp. 50–56, 116–19.

47 Brendsel, *Isaiah Saw His Glory*, 7–8, 71.

48 See Brendsel, *Isaiah Saw His Glory*, 117–18.

49 Evans, *To See and Not Perceive*, 133.

reveal his divine glory (12:37; cf. 1:11).[50] John explains that what looks like the failure of Christ's mission is actually the fulfillment of God's ancient plan revealed in Isaiah 6:10 and 53:1. Ironically, the Pharisees speak better than they know when they say, "Look, the world has gone after him" (John 12:19). John then records that some Greeks "wish to see Jesus" (v. 21), to which Christ responds that his time has come "to be glorified" (v. 23) and "lifted up," and so "draw all people to myself" (v. 32). This scene likely recalls Isaiah's final servant passage,[51] which opens by declaring that God's servant shall be "high and lifted up" and "exalted" (Isa. 52:13), which the Septuagint translates as "exceedingly glorified." Moreover, the Greeks' request to "see" Christ parallels Isaiah's prophecy that the nations and their kings will "see" and "understand" the servant's work (v. 15). These subtle links to Isaiah prepare for John's explicit citations of Isaiah 53:1 and 6:10, making clear that Jesus's suffering is the prophesied path to his exaltation and messianic mission to the nations.

John summons the prophet to testify as an eyewitness of Christ's glory: "Isaiah said these things because he saw his glory and spoke of him" (John 12:41).[52] Because this verse alludes to Isaiah's testimony that he "saw the Lord" and that "his glory" fills the earth (Isa. 6:1, 3), some interpreters conclude that the prophet beheld the glory of the preincarnate Son.[53] Jesus himself refers to the glory he had with the Father before the world began (John 17:5), and Andrew Lincoln reasons that "since Christ as the preexistent Logos shared God's glory (cf. 1:1, 14; 17:5), all previous sightings of God's glory were also visions of Christ's glory."[54] However, the preceding verses explicitly link Isaiah 6:10 with the prophecy of the suffering servant (53:1), who would be "exceedingly glorified" yet have no "glory" in people's

---

50 For a thorough discussion of the number and character of "signs" in John's Gospel, see Köstenberger, *The Missions of Jesus and the Disciples*, 54–70.

51 Johannes Beutler, "Greeks Come to See Jesus (John 12:20f)," *Bib* 71 (1990): 342–45.

52 Isaiah joins John the Baptist, Moses, and the evangelist as witnesses of Christ, according to Andreas Obermann, *Die christologische Erfüllung der Schrift im Johannesevangelium: eine Untersuchung zur johanneischen Hermeneutik anhand der Schriftzitate*, WUNT 2/83 (Tübingen: Mohr, 1996), 228.

53 See, for example, Rudolf Schnackenburg, "Joh 12,39–41: Zur christologischen Schriftauslegung des vierten Evangelisten," in *Neues Testament und Geschichte: Historisches Geschehen und Deutung im Neuen Testament: FS Oscar Cullmann*, ed. H. Baltensweiler and B. Reicke (Zürich: Theologischer Verlag, 1972), 176.

54 Lincoln, *John*, 358.

eyes (52:13; 53:2 LXX). It is likely that 52:13 stands behind the distinctive references to Jesus's exaltation ("lifted up") and glory.[55] John 1:14 asserts that "the Word became flesh and dwelt among us, and we have seen his glory"; at the close of the Book of Signs, John appeals to Isaiah's prophetic vision of Christ's glory as his own people fail to recognize his divine glory and reject him (12:37–41). Yet for those with eyes to see, Christ's rejection and suspension on the cross actually "*constitute* his messianic glory";[56] his shameful death is the "hour" of his glory, when he finishes his mission and draws all people to himself (12:23, 32–33; 19:30). Thus, John's argument in 12:41, the immediate context, and his distinctive use of terms such as "glory" and "lifted up" suggest that "his glory" includes the Son's *incarnate* glory as the suffering and exalted servant.[57]

The Sent Son Sends His Disciples (John 20:19–23)

The Gospel of John stresses the mission of the Son "sent" by his Father, but after his resurrection he also sends his followers with the Spirit's help. John 20:19–23 recounts Jesus's appearance to his gathered disciples on the day of his resurrection. He twice says, "Peace be with you," and he shows his followers his pierced hands and side, after which their fear turns to joy. Jesus then sends these disciples who have seen their risen Lord (v. 21). Finally, Christ breathes on them and says, "Receive the Holy Spirit" (v. 22). Let's reflect on the relationship between the missions of Jesus and his followers, as well as the biblical-theological significance of Jesus's symbolic action and commissioning in verses 21–22.

Jesus's initial resurrection appearance to his disciples in John 20:19–23 fulfills a number of specific promises made earlier in John's Gospel.[58] Jesus shows himself to his disciples after his resurrection (vv. 19–20), recalling his promise to return to them after going away (14:18–19). The risen Lord tells his fearful followers, "Peace be with you" (20:19, 21, 26), following through on his commitment to give them peace and reassure their troubled hearts (14:27). The disciples rejoice when they see the Lord (20:20), fulfilling

---

55 Richard Bauckham, *Gospel of Glory: Major Themes in Johannine Theology* (Grand Rapids, MI: Baker Academic, 2015), 54.

56 Brendsel, *Isaiah Saw His Glory*, 130.

57 Brendsel, *Isaiah Saw His Glory*, 130; cf. Carson, *The Gospel according to John*, 450.

58 Craig S. Keener, *The Gospel of John: A Commentary*, 2 vols. (Peabody, MA: Hendrickson, 2003), 2:1197.

his word that their sorrow would turn to joy (16:22). Further, the Lord commands them to receive the Holy Spirit (20:22), which recalls John the Baptist's claim that Jesus "baptizes with the Holy Spirit" (1:33), as well as Christ's promise to send the Helper from the Father (15:26).

Interpreters have long puzzled over how to relate John 20:22 to Luke's narrative of the Spirit's outpouring in Acts 2:1–4.[59] It is not necessary to equate the later action of the ascended Lord on the day of Pentecost with Jesus's command on the day of his resurrection, since Christ insists in John 20:17 that he has not yet ascended to the Father (cf. 14:12). Neither do we need to assume that Christ's imperative in 20:22 is exclusively a parable or symbolic anticipation of the disciples' later endowment of the Spirit. More likely, the risen Lord here commands the disciples to receive the Spirit as an initial fulfillment of his promise, turning their sorrow to joy and granting them spiritual power as he sends them on mission. John 7:39 anticipates believers receiving the Spirit when Jesus is "glorified." Since Jesus's glorification begins when he is "lifted up" at the cross (12:23, 32), it is fitting that he gives the Spirit after showing himself alive after death (20:20, 22).

In John 20:21, Jesus commissions his followers *as* he himself was sent by his Father: "As [*kathōs*] the Father has sent me, even so I am sending you." This comparison between the sending of Jesus and the sending of his disciples recalls Christ's prayer in 17:18: "As [*kathōs*] you sent me into the world, so I have sent them into the world." Earlier he clarifies that his followers will endure the world's hostility since they are not "of the world," just as he himself is not "of the world" (17:14, 16; cf. 15:18–19). While Jesus stresses in 17:18 that "the world" is the context for the disciples' mission, the risen Lord authorizes and legitimates his followers' mission as a continuation of his own in 20:21. Andreas Köstenberger summa-

---

59 Raymond Brown reads John 20:22 as the Fourth Gospel's version of Pentecost, in which the risen Christ fully bestows the Spirit on his followers. *The Gospel according to John*, 2 vols., AB 29–29A (Garden City, NY: Doubleday, 1966–1970), 2:1038–39. Alternatively, D. A. Carson interprets Jesus's breathing and command in John 20:22 "as a kind of acted parable pointing forward to the full enduement still to come." *The Gospel according to John*, 655. Still others argue that the disciples receive the Spirit in different ways on the day of Christ's resurrection and later at Pentecost; see, for example, Augustine, *The Trinity*, ed. Hermigild Dressler, trans. Stephen McKenna, The Fathers of the Church 45 (Washington, DC: The Catholic University of America, 1963), 15.26.46; and James M. Hamilton, *God's Indwelling Presence: The Holy Spirit in the Old and New Testaments*, NAC Studies in Bible and Theology 1 (Nashville: B&H Academic, 2006), 93–99.

rizes four overarching characteristics of Christ's mission as the sent Son: "(1) bringing glory and honor to the sender; (2) doing the sender's will, working his works, and speaking his words; (3) witnessing to the sender and representing him accurately; and (4) knowing the sender intimately, living in close relationship with the sender, and following his example."[60] Of course, Jesus alone is "the only Son of God," who reveals the Father and enacts salvation and judgment in the world (3:16–19; cf. 1:18). Yet he also presents himself as a model for his followers sent on mission.[61] The force of the adverb *kathōs* ("as") in 20:21 suggests that Christ's own experience of being sent provides the example and standard for his sending of his followers.[62] Thus, the sent disciples do not *replace* their Lord's central mission but *continue* his work in the world and follow his supreme example as the Son sent by the Father.[63] "Jesus deliberately makes his mission the *model* of ours. Thus the church should define its task in terms of its understanding of *Jesus'* task."[64]

John 20:22 adds that Jesus "breathed on them." The Greek verb *emphysaō* ("breathe on") occurs only here in the New Testament and likely alludes to Genesis 2:7 LXX: "God formed man, dust from the ground, and *breathed* [*enephysēsen*] into his face the breath of life."[65] Divine breath at creation makes Adam "a living creature" (v. 7). Wisdom of Solomon 15:11 castigates the one who fashions lifeless idols out of metal and clay, forgetting the Creator who fashioned him and "breathed [*emphysēsanta*] into him a life-giving spirit" (NETS), a deliberate allusion to the Genesis creation narrative. The same rare word occurs in the Greek translation of 1 Kings 17:21, when Elijah "breathed" (*enephysēsen*) on the widow's dead son three times and prayed that the boy's life would return to him. Breath is associated with returning life to dry bones in Ezekiel 37:9: "Prophesy to the breath; prophesy, son of man, and say to the breath, Thus says the Lord GOD: Come from the four

---

60 Köstenberger, *The Missions of Jesus and the Disciples*, 191; cf. Thompson, *John*, 422.

61 Craig S. Keener, "Sent like Jesus: Johannine Missiology (John 20:21–22)," *AJPS* 12 (2009): 27.

62 See Brown, *The Gospel according to John*, 2:1036.

63 Cf. Köstenberger, *The Missions of Jesus and the Disciples*, 141, 191.

64 Carson, *The Gospel according to John*, 648.

65 Many interpreters note John's allusion to Gen. 2:7, including Hamilton, *God's Indwelling Presence*, 171–73; Keener, *John*, 2:1204–5; and Craig R. Koester, *The Word of Life: A Theology of John's Gospel* (Grand Rapids, MI: Eerdmans, 2008), 158. Alternatively, Michaels calls this proposed allusion "doubtful" and argues that Jesus breathes because he is alive. *John*, 1010–11.

winds, O breath, and *breathe* [*emphysēson*] on these slain, that they may live." This connection between divine breath and life clearly draws on Genesis 2:7 and so casts the revival of lifeless, exiled Israel as "a recapitulation of God's first breathing into Adam and giving him life."[66]

Thus, the risen Lord's act of breathing on his disciples as he commands them to receive the Spirit reflects the biblical-theological association of breath with the giving or restoring of life, a link that goes all the way back to the creation narrative in Genesis 2:7. While Ezekiel 37:9 links God's creative breath with Israel's resurrection from death, in John 20:22 it is the resurrected Lord Jesus who breathes and bestows the divine Spirit. Thus, it is fitting to say that the risen Lord's breathing on his people signifies an act of "new creation."[67] Jesus not only inaugurates the age to come by rising from the tomb on the first day of the week, but he also imparts the life-giving Spirit to his followers called to carry out his commission.

John stresses that the sent Son reveals the Father and carries out his work (John 1:18; 4:34). Jesus's signs show forth his divine glory and summon people to believe and find life (2:11; 20:31), though most of Jesus's own people do not recognize the Son's glory (12:37–41). The Son's rejection may look like the end of his failed mission, but in fact it represents the fulfill-ment of Isaiah's prophecies about the people's spiritual blindness and the suffering and glory of the Lord's servant. The Greeks' request "to see Jesus" (v. 21) and Christ's announcement that he will be "glorified" (v. 23) and "lifted up" (v. 32) at the cross all recall Isaiah's prophecy about the servant's suffering and exaltation, which the nations and their kings would one day "see" and "understand" (Isa. 52:13–15).

The mission of the Son sent by the Father is central throughout the Fourth Gospel. Following his resurrection, Christ also commissions his disciples and commands them to receive the Spirit, just as he promised (John 20:21–22). As the Father sends the Son, so the Son sends his apostles. Jesus is both the supreme sent one and the sovereign sender who authorizes his servants for mission. Jesus does not simply compare their mission to his but sends and equips them to carry out his own mission as they make known the forgiveness of sins that he secured through his redemptive death. When

---

66 Beale, *A New Testament Biblical Theology*, 561.

67 See Beale, *A New Testament Biblical Theology*, 572; cf. George R. Beasley-Murray, *John*, 2 vols., 2nd ed., WBC 36 (Nashville: Thomas Nelson, 1999), 381.

Christ breathes on his disciples, this symbolic action recalls the creative activity of God to give and renew life (Gen. 2:7; Ezek. 37:9), and suggests that the risen Lord gives to his people the life of the new age.

The Hope of the Nations (Romans)

Paul expresses his eagerness to preach the gospel to the church in Rome (Rom. 1:15). He explains that this gospel was promised long ago by the Old Testament prophets and has now been revealed through the risen Lord Jesus, through whom the apostle to the Gentiles aims "to bring about the obedience of faith for the sake of his name among all the nations" (vv. 2–5). Careful study of the argument of Romans suggests that Paul penned this great letter with missionary, pastoral, and apologetic purposes in view.[68] These three aims are closely connected: the apostle shepherds the church through conflict between "the strong" and "the weak" (14:1–15:13), defends his gospel ministry in response to opposition and misunderstanding (e.g., 3:8; 16:17), and seeks "to further gospel mission in Rome and further afield."[69] Paul's pastoral and missionary aims converge in Romans 15 as he calls for Jewish and Gentile believers to welcome one another as Christ has welcomed them (v. 7) and then explains that his calling as "a minister of Christ Jesus to the Gentiles" compels him to preach the gospel where Christ is not yet known (vv. 16, 20). Significantly for the argument of this book, Paul grounds his pastoral exhortations and missionary ambitions with careful exposition of the Scriptures. He presents Christ himself as the model missionary to Jews and Gentiles, and casts his own apostolic ministry as the extension of his Lord's mission. Let's turn now to examine Paul's argument from the Scriptures to support his pastoral appeals and pioneering mission among the nations.

Christ, the Hope of Jews and Gentiles (Rom. 15:1–13)

In Romans 15:1–13, Paul urges believers in Rome to "please" their neighbors and "welcome one another," following Christ's example. These verses conclude his extended appeal for unity and mutual acceptance between "the strong" and "the weak" (14:1–15:13), and the Scripture-soaked section in

---

68 Will N. Timmins, "Why Paul Wrote Romans: Putting the Pieces Together," *Themelios* 43 (2018): 387.
69 Timmins, "Why Paul Wrote Romans," 403.

15:7–13 effectively serves as the climax of the entire letter.[70] Paul reasons that the Scriptures offer believers instruction and encouragement to live in harmony with one another for the purpose of glorifying God together (vv. 4–6), and he cites five Old Testament passages to this end (vv. 3, 9–12). These biblical citations poignantly express the sufferings and vindication of Christ and the hope of the nations.

Paul reasons that believers should please their neighbors, not themselves, because "Christ did not please himself, but as it is written, 'The reproaches of those who reproached you fell on me'" (Rom. 15:3). He cites Psalm 69:9 (68:10 LXX), where David's lament fittingly expresses and anticipates Jesus's consummate experience of suffering. Psalm 69 is frequently cited in the New Testament. John invokes this psalm to express Jesus's zeal for God's house (John 2:17; Ps. 69:9), the hostility he endured (John 15:25; Ps. 69:4), and his ironic thirst at the cross (John 19:28–29; Ps. 69:21).[71] Peter and Paul appeal to David's imprecatory prayers against God's enemies to explain God's judgment against Judas (Acts 1:20; Ps. 69:25) and unbelieving Israel's rejection of the Messiah (Rom. 11:9–10; Ps. 69:22–23).

Paul's extended quotation of the latter portion of Psalm 69 in Romans 11:9–10 demonstrates that when he cites Psalm 69:9 in Romans 15, he is mindful of the psalm's larger context.[72] Psalm 69 opens with a prayer for personal deliverance ("Save me," v. 1) and closes with confident hope that "God will save Zion" (v. 35). David describes his distress, dishonor, and despair as he cries out for God to rescue him and repay his persecutors. While the psalmist acknowledges his failings (v. 5), he insists that he has borne reproach and hatred for God's sake (vv. 4, 7, 9) and maintains hope in God (v. 3). Matthew Bates argues that the apostle places Psalm 69:9 in the Messiah's mouth in Romans 15:3.[73] He explains that "Paul was not interested

---

70 See Scott J. Hafemann, "Eschatology and Ethics: The Future of Israel and the Nations in Romans 15:1–13," *TynBul* 51 (2000): 161; J. Ross Wagner, *Heralds of the Good News: Isaiah and Paul 'in Concert' in the Letter to the Romans* (Leiden: Brill, 2002), 307; and Thomas R. Schreiner, *Romans*, 2nd ed., BECNT (Grand Rapids, MI: Baker Academic, 2018), 726.

71 See Brian J. Tabb, "Jesus's Thirst at the Cross: Irony and Intertextuality in John 19:28," *EvQ* 85 (2013): 338–51.

72 Mark Seifrid, "Romans," in *Commentary on the New Testament Use of the Old Testament*, 686.

73 He explains the "prosopological exegesis" of Ps. 69 in Matthew W. Bates, *The Hermeneutics of the Apostolic Proclamation: The Center of Paul's Method of Scriptural Interpretation* (Waco, TX: Baylor University Press, 2012), 240–55. For a similar interpretation, see Wagner, *Heralds of the Good News*, 312.

in David as the ascribed speaker, but rather David was a vehicle through whom the Spirit spoke in the prosopon [person] of the Christ."[74] However, it seems more likely that Paul applies the words of David typologically to Christ, who faithfully and fully endures the reproaches of God's enemies, following the pattern of the suffering psalmist.[75] Jesus refuses to please himself but willingly endures disdain and even death, offering believers the supreme ethical example to follow. In Psalm 69, David anticipates his vindication and the people's salvation on the other side of suffering, and Paul's argument similarly implies Christ's resurrection as he arises to rule over the Gentiles (Rom. 15:12), fulfilling Isaiah 11:10. Moreover, Romans 15:4 explains that the Scriptures (such as Ps. 69:9) offer believers "hope." This hope is anchored in Christ's own vindication after death and is extended to all peoples who welcome Christ's rule (Rom. 15:12).

Paul's argument in Romans 15:7–13 follows the same pattern as verses 1–6. He begins with a command ("welcome one another," v. 7), which he supports with the example of Christ ("For I tell you that Christ became a servant," v. 8). Paul then offers a biblical explanation ("as it is written," v. 9) followed by a concluding prayer ("May the God of hope fill you," v. 13).[76] The apostle develops his earlier point that "Christ did not please himself" (v. 3) with a key claim about the Messiah and his mission: "For I tell you that Christ became a servant to the circumcised to show God's truthfulness" (v. 8). Jesus's role as "servant to the circumcised" stresses his divine mission to bring salvation,[77] following the salvation-historical sequence Paul outlines in Romans 1:16: "to the Jew first and also to the Greek." Paul then articulates two purposes of Christ's servanthood: "in order to confirm the promises given to the patriarchs, and in order that the Gentiles might glorify God for his mercy" (15:8–9).[78] The second purpose builds on the first, since God's foundational "promises" concern not only Abraham's descendants but "all the families of the earth" who would be blessed in him (Gen. 12:3).[79] These

---

74 Bates, *The Hermeneutics of the Apostolic Proclamation*, 302.

75 Hafemann, "Eschatology and Ethics," 164–65; and Schreiner, *Romans*, 722n8.

76 Hafemann, "Eschatology and Ethics," 169; and Wagner, *Heralds of the Good News*, 308.

77 Eckhard J. Schnabel, *Der Brief des Paulus an die Römer: Kapitel 6–16*, HTA (Witten: Brockhaus, 2016), 787.

78 The syntax of these verses is debated. My analysis follows Hafemann, "Eschatology and Ethics," 170–72; and Schreiner, *Romans*, 726–29.

79 Paul develops this point further in Gal. 3:7–14.

verses in Romans explain how "Christ has welcomed" all believers—both the weak and the strong, Jews as well as Gentiles (Rom. 15:7).

A string of citations from the Law, Prophets, and Psalms (Rom. 15:9–12) unpacks the earlier reference to "the Scriptures" (v. 4) and offers biblical grounding for the Messiah's mission that extends God's saving mercy to Gentiles (vv. 8–9). First, Paul quotes Psalm 18:49 (17:50 LXX): "Therefore I will praise you among the Gentiles, and sing to your name."[80] This lengthy psalm of David praises God as the strength and shield of his people (vv. 1–2) who brings "great salvation" and shows his steadfast love to his anointed king (v. 50). The psalmist recounts that the Lord "made me the head of the nations," "subdued peoples under me," and "rescued me from my enemies" (vv. 43, 47, 48). For these reasons, he praises the Lord "among the nations" and confidently affirms God's commitment "to David and his offspring forever" (vv. 49–50), recalling the foundational covenant promises in 2 Samuel 7:12–16. Thus, "since David is God's anointed king, more is at stake in his rescue than simply his personal safety."[81] David's salvation from his foes confirms God's covenant with his king and anticipates the eternal reign of David's greater Son. Thus, Psalm 18 describes foreign peoples submitting to God's chosen king (vv. 43–45), who extols the Lord "among the nations" (v. 49). David's victories typologically anticipate Jesus's triumphs as David's messianic descendent,[82] whom God raised from the dead (Rom. 1:3–4). Paul cites Psalm 18:49 to show how Christ's victory and exaltation as ruler over the nations confirm God's promises to the patriarchs (Rom. 15:8).

The apostle's next two Scriptural citations summon the Gentiles to rejoice and praise the Lord.[83] "Rejoice, O Gentiles, with his people" in Romans 15:10 quotes Deuteronomy 32:43 LXX, the last verse of the famous Song of Moses. Deuteronomy 32 extols the Lord as "the Rock" of his people (vv. 4, 15, 18, 30, 31). Moses rehearses how God chose and cared for his people, yet they "forgot" their God and "stirred him to jealousy with strange gods" (vv. 16, 18). In response, the Lord promises to provoke Israel and warns that he will "heap disasters upon them" (vv. 21, 23). But judgment is not the final word,

---

80 The wording of this quotation also precisely parallels 2 Sam. 22:50 LXX.

81 Hafemann, "Eschatology and Ethics," 176.

82 Schreiner, *Romans*, 732. Alternatively, Bates argues that Paul engages in prosopological exegesis—not typology—by identifying Christ as the speaker in Ps. 18:49. *The Hermeneutics of the Apostolic Proclamation*, 293.

83 The unifying theme of praise is noted by Schnabel, *Der Brief des Paulus an die Römer*, 790.

as "the LORD will vindicate his people and have compassion on his servants" (v. 36). In conclusion, Moses calls for heavenly rejoicing and for the nations to "be glad . . . with his people" (v. 43 NETS). The apostle cites Deuteronomy 32:43 with clear awareness of the wider context of Moses's Song. Elsewhere in Romans, Paul appeals to Deuteronomy 32 to explain God's response to Israel's rebellion (Rom. 10:19; citing Deut. 32:21) and to stress that vengeance belongs to God alone (Rom 12:19; citing Deut. 32:35). Thus, Ross Wagner argues that "Paul reads the Song as a whole as a narrative of God's faithfulness to redeem Israel and, through Israel, the entire world."[84]

Paul next appeals to Psalm 117:1 (116:1 LXX): "Praise the Lord, all you Gentiles, and let all the peoples extol him" (Rom. 15:11). Psalm 117 is a brief psalm that begins and ends with a summons to "praise the LORD." The psalmist commands the peoples to worship God because of his prevailing "mercy upon us" (*eleos eph' hēmas*) and enduring "truth" (*alētheia*, v. 2 LXX). Paul may allude to this psalm when he speaks of "God's truthfulness" and "his mercy" in Romans 15:8–9.[85] Most interpreters read "us" in Psalm 117:2 as a reference to Israelites as the recipients of divine mercy. However, "The nations are called on by Israel here to praise YHWH because he has proved his love for Israel *and* for the nations."[86] Romans 15:9 makes clear that *the Gentiles* themselves are recipients of God's saving mercy through Christ. In Paul's argument, the citations of Deuteronomy 32:43 and Psalm 117:1 do not refer to the Gentiles' future praise at Jesus's second coming, but to the present reality of Gentile and Jewish believers in Christ worshipping together (Rom. 15:6).[87]

Paul calls on Isaiah to offer the concluding biblical argument for his claim about the Messiah and his mission:

And again Isaiah says,

> "The root of Jesse will come,
>   even he who arises to rule the Gentiles;
>   in him will the Gentiles hope." (Rom. 15:12)

---

84 Wagner, *Heralds of the Good News*, 317.

85 Hafemann, "Eschatology and Ethics," 183; Wagner, *Heralds of the Good News*, 315; and Hossfeld and Zenger, *Psalms 3*, 226.

86 Hossfeld and Zenger, *Psalms 3*, 224, emphasis original.

87 See Schreiner, *Romans*, 732; against Hafemann, "Eschatology and Ethics," 181–82.

Paul's introduction of this quotation of Isaiah 11:10 LXX marks the fifth time he names Isaiah in this letter.[88]

Isaiah 11:10 envisions a time of restoration "in that day," when the remnant of Israel will return from exile (10:20–22; 11:11) and praise God for his saving power and renewed presence with his people (12:1–6). Central to this future hope is Isaiah's prophecy of the Davidic Messiah (11:1), who will be endowed with the fullness of God's Spirit and rule with righteousness and wisdom (11:2–5). The Messiah's reign will lead to universal peace and renewal, as the knowledge of the Lord will fill the earth (11:6–9).[89] Some interpreters argue that "the root of Jesse" (v. 10) refers to the remnant of Israel that participates in the new era of restoration,[90] but this phrase more naturally refers to the Davidic Messiah introduced in verse 1 as a "shoot" from Jesse's stump and a "branch" from his roots (v. 1).[91] Isaiah 2:2–4 envisions all nations and peoples coming to God's mountain to receive instruction and submit to his rule in the last days, and 11:10 prophesies that these nations will hope in the messianic King.[92]

It is noteworthy that Romans 15:12 closely follows the Greek translation of Isaiah 11:10, which differs from the received Hebrew text in two key ways. The Hebrew states that the root of Jesse "shall stand as a signal for the peoples" and the nations shall "inquire" of him, but in the Septuagint, the root of Jesse "arises to rule nations," who "shall hope in him."[93] This prophecy of the Gentiles hoping in the Messiah illustrates Paul's earlier reference to the Scriptures offering believers "hope" (Rom. 15:4) and prepares for his prayer that "the God of hope" will enable his people to "abound in hope" (v. 13). Moreover, in light of Paul's argument and theological emphases

---

88 See Rom. 9:27; 10:16, 20.

89 The eschatological restoration described in Isa. 11:6–9 results from the direct action of God himself, not the promised ruler in 11:1, according to Greg Goswell, "Messianic Expectation in Isaiah 11," *WTJ* 79 (2017): 130. However, this presents a false choice between God and his anointed agent and also minimizes the significance of Isaiah's references to Jesse's offspring in verses 1 and 10 that frame verses 6–9.

90 For example, Childs, *Isaiah*, 105–6.

91 House, *Isaiah*, 1:333; and Joseph Blenkinsopp, *Isaiah 1–39*, AB 19 (New York: Doubleday, 1974), 267. For a discussion of early Jewish messianic interpretations of Isa. 11, see Wagner, *Heralds of the Good News*, 320–22.

92 House, *Isaiah*, 335–36.

93 The LXX translation *elpizō* ("hope") for the Hebrew *drš* ("seek") may reflect the influence of other passages in Isaiah that describe the nations' hope in the Lord's servant (42:1) and the Lord's arm (51:5); see Wagner, *Heralds of the Good News*, 319n46.

in this letter, the verb *anistēmi* ("arises") in verse 12 may refer to Christ's resurrection, which Paul ties to the Son's enthronement as messianic King (1:4).[94] Isaiah 11:10 effectively sums up Paul's argument, as "all the elements of Romans 15:8–9 are present here in one scriptural quotation."[95]

Thus, Paul shows from the Law, Prophets, and Psalms that the risen Lord Jesus has fulfilled God's ancient promises and extended God's saving mercy to the Gentiles, who join with Jewish believers in glorifying God. Paul urges the strong and weak to follow Christ's example of enduring reproach rather than seeking to please himself (Rom. 15:2–3; Ps. 69:9). The ancient Scriptures offer believers instruction that "we might have hope" (Rom. 15:4). This hope is anchored in the risen messianic King Jesus and shared by all believers—Jews and Gentiles, the weak and strong alike—who may now live in harmony with one another and glorify God "with one voice" (v. 6).

Paul's Mission to Proclaim the Servant (Rom. 15:21)

Paul identifies himself as "a minister of Christ Jesus to the Gentiles" (Rom. 15:16). The apostle carries out "the priestly service of the gospel of God," and the Gentiles are his acceptable "offering" to God (v. 16). Thus, he endeavors "to bring the Gentiles to obedience" by preaching the gospel wherever Christ is not named (vv. 18, 20). The apostle explains in verse 21 that his mission to the nations aligns with what "is written," and cites Isaiah 52:15 LXX: "Those who have never been told of him will see, and those who have never heard will understand."

This is the fourth time in Romans that Paul directly quotes a passage from Isaiah 52–53. Romans 2:24 cites Isaiah 52:5 to explain that Israel's sins have dishonored God and led to his name being "blasphemed among the Gentiles." In Romans 10:15, Paul appeals to Isaiah 52:7: "And how are they to preach unless they are sent? As it is written, 'How beautiful are the feet of those who preach the good news!'" Isaiah announces the Lord's "return" to Zion (52:8) and heralds the good news that "God reigns" and brings salvation and comfort to his people "before the eyes of all the nations" (vv. 7, 9–10). The apostle who has been "set apart for

---

94 Douglas J. Moo, *The Letter to the Romans*, 2nd ed., NICNT (Grand Rapids, MI: Eerdmans, 2018), 896–97; and Schreiner, *Romans*, 733. Similarly, Wagner suggests "a delicious double-entendre" in the verb *anistēmi*. *Heralds of the Good News*, 319.

95 Wagner, *Heralds of the Good News*, 317.

the gospel of God" (Rom. 1:1) cites Isaiah 52:7 in Romans 10 to situate his own mission among the Gentiles in the context of God's unfolding plan.[96] While Paul and other missionaries herald the good news of salvation through the Lord Jesus, he explains that "they have not all obeyed the gospel" (v. 16). Paul explains that this response of rejection is an outworking of prophecy, appealing to Isaiah 53:1: "For Isaiah says, 'Lord, who has believed what he has heard from us?'"

In Romans 15:21, as in 10:16, the apostle cites Isaiah's famous prophecy of the Lord's servant, who will be greatly exalted yet greatly despised as he suffers for the sins of others. We have seen that Jesus emphatically applies Isaiah 53 to himself in Luke 22:37, and his first followers similarly explain the significance of Jesus's suffering and exaltation from Isaiah's servant prophecy (e.g., Acts 8:32–35; 1 Pet. 2:22–25).[97] While Paul does not explicitly quote this servant prophecy to explain the necessity and significance of Jesus's suffering and vindication, interpreters have suggested allusions to Isaiah 53 elsewhere in Romans,[98] and it is "a virtually unavoidable implication" of Paul's argument from Scripture that he understands Christ to be the suffering servant.[99] Isaiah 52:15 LXX refers to an announcement "concerning *him*," clearly referring to the Lord's servant in verse 13. In context, "those who have never been told" are the "many nations" and "kings" mentioned earlier in the verse. The promise that these nations "will see" and "understand" contrasts sharply with Paul's earlier description of Israel's spiritual hardening in Romans 11:8:

As it is written,

"God gave them a spirit of stupor,
    eyes that would not see
    and ears that would not hear,
down to this very day." (Citing Deut. 29:4 with Isa. 29:10)

---

96 Wagner, *Heralds of the Good News*, 170.

97 For additional discussion of Isa. 53, see chap. 2, pp. 50–56; chap. 5, pp. 116–19; and the exposition of Matt. 8:17 in this chapter, pp. 169–72.

98 For example, Rom. 4:25 may allude to Isa. 53:11–12, as noted by Moo, *The Letter to the Romans*, 314; cf. James D. G. Dunn, *Romans*, 2 vols., WBC 38A–B (Dallas: Word, 1988), 1:241.

99 Wagner, *Heralds of the Good News*, 335.

This contrast parallels Paul's argument in Acts 28:25–28, where he draws upon Isaiah 6:9–10 and 40:5 to explain the Jews' unbelief and the Gentiles' favorable response to "this salvation of God."[100]

We see in Romans 15 that Paul proclaims Christ wherever he is not named and thereby extends Christ's servant mission to the nations. The apostle earlier explains that Christ "became a servant to the circumcised . . . in order that the Gentiles might glorify God for his mercy" (vv. 8–9). Thus, Christ is the model missionary to Jews and Gentiles, and Paul understands his own apostolic work as "nothing less than the continuation of Christ's own mission."[101] In sum, Isaiah 52:15 sets forth the marching orders for Paul's pioneering mission to announce the good news about Christ Jesus to the Gentiles who have never heard.

A Royal Priesthood Proclaiming God's Excellencies (1 Pet. 2:4–10)

Peter explains the identity and mission of Christ and his people by employing one of the New Testament's "most extensive chains of OT citations" in 1 Peter 2:6–10.[102] The apostle previews his argument from the Scriptures in verses 4–5. Jesus is "a living stone rejected by men but in the sight of God chosen and precious" (v. 4), a claim supported by three scriptural "stone" (*lithos*) texts (vv. 6–8).[103] "Chosen and precious" corresponds to Isaiah 28:16, "rejected" anticipates Psalm 118:22, and Isaiah 8:14 explains that this "stone" causes some to stumble. Peter then explains that his readers who come to Christ are "like living stones . . . being built up as a spiritual house, to be a holy priesthood, to offer spiritual sacrifices acceptable to God through Jesus Christ" (1 Pet. 2:5). This description of believers prepares for verse 9, where Peter alludes to multiple Old Testament passages (Isa. 43:20–21; Ex. 19:6; Hos. 2:23) to illuminate the election and priestly vocation of God's people.

---

100 See chap. 6, pp. 161–64.

101 Wagner, *Heralds of the Good News*, 331.

102 John H. Elliott, *1 Peter: A New Translation with Introduction and Commentary*, AB 37B (New Haven: Yale University Press, 2000), 423.

103 Peter's combination of these three texts reflects the interpretive principle of *gezerah shawah* (argument from analogy). For detailed analysis of the textual interconnections within 1 Pet. 2:4–10, see Richard Bauckham, "James, 1 and 2 Peter, Jude," in *It Is Written: Scripture Citing Scripture: Essays in Honour of Barnabas Lindars*, ed. D. A. Carson and H. G. M. Williamson (Cambridge: Cambridge University Press, 1988), 310–11.

Peter begins his explanation of Jesus as the "stone" by appealing to Isaiah 28:16: "For it stands in Scripture: 'Behold, I am laying in Zion a stone, a cornerstone chosen and precious, and whoever believes in him will not be put to shame'" (1 Pet. 2:6). This citation "reintroduces, reinforces, and establishes by scriptural authority the themes of 2:4."[104] Isaiah 28:16 in Hebrew concludes with the line, "Whoever believes will not be *in haste*," but the Septuagint reads, "Whoever believes *in him* will not be *put to shame*." Peter's quotation substantially agrees with Isaiah 28:16 LXX, which specifies the "cornerstone" as the object of faith.[105]

Scholars have variously explained the "cornerstone" in Isaiah 28:16 as the Lord himself (as in 8:14), Zion, the messianic King, or the remnant of God's people.[106] The Dead Sea Scrolls apply this passage to the community of faithful Israelites,[107] while the Aramaic Targum explicitly refers to "a king" in Zion, and the Septuagint translation "believes *in him*" suggests a messianic interpretation. The overall context of the book, the Aramaic and Greek renderings of Isaiah 28:16, and the New Testament application of this prophecy to Christ cumulatively support identifying the stone laid in Zion as the Messiah.[108]

Peter identifies Jesus Christ as "a living stone," who fulfills Isaiah's "cornerstone" prophecy through his resurrection from the dead (1 Pet. 2:4, 6; cf. 1:3). He offers additional scriptural support for this Christological claim in 2:7–8 by citing Psalm 118:22 and Isaiah 8:14, texts that Jesus references in the Gospels to identify himself as the "stone."[109] Christ says, "What then is this that is written: 'The stone that the builders rejected has become the cornerstone'? Everyone who falls on that stone will be broken to pieces, and when it falls on anyone, it will crush him" (Luke 20:17–18; cf.

---

104 D. A. Carson, "1 Peter," in *Commentary on the New Testament Use of the Old Testament*, 1026.
105 For additional textual comparison between 1 Pet. 2:6 and Isa. 28:16, see Carson, "1 Peter," 1025–26. Paul also cites Isa. 28:16 LXX in Rom. 9:33 (in combination with Isa. 8:14) and 10:11.
106 For a survey of these and other interpretations, see Oswalt, *The Book of Isaiah*, 1:518.
107 "When such men as these come to be in Israel, then shall the party of the Yahad truly be established. . . . They will be 'the tested wall, the precious cornerstone.'" 1QS 8:4–7.
108 Paul House writes, "In Isaiah, only Yahweh and His chosen Messiah merit belief. No place but Zion is ultimately a permanent home of righteousness, justice, and peace. Only the believing remnant will reside in Zion. . . . Yahweh's word and the messianic promise are the stone that tests all people and all ideas." *Isaiah*, 2:44.
109 See Carson, "1 Peter," 1024. Peter and John also allude to Ps. 118:22 in Acts 4:11, as discussed in chap. 5, pp. 109–11.

Matt. 21:42, 44). This appeal to Psalm 118 is crucial to understanding the significance of Jesus's parable about the tenants who murder the master's son.[110] This psalm anticipates Christ's rejection by the Jewish leaders and also his vindication by God as "the foundation stone of the new temple."[111] Jesus's allusion to Isaiah 8:14–15 in Luke 20:18 illustrates Simeon's earlier prophecy that Mary's son "is appointed for the fall and rising of many in Israel" (Luke 2:34).

Peter's third "stone" citation underscores the disastrous consequences of rejecting Christ as the chosen and precious "living stone" (1 Pet. 2:4). In verse 8, he loosely quotes a portion of Isaiah 8:14: "A stone of stumbling, and a rock of offense."[112] In this verse, the LORD of hosts identifies himself as both "a sanctuary and a stone of offense," stressing that his unchanging holiness offers security and comfort to some but scandalizes others.[113] The prophet warns that those who do not fear God "shall stumble" on the divine rock and "shall fall and be broken" (v. 15), yet he resolves to "wait for the LORD" (v. 17). This "double-edged nature of God's self-revelation becomes most pointed" in Christ:[114] some recognize him as the chosen cornerstone and share in his honor, while others stumble in unbelief.

According to 1 Peter 2:4, Christ is "a living stone" who is "chosen" (*eklektos*) and "precious" (*entimos*), and the apostle describes Christ's followers in similar terms. Peter likens believers to "living stones" who "are being built up as a spiritual house" (v. 5). Christians share in Christ's resurrection life, having been "born again to a living hope" through his resurrection (1:3), and they themselves are stones in God's end-time temple founded on Christ as the cornerstone. Moreover, believers, like Christ, are chosen by God and honored in his sight. The apostle writes to "elect exiles" (*eklektois parepidēmois*, 1:1) and identifies this group of mostly Gentile Christians as "a chosen race" (*genos eklekton*, 2:9), alluding to Isaiah 43:20. Similarly, Christians' faith is "more precious [*polytimoteron*] than gold" and will result in "honor" (*timē*) at Christ's return (1 Pet. 1:7), and Peter specifies that "the honor [*timē*] is for you who believe" (2:7). Thus, he reminds suffering

---

110 Snodgrass, *Stories with Intent*, 290.
111 Beale, *The Temple and the Church's Mission*, 184.
112 For textual details of this citation, see Carson, "1 Peter," 1028–29.
113 See Motyer, *Isaiah*, 97.
114 Oswalt, *The Book of Isaiah*, 1:234. See Carson, "1 Peter," 1029.

followers of Christ that they "share in the honor God has shown to him as honored and elect cornerstone."[115]

Peter contrasts those who "stumble because they disobey the word" (1 Pet. 2:8) with believers who have a new identity and glorious mission in Christ:

> But you are a chosen race, a royal priesthood, a holy nation, a people for his own possession, that you may proclaim the excellencies of him who called you out of darkness into his marvelous light. Once you were not a people, but now you are God's people; once you had not received mercy, but now you have received mercy. (vv. 9–10)

Strikingly, the apostle here applies Old Testament language for Israel's election and vocation to his readers, who are most likely Gentile Christians.[116]

Isaiah 43:20–21 stands behind the description of the believers' identity as "a chosen race" and "a people for his own possession" and their calling to declare God's "excellencies." In Isaiah 43, the Lord declares that he is "doing a new thing" in contrast to the "former things" (vv. 18–19). He promises to make a way in the wilderness and provide water for Israel, "my chosen race, my people whom I have acquired to set forth my excellences" (vv. 19–21 NETS).[117] The word *genos* ("race") refers to "a stock or 'line' of persons descended from a common ancestor,"[118] specifically "Jacob" in Isaiah's prophecy (see 43:1, 22; 44:1). Yet Peter calls Christians "a chosen race" because of their identification with Christ, God's "chosen" stone laid in Zion (1 Pet. 2:4, 6). Thus, these scattered, suffering followers of Christ "are part of the restored Israel of the latter days."[119]

---

115 Paul J. Achtemeier, *1 Peter: A Commentary*, Hermeneia (Minneapolis: Fortress, 1996), 161.

116 Elsewhere, Peter refers to the readers' "former ignorance" and "futile ways," and argues that "the time that is past suffices for doing what the Gentiles want to do" (1 Pet. 1:14, 18; 4:3). These and other passages suggest that most of these readers are Gentiles, as explained by Elliott, *1 Peter*, 50–51. Alternatively, some commentators maintain that Peter addresses a largely Jewish audience, and "it makes little difference whether the original readers were Jews or Gentiles," according to Karen H. Jobes, *1 Peter*, BECNT (Grand Rapids, MI: Baker Academic, 2005), 24.

117 1 Pet. 2:9 may also reflect the influence of Isa. 42:12 LXX ("they will *declare his excellences* in the islands"), according to Beale, *A New Testament Biblical Theology*, 741.

118 Elliott, *1 Peter*, 435. The term *genos* "implies a specifically 'ethnic' type of identity," according to David G. Horrell, "'Race,' 'Nation,' 'People': Ethnic Identity-Construction in 1 Peter 2.9," *NTS* 58 (2012): 130.

119 Beale, *A New Testament Biblical Theology*, 741.

Next, Peter identifies these elect exiles as "a royal priesthood" and "a holy nation" (1 Pet. 2:9), which precisely recalls the language of Exodus 19:6 LXX: "You shall be for me a royal priesthood and a holy nation" (NETS). Ross Blackburn calls verses 4–6 Israel's "mission statement."[120] Verse 4 recounts how the Lord executes judgments on the Egyptians and bears Israel "on eagles' wings" in the exodus, delivering his people "for *relationship with him*."[121] The Lord then summons Israel to heed his voice and keep his covenant, and so be his special people out of all nations (v. 5). The phrase "kingdom of priests" (v. 6) fittingly expresses Israel's God-given vocation to be priestly mediators of God's presence, blessing, and revelation to the nations around them.[122] By representing the Lord and reflecting his holiness as a holy people, "Israel makes him known to the world."[123] This summary of Israel's identity and calling may recall God's foundational promises to make Abraham a great "nation" and bless the earth's families through him (Gen. 12:2–3).[124]

According to Peter, Jesus's followers typologically fulfill this description of the nation of Israel in Exodus 19:6.[125] Believers in Christ have received God's mercy and experienced a kind of new exodus out of darkness into light, and they now have a new identity as God's holy people (1 Pet. 2:9–10). The apostle presents believers as stones in God's "spiritual house" and as priests offering "spiritual sacrifices acceptable to God through Jesus Christ" (v. 5). Thus, Christians have a new vocation to offer true worship to God rightly and to proclaim God's excellencies in the world and for the world.[126] Peter urges believers to carry out their mission as "sojourners and exiles" in this world by conducting themselves honorably "among the Gentiles," in hopes that they, too, may "glorify God" (vv. 11–12).

---

120 W. Ross Blackburn, *The God Who Makes Himself Known: The Missionary Heart of the Book of Exodus*, NSBT 28 (Downers Grove, IL: InterVarsity Press, 2012), 87.

121 Blackburn, *The God Who Makes Himself Known*, 88, emphasis original.

122 The Levitical priesthood does not replace the nation's collective calling as a royal priesthood; rather, the Levites provide "a visual model of that vocation," according to John A. Davies, *A Royal Priesthood: Literary and Intertextual Perspectives on an Image of Israel in Exodus 19.6*, JSOTSup 395 (London: T&T Clark, 2004), 240.

123 Blackburn, *The God Who Makes Himself Known*, 92.

124 William J. Dumbrell, *Covenant and Creation: An Old Testament Covenantal Theology* (Exeter: Paternoster, 1984), 89–90.

125 See Carson, "1 Peter," 1030–31.

126 Horrell, "Ethnic Identity-Construction in 1 Peter 2.9," 142.

Further, in 1 Peter 2:10, the apostle clarifies how his Gentile readers came to be "a *people* for his own possession" (v. 9): "Once you were not a people, but now you are God's people; once you had not received mercy, but now you have received mercy." The repeated phrase "but now" contrasts these believers' bleak past with their present status before God.[127] Peter articulates the radical transformation of his readers by alluding to Hosea 2:23 (2:25 LXX):

> And I will have mercy on No Mercy,
>> and I will say to Not My People, "You are my people";
>> and he shall say, "You are my God."

To appreciate this stunning promise of divine mercy, we must remember that Hosea indicts Israel for committing "great whoredom by forsaking the LORD" and worshipping false gods (1:2; 2:8, 13). The Lord charges that "the northern kingdom . . . has become a brothel," and the names of Hosea's three children—Jezreel, No Mercy, and Not My People (1:4, 6, 9)—signify "God's profound opposition to his people's whoredom."[128] In fact, the Lord's chilling pronouncement, "You are not my people, and I am not your God" (1:9), signals that God has revoked Israel's covenantal status as "my people" (cf. Ex. 6:7; Lev. 26:12).[129] The Lord warns that he will "uncover her lewdness in the sight of her lovers" (Hos. 2:10) and "punish her for the feast days of the Baals" (v. 13). However, judgment is not God's final goal. He promises to "allure" Israel (v. 14) and "betroth" her to himself forever in righteousness and faithfulness (v. 19), so that the people "shall know the LORD" (v. 20).

Strikingly, Peter relates Hosea's prophecy about *Israel's* end-time restoration after exile to his predominantly *Gentile* readers.[130] In Hosea, Israel's covenant unfaithfulness renders her "Not My People," just like the nations around her, who do not know the true God. Yet the Lord promises to once again show mercy and enter into covenant with Israel. Peter applies Hosea

---

127 See J. Ramsey Michaels, *1 Peter*, WBC 49 (Waco, TX: Word, 1988), 112; and Achtemeier, *1 Peter*, 168.

128 Raymond C. Ortlund, *God's Unfaithful Wife: A Biblical Theology of Spiritual Adultery*, NSBT 2 (Downers Grove, IL: InterVarsity Press, 1996), 50, 53.

129 The announcement in Hos. 1:9 is "the equivalent to a divorce," according to Ortlund, *God's Unfaithful Wife*, 54.

130 Beale, *A New Testament Biblical Theology*, 742.

2:23 typologically to Gentile Christians whose former situation as "not a people" corresponds to exiled Israel, standing outside of God's covenant and saving mercy.[131] The apostle's use of Hosea highlights God's extravagant mercy that extends not only to "Gentile" Israel but also to the rest of the nations, which were in spiritual darkness before the Creator God called them into his marvelous light to declare his praises.

Thus, 1 Peter 2:4–10 expounds the identity and mission of the Messiah and his people by drawing on at least six Old Testament passages. Peter explains that Christ was rejected by men yet chosen by God; by virtue of his resurrection, he is "a living stone" and the foundational cornerstone for God's temple in the last days (Ps. 118:22). Jesus is the messianic "stone" of Isaiah 8:14 and 28:16. People respond to this Christ stone in one of two ways: believers recognize him as the chosen cornerstone and will not be put to shame, while others stumble and fall in unbelief (1 Pet. 2:6–8). Peter presents Christ's followers as "living stones" in God's spiritual house, who offer true worship and proclaim God's excellencies (vv. 5, 9). Through faith in the risen Messiah, these Gentile Christians typologically fulfill Israel's original vocation as "a royal priesthood" and "a holy nation" (Ex. 19:6) and also God's prophecies of end-time restoration for his "chosen race," who will receive his saving mercy and be called his people (Isa. 43:20–21; Hos. 2:23).

Summary

George Lucas's original *Star Wars* trilogy (1977–1983) was a blockbuster success and remains hugely popular. Three prequel films (released in 1999–2005) recount the rise and fall of Anakin Skywalker, who becomes Darth Vader, and a later sequel trilogy (2015–2019) concludes the epic series. While these films develop various major characters, such as Anakin, Luke Skywalker, Han Solo, Kylo Ren, and Rey, it is John Williams's musical scores that masterfully tie the story together. The ominous "Imperial March" accompanies Darth Vader's scenes in the original trilogy, and this theme returns in Episodes 7–9 when Kylo Ren clutches Vader's charred mask and is likened to a new Vader. Likewise, the more hopeful "Star Wars Main

---

131 See Carson, "1 Peter," 1032; and David I. Starling, *Not My People: Gentiles as Exiles in Pauline Hermeneutics*, BZNW 184 (Berlin: de Gruyter, 2011), 200. Starling's comments on the use of Hos. 1–2 in Rom. 9:25–26 are fitting for 1 Pet. 2:10 as well: "Gentiles can become 'my people' because Israel has first become 'not my people'" (p. 164).

Title" opens all nine movies, serves as Luke Skywalker's theme song, and recurs in the "Reunion" track in the final episode, *The Rise of Skywalker*. Similarly, the Lord Jesus's climactic exposition of the Scriptures in Luke 24:44–49 serves as the "main title" track or "melodic line" for his teaching and that of his followers in Luke's two episodes.[132]

This chapter has considered representative passages in Matthew, John, Romans, and 1 Peter that expound the biblical hopes concerning the Messiah and his mission. I have argued that Jesus's scriptural summary about his suffering, resurrection, and mission to all nations (Luke 24:46–47) is a melody that recurs in other New Testament books. These apostolic voices sound distinctive notes, yet they sing in harmony with Luke's Gospel and Acts, which I examined in detail in chapters 1–6.

While Jesus interpreted *all* the Scriptures in light of himself (Luke 24:27), certain Old Testament texts are particularly prominent in his teaching and that of his followers, such as the Psalms and Isaiah's prophecies concerning the new exodus and the Lord's servant. We have seen that the servant prophecies in Isaiah 49:6 and 52:13–53:12 provide a crucial biblical rationale for Christ's suffering and resurrection, as well as the mission "to the end of the earth" that his followers take up. Matthew 8:17 and 12:17–21 also stress that Jesus "fulfills" Isaiah's prophecies about the Lord's servant, bearing sins and sicknesses and offering healing and hope for the nations. Similarly, John 12:37–41 presents Jesus's rejection as the fulfillment of Isaiah's final Servant Song and consistent with the prophetic pattern of God's word falling on deaf ears, even as Isaiah himself saw and spoke of the Messiah's glory. Jesus is the model missionary sent to do the Father's will, and he also sends his followers to carry out his mission with the Spirit's help (John 20:19–23). Romans 15:1–13 appeals to the Law, Prophets, and Psalms to offer biblical grounding for the Messiah's mission that extends God's mercy to the Gentiles, as well as motivation for believers to welcome one another as they have received Christ's welcome. Paul then strikingly quotes Isaiah 52:15 as a rationale for his own apostolic mission to the nations, which continues Christ's servant mission (Rom. 15:21). Finally, 1 Peter 2:4–10 cites three Old Testament stone passages (following Jesus's own example in Luke 20:17–18). Peter

---

132 On the "melodic line" of a biblical book, see David R. Helm, *Expositional Preaching: How We Speak God's Word Today*, 9Marks (Wheaton, IL: Crossway, 2014), 47–51.

establishes that Jesus is the rejected yet chosen living stone, the cornerstone of God's new temple. He also remarkably applies Old Testament language for Israel's identity and vocation as God's holy people and royal priesthood to Gentile followers of Jesus, who have received mercy and been called to proclaim Christ's excellencies.

These soundings from the writings of Matthew, John, Paul, and Peter illustrate this book's argument that the risen Lord's summary of the Scriptures in Luke 24 provides a hermeneutical lens with which to interpret the biblical story after Emmaus. The apostles and their associates appeal to the Old Testament to show that Jesus had to suffer and rise again and that the gospel's advance among the nations is the fulfillment of biblical expectation. Christ models for his followers this focus on the Messiah's suffering, resurrection, and mission, and he empowers them to carry out his mission among the nations. The next chapter urges Christian readers today to follow the risen Lord's example for reading the Scriptures and to participate in his mission in the world.

8

Participating in the Messiah's Mission

And Paul went in, as was his custom, and on three Sabbath
days he reasoned with them from the Scriptures,
explaining and proving that it was necessary for the
Christ to suffer and to rise from the dead, and saying,
"This Jesus, whom I proclaim to you, is the Christ."

ACTS 17:2–3

A VISION OF A MACEDONIAN MAN asking for help moves Paul and his friends to pack their bags for Philippi (Acts 16:9–10, 12). While the missionaries are confident in God's call to go to Macedonia, this vision does not detail all the troubles coming their way. Paul and Silas are attacked, publicly beaten with rods, and thrown into prison in Philippi (vv. 19–24). Their reception is not much warmer in Thessalonica, the city called "the mother of all Macedonia."[1] Paul opens the Scriptures and explains that "it was necessary for the Christ to suffer and to rise from the dead" (17:3). He persuades some people but encounters stiff opposition from the Jewish leaders, who form a mob and start a riot (vv. 4–5). They accuse Paul and Silas of turning the world upside down as they speak about "another king, Jesus" (vv. 6–7). The missionaries' work in Thessalonica ends abruptly as they have to flee by night (v. 10).

---

1   Antipater of Thessalonike, *Anthologia Palatina*, 4:428, cited in Schnabel, *Early Christian Mission*, 2:1160.

Luke's account of Paul and Silas's visit to Thessalonica offers a poignant example of what it looks like to participate in the Messiah's mission after Emmaus. First, we see that Paul proclaims the necessity of Christ's suffering and resurrection from the Scriptures (Acts 17:2–3). Luke summarizes Paul's message in a way that closely parallels the Lord's own exposition of the Old Testament (Luke 24:26–27, 46). Notably, the Greek verb *dianoigō*, rendered as "explaining" in Acts 17:3, repeatedly occurs in Luke 24, where the disciples' eyes are "opened" to recognize their Lord (v. 31), and Christ "opened" the sacred text (v. 32) and also "opened their minds to understand the Scriptures" (v. 45).[2] Of course, neither Paul nor Silas journeyed with Jesus on the Emmaus Road or gathered with the apostles to hear the Lord's teaching for forty days before his ascension, yet they preach the same message from the same Scriptures.

Further, they carry out the Lord's mission far beyond Jerusalem. Some Jews and a large number of Greeks respond favorably to the missionaries' message about the Messiah (Acts 17:4). This recalls Paul's foundational calling to bring Jesus's name before Gentiles and Jews (9:15) and to turn to the Gentiles in obedience to prophecy (13:46–47; Isa. 49:6).

Third, Paul and Silas experience significant opposition to their gospel ministry, just as Jesus promised (Acts 9:16). As the apostle reflects in his first letter to this church, "we had boldness in our God to declare to you the gospel of God in the midst of much conflict" (1 Thess. 2:2). Likewise, Paul recalls how the Thessalonian believers "turned to God from idols" and soon experienced intense suffering from their compatriots (1:9; 2:14). Opponents attack Christians' homes and accuse the missionaries of violating Caesar's decrees and upending the social order as they herald "another king, Jesus" (Acts 17:5–8). Luke's account illustrates Paul House's observation that "the gospel moves, but never without pain."[3] Paul and Silas proclaim a suffering Messiah and experience suffering as they participate in his mission.[4]

Luke 24 as a Biblical-Theological Lens

The risen Lord's last words in Luke's Gospel offer a hermeneutical lens through which to see the Messiah and his mission in the biblical story.

2 This link is also noted by Tannehill, *The Narrative Unity of Luke-Acts*, 2:206–7.
3 Paul R. House, "Suffering and the Purpose of Acts," *JETS* 33 (1990): 326.
4 See further Tabb, "Salvation, Spreading, and Suffering," 51–54.

The book of Acts and other New Testament books show that the apostles and their associates follow Christ's model of biblical interpretation as they proclaim the gospel in Jesus's name among the nations. That's the thesis of this book. My hope is that this study clarifies your Bible reading and compels you to participate in Christ's mission.

Let's recap the book's argument thus far and then draw out some implications for the church's message, mission, and motivation. The first chapter offers six guiding observations about Jesus's expositions of Scripture on the Emmaus Road and with his gathered disciples in Luke 24. The risen Lord reviews the Gospel's narrative of his necessary suffering and glorious resurrection, and also previews the disciples' mission as his witnesses in Acts. Christ's resurrection in Luke 24 also validates that he is a true prophet, whose predictions come to pass. He is not just a prophet, however, since he is the one who fulfills prophecy, carrying out God's revealed plan. Further, the risen Lord not only "opens" the Scriptures but also "opens" his disciples' eyes and minds, so that they might receive his remarkable revelation about himself (24:31–32, 45). Christ identifies the disciples as his witnesses and promises them divine power to carry out their mission in his name. Moreover, his last words are both *programmatic*—outlining the plan for Luke's second book—and also *paradigmatic*—providing a model by which his people should read the Bible. This leads to a final, crucial insight about Luke 24: Jesus summarizes the messianic and missiological thrust of the biblical story, explaining that the Scriptures find their central focus and climactic fulfillment in his death and resurrection *and* in the universal mission in his name. Paul's speech before King Agrippa mirrors the Lord's threefold summary of the Scriptures (Acts 26:22–23) and shows that Luke 24:44–47 sets the agenda for the message and mission of Christ's witnesses in Acts.

The Suffering, Resurrection, and Mission of the Messiah

Building on the opening chapter's reflections on Luke 24, the next six chapters study how Jesus and the apostles express the necessity of the Messiah's suffering, vindication, and mission in the biblical story.

Chapter 2 examines how Jesus's biblical exposition in Luke's Gospel anticipates his climactic claims that he must suffer to fulfill the Scriptures (Luke 24:26, 46). Christ presents himself as the dishonored prophet whose message falls on deaf ears (Luke 8:10; cf. 4:24; Isa. 6:10). Jesus also appeals to Psalm 118:22 to offer scriptural support for his rejection and resurrection as the chosen cornerstone of God's new temple. Further, he explains the saving purpose of his suffering at the Last Supper, as his shed blood initiates the new covenant promised in Jeremiah 31:31 (Luke 22:20). Christ emphatically cites Isaiah 53:12 to present his passion as the fulfillment of the mission of the suffering servant (Luke 22:37). He then calls out from the cross, "Father, into your hands I commit my spirit" (23:46), expressing his confident trust in God in the words of Psalm 31:5. Jesus's shameful crucifixion does not prove that he is a messianic imposter, but that he is the righteous King in David's line who suffers according to God's plan.

Chapter 3 considers how Luke's Gospel anticipates the risen Lord's assertion that the Messiah had to rise from the dead on the third day according to the Scriptures (Luke 24:46). Simeon prophesies that the Christ child will bring about a fundamental division within Israel: those who reject him will "fall" into judgment, while those who respond rightly to him will "rise" (2:34). Then Jesus's transfiguration and promised "departure" (or "exodus") preview his resurrection glory (9:29–35). Christ's teaching about "the sign of Jonah" in 11:29–32 stresses that Jesus himself will be "the sign" for his generation, a claim that is confirmed in his vindication after death. Further, Jesus predicts that he will rise on the third day (9:22; 18:33; 24:7), probably recalling the promise of resurrection after exile in Hosea 6:2. He also appeals to Exodus 3:6 to anchor resurrection hope on God's identity, reputation, and secure promise to his covenant people (Luke 20:34–38). Finally, Jesus's riddle about the Messiah as David's son and his Lord finds resolution in his apostles' preaching about his resurrection and heavenly enthronement (Luke 20:41–44; Acts 2:34–36; Ps. 110:1).

Chapter 4 focuses on four key passages in Luke that reference Old Testament prophecy to explain Jesus's identity, mission, and saving work. First, Simeon identifies the Christ child as the Lord's servant who brings the light of salvation to Israel and the nations (Luke 2:30–32; Isa. 49:6). Second, the evangelist quotes Isaiah 40:3–5 to clarify the scope of the new exodus salvation that the Lord Jesus brings (Luke 3:4–6). Third, Jesus announces that he is the Lord's Spirit-anointed agent sent to proclaim good news to the poor and oppressed (Luke 4:18–19; Isa. 61:1–2). Christ's hometown rejection aligns him with the Old Testament prophets, while his message of "liberty" (*aphesis*) prepares for Jesus's witnesses proclaiming "the forgiveness of sins [*aphesin hamartiōn*] . . . in his name to all nations" (Luke 24:47). Finally, Jesus presents his mission "to seek and save the lost" in terms that recall God's own commitment as Israel's true shepherd (Luke 19:10; Ezek. 34:16, 22). The conversion of Zacchaeus (Luke 19:1–10) illustrates Christ's mission to rescue lost sinners and anticipates the narrative of Acts, as Jesus's witnesses proclaim good news in his name to lost Jews and Gentiles.

Chapter 5 shows how the apostles and their associates proclaim Christ's suffering and resurrection with Spirit-brought courage and Christ-taught clarity after Emmaus, following the pattern that they learned from their Lord. They expound the Scriptures to explain that Christ is the rejected cornerstone of Psalm 118:22 (Acts 4:11), the Lord's anointed against whom the Gentiles and Israel plotted (Acts 4:25–28; Ps. 2:1), the cursed one hung on the tree (Acts 5:30; 10:39; Deut. 21:23), and the lamb-like servant led to the slaughter (Acts 8:30–35; Isa. 53:7–8). The witnesses also testify to the radical reversal brought about by the resurrection, which confirmed Jesus as the incorruptible Christ in David's line (Acts 2:24–32; 13:35; Ps. 16:8–11), the exalted Lord enthroned in heaven (Acts 2:34–35; Ps. 110:1), and God's Son, who reigns forever (Acts 13:32–33; cf. Ps. 2:7). This Jesus is the promised Lord and Messiah, who has poured out the promised Spirit on his people in the last days and offers salvation and forgiveness for all who call upon his name (Acts 2:16–21, 36; cf. Joel 2:28–32).

Chapter 6 addresses the biblical rationale for the disciples' mission to all nations in Acts. The risen Lord's foundational promise in Acts 1:8 previews the unfolding mission of Christ's witnesses in Jerusalem, Judea and Samaria, and beyond. Significantly, this mission plan draws upon Isaiah's prophecies that the Lord would pour out his Spirit, call his people as witnesses, and commission his servant to bring salvation "to the end of the earth" (Isa. 32:15; 43:10; 49:6). Peter proclaims that Christ is Abraham's promised offspring, through whom God's blessing would flow to Israel and all families of the earth (Acts 3:25–26; Gen. 12:3; 22:18). James shows that Jesus's exaltation to heaven's throne leads to Israel's restoration and the inclusion of Gentiles as full members of God's people, in harmony with the prophets' words (Acts 15:16–18; Amos 9:11–12). Paul and Barnabas cite Isaiah 49:6 as the biblical basis for their outreach to Gentiles (Acts 13:46–47). I argue that Jesus is the Lord's servant who would be "a light . . . to the Gentiles" (Luke 2:32), and the missionaries participate in and carry out Christ's mission through corporate solidarity. Finally, the Jews' divided response to Paul's preaching continues the pattern of spiritual deafness to the prophetic word (Isa. 6:9–10; Luke 8:10), yet this does not hinder the word's advance but serves as a catalyst for the message of salvation to reach the Gentiles, just as God promised (Acts 28:28; cf. Luke 3:6; Isa. 40:5).

Chapter 7 moves beyond Luke and Acts to consider how representative passages in Matthew, John, Romans, and 1 Peter expound the biblical hopes concerning the Messiah and his mission. Matthew presents Jesus fulfilling Isaiah's prophecies about the Lord's servant, who bears sins and sicknesses and offers healing and also hope for the Gentiles (Matt. 8:17; 12:17–21; cf. Isa. 42:1–4; 53:4). John's Gospel presents Jesus as the Son sent by the Father into the world to bring salvation and speak God's words. John 12:37–41 casts Jesus's rejection as an example of the prophetic pattern of God's word falling on deaf ears (Isa. 6:10) and as the fulfillment of the servant prophecy in Isaiah 53:1. After his resurrection, Jesus the paradigmatic missionary also sends his disciples to carry out his mission with the Spirit's aid (John 20:21–22). Next, Paul quotes texts from the Law, Prophets, and Psalms at the climax of his letter to the Romans to explain that Christ's mission extends God's mercy to the Gentiles (Rom. 15:8–13) and to motivate Jewish and Gentile believers to welcome one another as they have received Christ's welcome (v. 7). The apostle then cites Isaiah 52:15 as justification for his pioneering mission to the nations, which continues Christ's own servant mission (Rom. 15:21). Finally, 1 Peter 2:4–10 appeals to several Old Testament texts to establish that Jesus is the rejected yet chosen living stone, the cornerstone of God's new temple. Peter also remarkably transfers biblical descriptions of Israel's identity and vocation as God's holy people and royal priesthood to Gentile followers of Jesus, who have received mercy and now herald Christ's excellencies.

Thus, Jesus and the apostles appeal to the Law, Prophets, and Psalms to show that the Messiah and his mission to the nations are central to the biblical story. Luke 24:44–49 is a key summary of this melodic line of the Scriptures, a hermeneutical lens that helps Christ's followers see clearly what our Lord himself emphasizes. Jesus interprets "*in all the Scriptures* the things concerning himself" for the disciples on the Emmaus Road (v. 27). Christ's own biblical exposition in Luke's Gospel *anticipates* his climactic summary of the Scriptures in Luke 24, and the apostles and their associates *apply* the hermeneutical model they learned from the Lord Jesus as they proclaim the significance of his messianic suffering and resurrection, and also participate in his servant mission.

While Christ and his followers cite and allude to a wide range of Old Testament texts, we have seen that Isaiah plays a central role in linking the Messiah's suffering and vindication to the hope for the nations. Jesus announces that he is the Lord's Spirit-anointed agent sent to proclaim good news to the poor and liberty to the captives (Luke 4:18–19; Isa. 61:1–2). Simeon likewise identifies him as "a light for revelation to the Gentiles" (Luke 2:32), alluding to the mission of the Lord's servant in Isaiah 49:6. Christ also insists that his calling as the promised servant requires that he be numbered with the transgressors (Luke 22:37; Isa. 53:12) and also delivered over, spat upon, scourged, and punished for others (Luke 18:32–33; 23:16, 22; Isa. 50:6; 53:5, 12). Throughout the New Testament, the apostles and their associates repeatedly proclaim that Jesus is the suffering and vindicated servant of Isaiah.[5] But Isaiah also sets forth the servant's mission that Christ's followers carry out to the end of the earth. As the Lord's servant, Jesus acts as true "Israel" to restore Israel and bring God's salvation to the nations (Isa. 49:3, 5–6), and his followers partake in his mission through the principle of corporate solidarity (Acts 1:8; 13:47; cf. Isa. 49:6). Thus, the risen Lord accomplishes his mission *through* the work of his Spirit-empowered people, who act as *his* witnesses unto the outermost regions of the world.[6] Similarly, Paul describes Christ as a model missionary and presents his own pioneering gospel ministry among the Gentiles as an extension of Christ's servant mission (Rom. 15:8–9, 20–21; Isa. 52:15).[7]

Participating in Christ's Mission

Throughout this book, I emphasize that the Lord Jesus's biblical exposition in Luke 24:44–47 provides a hermeneutical model or lens for his followers to see how the Scriptures comprehensively testify to the Messiah *and* his mission. Patient readers who have made it this far may rightly ask, *So what?* The risen Lord does not open the Scriptures to give his disciples merely

---

5 See, for example, Matt. 8:17; John 12:38; Acts 3:13; 8:27–35; 1 Pet. 2:22–25.

6 Schnabel, *Early Christian Mission*, 1:372–75. I discuss Acts 1:8 further in chap. 6, pp. 136–41.

7 I discuss Paul's use of Scripture in Rom. 15 in chap. 7, pp. 185–93; see also Wagner, *Heralds of the Good News*, 331.

academic knowledge but to prepare his people to participate in his work in the world. The central teaching of Jesus and the apostles concerning the Messiah's suffering, resurrection, and mission according to the Scriptures provides us with a coherent, Christ-centered *message* and a compelling *mission* among the nations. Examining Jesus's mission in the Scriptures also supplies us with a powerful *motivation* to proclaim Christ with clarity and courage, and to pray with confidence for the advance of God's word in the world.

The Church's Message

See how the biblical story coheres and culminates in the Messiah and his mission among the nations. Jesus's last words in Luke's Gospel offer us a hermeneutical lens with which to read the Scriptures with the proper focus. Luke 24:44–47 also serves as the canonical fulcrum, the pivot point in the Bible's narrative.[8] Jesus here summarizes how his suffering and resurrection and the mission to the nations fulfill the Old Testament and offers his people a model for reading the Scriptures after Emmaus.

Jesus's teaching in Luke 24 not only helps us to grasp the Bible's "big picture" and unity amid the diversity of authors, historical contexts, and genres. It also helps us guard against truncated or distorted gospel presentations. Consider two recent examples.

Andy Stanley argues that we should "consider unhitching" our teaching about "what it means to follow Jesus from all things old covenant."[9] He claims that we should focus on "the life, death, and resurrection of Jesus" rather than insisting on what "the Bible says" in our post-Christian culture.[10] Stanley's desire to communicate the gospel in an intelligible and compelling way to today's generation is commendable, and he rightly insists that "something genuinely new happens with Jesus, and that changes the course of history."[11] However, Christ and his followers consistently appealed to the authoritative Scriptures to explain *why* the Messiah had

---

8   Daniel Marguerat calls Christ's resurrection "the lever" (le levier) that opens the meaning of the biblical texts, in "Quand la résurrection se fait clef de lecture de l'histoire (Luc-Actes)," 189.

9   Andy Stanley, *Irresistible: Reclaiming the New That Jesus Unleashed for the World* (Grand Rapids, MI: Zondervan, 2018), 315.

10 Stanley, *Irresistible*, 313.

11 Andy Stanley, "Jesus Ended the Old Covenant Once and for All," *Christianity Today*, October 18, 2018, http://www.christianitytoday.com/.

to suffer, die, and rise again to fulfill God's plan and *how* all the nations are included in God's plan. The call to unhitch from the Old Testament to focus on Christ's new work has similarities with the view of Marcion in the second century, who rejected the Old Testament as irreconcilable with the New Testament.[12] This approach reflects an inadequate perspective on the unity and coherence of the biblical story and results in a truncated gospel presentation.

Alternatively, Matthew Bates calls readers to "rethink the gospel, faith, and other matters pertaining to salvation."[13] He insists that while Christ "died for our sins," this is "only a small but vital portion of the gospel," which "climaxes with the enthronement of Jesus as the cosmic king."[14] While it is not possible to engage fully with Bates's proposal here,[15] I note that his shift in emphasis from Christ's past work through his suffering and resurrection to his present work as ascended Lord does not align with Christ's own explanation of "what is written" in Luke 24, which is paradigmatic for his followers. Further, Bates's presentation of "the full gospel" surprisingly fails to discuss how the gospel proclamation of Jesus and the apostles draws heavily on Old Testament prophecy, particularly the book of Isaiah.[16]

D. A. Carson asserts, "The heart of the gospel is what God has done in Jesus, supremely in his death and resurrection. Period."[17] This is the gospel that witnesses proclaim throughout Acts, and they consistently explain that this message fulfills the Scriptures. For example, Philip tells the eunuch "the good news about Jesus" beginning with Isaiah's prophecy about the suffering servant (Acts 8:35). Likewise, Paul recounts "the good news that what God promised to the fathers, this he has fulfilled to us their children by raising Jesus" (13:32–33). It is this good news about the crucified and risen Lord that the first Christians proclaim to Jews, Samaritans, and Gentiles beginning

---

12 For discussion of Marcion's view of the Old Testament, see Michael J. Kruger, *Christianity at the Crossroads: How the Second Century Shaped the Future of the Church* (Downers Grove, IL: InterVarsity Press, 2018), 117–18.

13 Matthew W. Bates, *Salvation by Allegiance Alone: Rethinking Faith, Works, and the Gospel of Jesus the King* (Grand Rapids, MI: Baker Academic, 2017), 5.

14 Bates, *Salvation by Allegiance Alone*, 39, 77.

15 See the incisive evaluation by Will N. Timmins, "A Faith Unlike Abraham's: Matthew Bates on Salvation by Allegiance Alone," *JETS* 61 (2018): 595–616.

16 See, for example, Isa. 40:9; 52:7; 61:1; cf. chap. 4, pp. 94–101.

17 D. A. Carson, "What Is the Gospel?—Revisited," in *For the Fame of God's Name: Essays in Honor of John Piper*, ed. C. Samuel Storms and Justin Taylor (Wheaton, IL: Crossway, 2010), 162.

in Jerusalem and extending to all nations. The church must continue to herald the same message about Christ as we carry out his mission today.

The Church's Mission

Participate in Christ's kingdom-extending work. Our Lord expounded the Scriptures in Luke 24:44–47 not only to explain the outworking of God's revealed plan but also to move his people to action. Jesus declares "that repentance for the forgiveness of sins *should be proclaimed* [*kērychthēnai*] in his name to all nations, beginning from Jerusalem" (v. 47), clearly implying that *preachers* will herald the message of repentance for the forgiveness of sins in Christ's name to all the nations. While he imprecisely calls verses 46–49 "the Lucan Great Commission," Thomas Moore rightly recognizes that Jesus's teaching implicitly summons his disciples to carry out their mission.[18] The narrative of Acts suggests this connection as various witnesses "proclaim" (*kēryssō*) the Messiah and the kingdom of God.[19] Peter recounts that Jesus commanded his apostles "to preach to the people" (Acts 10:42)—that is, the Jewish people[20]—though here he proclaims the message of forgiveness of sins in Christ's name to Cornelius, a God-fearing Gentile (v. 43). The apostles were in the room to hear the risen Lord open the Scriptures, but it is other disciples, such as Philip and Paul, who proclaim Christ and carry out his mission to Samaria (8:5) and as far as Rome in the very heart of the Gentile world (28:31). The open ending of Luke's narrative not only encourages readers by the unhindered progress of the gospel but also invites us "to participate in this universal mission."[21]

There is a long-standing debate among theologians and missiologists over *what* the mission of the church is and *how* to carry it out in the world today.[22] Some stress that Christ outlines the church's unique, central task to proclaim the gospel message and make disciples of all nations.[23] Others

---

18 Moore, "The Lucan Great Commission," 51.

19 See, for example, Acts 8:5; 9:20; 20:25; 28:31.

20 Jervell, *Apostelgeschichte*, 312; and Schnabel, *Acts*, 503.

21 Keener, *Acts*, 1:708.

22 Consider the range of perspectives in Jason S. Sexton, ed., *Four Views on the Church's Mission*, Counterpoints (Grand Rapids, MI: Zondervan, 2017); and Craig Ott, ed., *The Mission of the Church: Five Views in Conversation* (Grand Rapids, MI: Baker Academic, 2016).

23 Kevin DeYoung and Greg Gilbert, *What Is the Mission of the Church? Making Sense of Social Justice, Shalom, and the Great Commission* (Wheaton, IL: Crossway, 2011), 26. They reference the following "Great Commission passages" in support: Matt. 28:16–20; Mark 13:10; 14:9;

argue that the church's "mission" constitutes "all that God has called the church into existence for and all that God has sent the church into the world to do."[24] Thus, the mission includes not only evangelism and teaching but also activities such as doing good, pursuing justice, and stewarding creation.[25] Still others minimize the call to proclaim the gospel *to* the world and instead emphasize the socioeconomic and political thrust of the church's witness *in* society.[26] While a full discussion of such important questions is beyond the scope of this book, I have focused considerable attention on the risen Lord's climactic exposition of the messianic and missiological thrust of the Scriptures in Luke 24:44–47, which distills Jesus's teaching elsewhere and provides a model and marching orders for his disciples. Christ's people participate in *his* mission as the promised servant as they preach forgiveness in his name among all nations as Christ's "witnesses" (Luke 24:48; Acts 1:8).

The reference to proclamation in Luke 24:47 clearly anticipates the mission of the apostles and their associates in Acts; it also recalls Jesus's explanation of his own mission in terms of Isaiah 61:1–2: "to *proclaim good news* to the poor . . . to *proclaim* [*kēryxai*] liberty to the captives . . . to *proclaim* [*kēryxai*] the year of the Lord's favor" (Luke 4:18–19). Jesus preaches in the Judean synagogues (4:44), proclaims good news about the kingdom in various cities and villages and even in the temple (8:1; 20:1), and also sends the twelve "to proclaim the kingdom of God and to heal" (9:2; cf. v. 6). Of course, Jesus also does good and heals "all who were oppressed by the devil" (Acts 10:38; cf. 2:22), and his mighty deeds confirm his messianic identity and signal the inbreaking of the eschatological era of salvation (Luke 7:18–23; cf. Isa. 35:4–6). But Jesus does not simply perform mighty works or set an example of compassionate action for his followers; he fulfills the script of the Scriptures by suffering, dying, and rising on the third day. This is why his witnesses proclaim "repentance for

---

Luke 24:44–49; Acts 1:8. Jonathan Leeman offers a nuanced version of this view, distinguishing between the narrow mission of the organized church to *make* disciples and the broad mission of individual church members to *be* disciples. "Soteriological Mission," in *Four Views on the Church's Mission*, 41.

24 Christopher J. H. Wright, "Participatory Mission," in *Four Views on the Church's Mission*, 91.

25 Wright, "Participatory Mission," 80–90.

26 Amos Yong, *Mission after Pentecost: The Witness of the Spirit from Genesis to Revelation*, The Mission in Global Community (Grand Rapids, MI: Baker Academic, 2019), 278. Yong reasons that the biblical call is "less the verbal proclamation to nations as such than the call to believing faithfulness amid a watching world" (p. 279).

the forgiveness of sins" and "salvation" in Jesus's name alone (Luke 24:47; Acts 4:12; cf. 13:26–39). Thus, Christians herald the servant's saving work and extend the servant's mission among the nations.[27] As we participate in Christ's mission, we should maintain—or perhaps recover—the New Testament's understanding of what the gospel *is* and the central priority of *proclamation* in that mission.

The Church's Motivation

Speak about Christ with courage and clarity. Acts records the remarkable transformation of Jesus's disciples after Emmaus, as these uncredentialed men boldly testify to their risen Lord in the face of stiff opposition. Peter and John are arrested, Stephen is stoned, James is beheaded, and the church is threatened and scattered. Then Paul—who formerly persecuted the church with violent zeal—endures all manner of hardships for Christ's sake as he carries out Christ's mission in every city. Ancient philosophers reason that adversity offers an opportunity for good people "to perform a brave and courageous action."[28] But the "courage" and calmness of Jesus's witnesses does not highlight their own virtue but the Holy Spirit's presence and power in their preaching, just as Jesus promises in Luke 12:11–12:

> And when they bring you before the synagogues and the rulers and the authorities, do not be anxious about how you should defend yourself or what you should say, for the Holy Spirit will teach you in that very hour what you ought to say.

Tim Keesee recounts the audacity and adversities of Christ's ambassadors on the front lines of gospel advance. He tells about a Bengalese believer named Hasan, who was beaten, slapped with sandals, and threatened by a mob after proclaiming Christ in a house meeting.[29] Keesee also describes

---

27 Harmon puts it well: "While the work of Jesus the servant to atone for our sins is entirely finished, the proclamation of that good news has yet to reach every corner of this planet. It is through his people the church that Jesus continues the servant's mission of being a light of salvation to the nations." *The Servant of the Lord and His Servant People*, 226.

28 Seneca, *On Providence*, in *Dialogues and Essays*, trans. John N. Davie and Tobias Reinhardt, OWC (Oxford: Oxford University Press, 2007), 4.5.

29 Tim Keesee, *Dispatches from the Front: Stories of Gospel Advance in the World's Difficult Places* (Wheaton, IL: Crossway, 2014), 133.

his hospital visit with a young Pakistani pastor named Indriaz, who lost an ear and an eye when he was severely beaten by Muslims in his village.[30] These accounts offer sober yet hopeful examples of the cost of following a crucified King, and they reiterate the church's call to carry out Christ's mission to the farthest reaches of the earth, come what may. Keesee's stories also stir Christians to pray persistently for the gospel's advance among the nations and to be personally involved in the cause of global missions. While few readers of this book have endured beatings for their bold testimony to Christ, you may have experienced eye rolls, dismissive comments, or relational strain when sharing the gospel with family members and friends. Remember that "God ordains that the mission of his church move forward . . . at the price of suffering."[31] Studying Christ's mission in the Scriptures and hearing stories of believers' suffering for the sake of Christ's name should move us to proclaim Christ with clarity and courage and to pray with confidence for the advance of God's word in the world (Acts 4:29–30; Col. 4:2–3; 2 Thess. 3:1).

Acts concludes with Paul under house arrest in Rome, far away from his hometown of Tarsus, "proclaiming the kingdom of God and teaching about the Lord Jesus Christ with all boldness and without hindrance" (28:31). The book's open ending does not recount the missionary's fate as he awaits trial before Caesar but instead highlights the bold, clear testimony about the Lord Jesus. After Emmaus, Christ sums up the central message of the Scriptures about his suffering, resurrection, and mission to all nations. The last words of our risen Lord summon the church today to continue proclaiming this gospel message and carrying out his global mission with courage, clarity, and confidence.

---

30 Keesee, *Dispatches from the Front*, 152.

31 John Piper, "Let the Nations Be Glad! The Supremacy of God in Missions," in *The Collected Works of John Piper, Volume 3*, ed. David Mathis and Justin Taylor (Wheaton, IL: Crossway, 2017), 693.

Acknowledgments

I WANT TO ACKNOWLEDGE and thank many of the people who offered support and encouragement for this book. The original idea for it stems from reflecting on the Lord Jesus's teaching in Luke 24 with the wonderful students at Bethlehem College & Seminary in my courses on the use of the Old Testament in the New Testament and principles of biblical interpretation.

Special thanks are due to Justin Taylor and the Crossway publishing committee members, who expressed enthusiastic support for this project. Claire Cook and the design team produced a beautiful book cover that incorporates vignettes of Velázquez's painting *The Supper at Emmaus*, Greg Bailey skillfully edited the book, and Amy Kruis, Lauren Wills, and others coordinated marketing efforts.

It is a great privilege to serve on the Bethlehem College & Seminary faculty. President Tim Tomlinson graciously granted me a research sabbatical during the 2020 spring semester, during which I conducted most of the research and writing for this book. Chris Bruno admirably served as acting academic dean in my absence during a very challenging season due to the COVID-19 pandemic. Barbara Winters also provided wonderful assistance securing needed books and articles, even when many libraries were closed to patrons.

Many coworkers and friends offered encouragement for this project at the proposal stage, including the following individuals who graciously read portions of the manuscript and offered valuable feedback: Mark Batluck, Leah Bruneau, Jared Compton, Jason DeRouchie, Alex Kirk, Andy Naselli, Sarah Todd, Matthew Westerholm, and Hernan Wu.

I also thank God for my dear family—Kristin, Jeremiah, Julia, Judson, and Jonah—who bring incredible joy to me and offer constant love and patient support day after day. "The lines have fallen for me in pleasant places" (Ps. 16:6).

I dedicate this book to my father, Professor William Murray Tabb, who has been a faithful example to me and continues to give much wise counsel and timely encouragement. He also read the entire manuscript and offered insightful comments that strengthened the final product. "Hear, O sons, a father's instruction, and be attentive, that you may gain insight" (Prov. 4:1).

Soli Deo gloria.

Brian J. Tabb
Advent, 2020

Works Cited

Abernethy, Andrew T. *The Book of Isaiah and God's Kingdom: A Thematic-Theological Approach*. NSBT 40. Downers Grove, IL: InterVarsity Press, 2016.

Achtemeier, Paul J. *1 Peter: A Commentary*. Hermeneia. Minneapolis: Fortress, 1996.

Adams, Sean A., and Seth M. Ehorn, eds. *Composite Citations in Antiquity, Volume Two: New Testament Uses*. LNTS 593. London: Bloomsbury T&T Clark, 2018.

Aeschylus. *Oresteia: Agamemnon, Libation-Bearers, Eumenides*. Translated by Alan H. Sommerstein. LCL 146. Cambridge, MA: Harvard University Press, 2009.

Allen, Leslie C. *The Books of Joel, Obadiah, Jonah and Micah*. NICOT. Grand Rapids, MI: Eerdmans, 1976.

Andersen, Francis I., and David Noel Freedman. *Amos: A New Translation with Introduction and Commentary*. AB 24A. New Haven: Yale University Press, 1989.

Anderson, Kevin L. *'But God Raised Him from the Dead': The Theology of Jesus' Resurrection in Luke-Acts*. Paternoster Biblical Monographs. Bletchley: Paternoster, 2006.

Andrews, Michael W. "The Sign of Jonah: Jesus in the Heart of the Earth." *JETS* 61 (2018): 105–19.

Augustine. *The City of God*. Edited by Hermigild Dressler. Translated by Gerald G. Walsh et al. 3 vols. The Fathers of the Church 8, 14, 24. Washington, DC: The Catholic University of America Press, 1950–1954.

Augustine. *The Trinity*. Edited by Hermigild Dressler. Translated by Stephen McKenna. The Fathers of the Church 45. Washington, DC: The Catholic University of America Press, 1963.

Augustus. *Res Gestae Divi Augusti*. Translated by Frederick W. Shipley. LCL 152. Cambridge, MA: Harvard University Press, 1924.

Barrett, C. K. *The Acts of the Apostles*. 2 vols. ICC. London: T&T Clark, 1994–1998.

Bates, Matthew W. "Closed-Minded Hermeneutics? A Proposed Alternative Translation for Luke 24:45." *JBL* 129 (2010): 537–57.

Bates, Matthew W. *The Hermeneutics of the Apostolic Proclamation: The Center of Paul's Method of Scriptural Interpretation*. Waco, TX: Baylor University Press, 2012.

Bates, Matthew W. *Salvation by Allegiance Alone: Rethinking Faith, Works, and the Gospel of Jesus the King*. Grand Rapids, MI: Baker Academic, 2017.

Batluck, Mark. "Visions of Jesus Animate Israel's Tradition in Luke." *ExpTim* 129 (2018): 408–15.

Bauckham, Richard. *Gospel of Glory: Major Themes in Johannine Theology*. Grand Rapids, MI: Baker Academic, 2015.

Bauckham, Richard. "James, 1 and 2 Peter, Jude." Pages 303–17 in *It Is Written: Scripture Citing Scripture: Essays in Honour of Barnabas Lindars*. Edited by D. A. Carson and H. G. M. Williamson. Cambridge: Cambridge University Press, 1988.

Bauckham, Richard. "James and the Gentiles (Acts 15.13–21)." Pages 154–84 in *History, Literature, and Society in the Book of Acts*. Edited by Ben Witherington III. New York: Cambridge University Press, 1996.

Bayer, Hans F. *Jesus' Predictions of Vindication and Resurrection: The Provenance, Meaning, and Correlation of the Synoptic Predictions*. WUNT 2/20. Tübingen: Mohr Siebeck, 1986.

Beale, G. K. "Finding Christ in the Old Testament." *JETS* 63 (2020): 25–50.

Beale, G. K. *Handbook on the New Testament Use of the Old Testament: Exegesis and Interpretation*. Grand Rapids, MI: Baker Academic, 2012.

Beale, G. K. *A New Testament Biblical Theology: The Unfolding of the Old Testament in the New*. Grand Rapids, MI: Baker Academic, 2011.

Beale, G. K. *The Temple and the Church's Mission: A Biblical Theology of the Dwelling Place of God*. NSBT 17. Downers Grove, IL: InterVarsity Press, 2004.

Beale, G. K. *We Become What We Worship: A Biblical Theology of Idolatry*. Downers Grove, IL: IVP Academic, 2008.

Beasley-Murray, George R. *John*. 2nd ed. 2 vols. WBC 36. Nashville: Thomas Nelson, 1999.

Beaton, Richard. *Isaiah's Christ in Matthew's Gospel*. SNTSMS 123. Cambridge: Cambridge University Press, 2002.

Beaton, Richard. "Isaiah in Matthew's Gospel." Pages 63–78 in *Isaiah in the New Testament*. Edited by M. J. J. Menken and Steve Moyise. London: T&T Clark, 2005.

Beaton, Richard. "Messiah and Justice: A Key to Matthew's Use of Isaiah 42.1–4?" *JSNT* 22 (1999): 5–23.

Beers, Holly. *The Followers of Jesus as the "Servant": Luke's Model from Isaiah for the Disciples in Luke-Acts*. LNTS 535. New York: Bloomsbury T&T Clark, 2015.

Beutler, Johannes. "Greeks Come to See Jesus (John 12:20f)." *Bib* 71 (1990): 333–47.

Blackburn, W. Ross. *The God Who Makes Himself Known: The Missionary Heart of the Book of Exodus*. NSBT 28. Downers Grove, IL: InterVarsity Press, 2012.

Blenkinsopp, Joseph. *Isaiah 1–39*. AB 19. New York: Doubleday, 1974.

Blenkinsopp, Joseph. *Opening the Sealed Book: Interpretations of the Book of Isaiah in Late Antiquity*. Grand Rapids, MI: Eerdmans, 2006.

Block, Daniel I. *The Book of Ezekiel*. 2 vols. NICOT. Grand Rapids, MI: Eerdmans, 1997–1998.

Block, Daniel I. "Christotelic Preaching: A Plea for Hermeneutical Integrity and Missional Passion." *SBJT* 22.3 (2018): 7–34.

Blomberg, Craig L. *A New Testament Theology*. Waco, TX: Baylor University Press, 2018.

Blumhofer, Chris. "Luke's Alteration of Joel 3.1–5 in Acts 2.17–21." *NTS* 62 (2016): 499–516.

Bock, Darrell L. *Acts*. BECNT. Grand Rapids, MI: Baker, 2007.

Bock, Darrell L. *Luke*. 2 vols. BECNT. Grand Rapids, MI: Baker, 1994–1996.

Bock, Darrell L. *Proclamation from Prophecy and Pattern: Lucan Old Testament Christology*. JSNTSup 12. Sheffield: JSOT Press, 1987.

Bock, Darrell L. *A Theology of Luke and Acts*. Biblical Theology of the New Testament. Grand Rapids, MI: Zondervan, 2012.

Bock, Darrell L. "The Use of Daniel 7 in Jesus' Trial, with Implications for his Self-Understanding." Pages 78–100 in *'Who Is This Son of Man?': The Latest Scholarship on a Puzzling Expression of the Historical Jesus*. Edited by Larry W. Hurtado and Paul L. Owen. LNTS 390. London: T&T Clark, 2011.

Bøe, Sverre. *Cross-Bearing in Luke.* WUNT 2/278. Tübingen: Mohr Siebeck, 2010.

Bolt, Peter G. "Mission and Witness." Pages 191–214 in *Witness to the Gospel.* Edited by I. Howard Marshall and David G. Peterson. Grand Rapids, MI: Eerdmans, 1998.

Bovon, François. *Luke 1: A Commentary on the Gospel of Luke 1:1–9:50.* Translated by Christine M. Thomas. Hermeneia. Minneapolis: Fortress, 2002.

Bovon, François. *Luke 2: A Commentary on the Gospel of Luke 9:51–19:27.* Translated by Christine M. Thomas. Hermeneia. Minneapolis: Fortress, 2013.

Brendsel, Daniel J. *Isaiah Saw His Glory: The Use of Isaiah 52–53 in John 12.* BZNW 208. Berlin: de Gruyter, 2014.

Brown, Raymond E. *The Gospel according to John.* 2 vols. AB 29–29A. Garden City, NY: Doubleday, 1966–1970.

Bruce, F. F. *The Book of the Acts.* Rev. ed. NICNT. Grand Rapids, MI: Eerdmans, 1988.

Brueggemann, Walter, and William H. Bellinger Jr. *Psalms.* NCBC. Cambridge: Cambridge University Press, 2014.

Bruno, Chris. "Jesus Is Our Jubilee . . . But How? The OT Background and Lukan Fulfillment of the Ethics of Jubilee." *JETS* 53 (2010): 81–101.

Bruno, Chris, Jared Compton, and Kevin McFadden. *Biblical Theology according to the Apostles: How the Earliest Christians Told the Story of Israel.* NSBT 52. London: Apollos, 2020.

Bullard, Collin Blake. *Jesus and the Thoughts of Many Hearts: Implicit Christology and Jesus' Knowledge in the Gospel of Luke.* LNTS 530. London: Bloomsbury T&T Clark, 2015.

Calvin, John. *Commentary upon the Acts of the Apostles.* Translated by Henry Beveridge. Repr. ed. Bellingham, WA: Logos Bible Software, 2010.

Calvin, John. *Institutes of the Christian Religion.* Edited by John T. McNeill. Translated by Ford Lewis Battles. Library of Christian Classics. Philadelphia: Westminster John Knox Press, 1960.

Carson, D. A. "1 Peter." Pages 1015–46 in *Commentary on the New Testament Use of the Old Testament.* Edited by G. K. Beale and D. A. Carson. Grand Rapids, MI: Baker Academic, 2007.

Carson, D. A. *The Gospel according to John.* PNTC. Grand Rapids, MI: Eerdmans, 1991.

Carson, D. A. *Jesus the Son of God: A Christological Title Often Overlooked, Sometimes Misunderstood, and Currently Disputed.* Wheaton, IL: Crossway, 2012.

Carson, D. A. "Matthew." Pages 25–670 in *Matthew-Mark*. Edited by Tremper Longman III and David E. Garland. Rev. ed. EBC 9. Grand Rapids, MI: Zondervan, 2010.

Carson, D. A. "What Is the Gospel?—Revisited." Pages 147–70 in *For the Fame of God's Name: Essays in Honor of John Piper*. Edited by C. Samuel Storms and Justin Taylor. Wheaton, IL: Crossway, 2010.

Cartlidge, David R., and David L. Dungan. *Documents and Images for the Study of the Gospels*. 3rd ed. Minneapolis: Fortress, 2015.

Chapman, David W. *Ancient Jewish and Christian Perceptions of Crucifixion*. Grand Rapids, MI: Baker Academic, 2010.

Charlesworth, James H., ed. *The Old Testament Pseudepigrapha*. 2 vols. Garden City, NY: Doubleday, 1983–1985.

Chase, Mitchell L. *40 Questions about Typology and Allegory*. Grand Rapids, MI: Kregel, 2020.

Chase, Mitchell L. "The Genesis of Resurrection Hope: Exploring Its Early Presence and Deep Roots." *JETS* 57 (2014): 467–80.

Chavez, Chris. "Kobe Bryant, Daughter Die in California Helicopter Crash." *Sports Illustrated*, January 28, 2020. http://www.si.com/.

Childs, Brevard S. *Isaiah: A Commentary*. OTL. Louisville: Westminster John Knox, 2001.

Chou, Abner. *The Hermeneutics of the Biblical Writers: Learning to Interpret Scripture from the Prophets and Apostles*. Grand Rapids, MI: Kregel, 2018.

Cicero. *On Duties*. Translated by Walter Miller. LCL 30. Cambridge, MA: Harvard University Press, 1913.

Cicero. *The Orations of Marcus Tullius Cicero*. Translated by C. D. Yonge. London: George Bell & Sons, 1903.

Clark, Andrew C. "The Role of the Apostles." Pages 169–90 in *Witness to the Gospel*. Edited by I. Howard Marshall and David G. Peterson. Grand Rapids, MI: Eerdmans, 1998.

Compton, Jared. *Psalm 110 and the Logic of Hebrews*. LNTS 537. London: Bloomsbury T&T Clark, 2015.

Cosgrove, Charles H. "The Divine ΔEI in Luke-Acts: Investigations into the Lukan Understanding of God's Providence." *NovT* 26 (1984): 168–90.

Craigie, Peter. *The Book of Deuteronomy*. NICOT. Grand Rapids, MI: Eerdmans, 1976.

Crenshaw, James L. *Joel*. AB 24C. New York: Doubleday, 1995.

Crowe, Brandon D. "Fulfillment in Matthew as Eschatological Reversal." *WTJ* 75 (2013): 111–27.

Crowe, Brandon D. *The Hope of Israel: The Resurrection of Christ in the Acts of the Apostles.* Grand Rapids, MI: Baker Academic, 2020.

Cuany, Monique. "The Divine Necessity of the Resurrection: A Re-Assessment of the Use of Psalm 16 in Acts 2." *NTS* 66 (2020): 392–405.

Cuany, Monique. "'Today, Salvation Has Come to This House': God's Salvation of God's People in Luke's Gospel." *CurTM* 45.4 (2018): 12–17.

Cunningham, Scott S. *"Through Many Tribulations": The Theology of Persecution in Luke-Acts.* JSNTSup 142. Sheffield: Sheffield Academic, 1997.

Dautzenberg, Gerhard. "Psalm 110 im Neuen Testament." Pages 141–71 in *Liturgie und Dichtung: Ein interdisziplinäres Kompendium.* Edited by Hansjakob Becker and Reiner Kaczynski. Pietas liturgica 2. Sankt Ottilien: EOS Verlag, 1983.

Davies, John A. *A Royal Priesthood: Literary and Intertextual Perspectives on an Image of Israel in Exodus 19.6.* JSOTSup 395. London: T&T Clark, 2004.

Davies, W. D. and Dale C. Allison. *A Critical and Exegetical Commentary on the Gospel according to Saint Matthew.* 3 vols. ICC. Edinburgh: T&T Clark, 1988–1997.

Day, John. *Yahweh and the Gods and Goddesses of Canaan.* JSOTSup 265. Sheffield: Sheffield Academic, 2002.

DeClaissé-Walford, Nancy L., Rolf A. Jacobson, and Beth LaNeel Tanner. *The Book of Psalms.* NICOT. Grand Rapids, MI: Eerdmans, 2014.

Dempster, Stephen G. *Dominion and Dynasty: A Biblical Theology of the Hebrew Bible.* NSBT 15. Downers Grove, IL: InterVarsity Press, 2003.

Dempster, Stephen G. "From Slight Peg to Cornerstone to Capstone: The Resurrection of Christ on 'the Third Day' according to the Scriptures." *WTJ* 76 (2014): 371–409.

DeRouchie, Jason S. "The Mystery Revealed: A Biblical Case for Christ-Centered Old Testament Interpretation." *Themelios* 44 (2019): 226–48.

DeRouchie, Jason S. "Why the Third Day? The Promise of Resurrection in All of Scripture." Desiring God, June 11, 2019. http://www.desiringgod.org/.

DeRouchie, Jason S., and Jason C. Meyer. "Christ or Family as the 'Seed' of Promise? An Evaluation of N. T. Wright on Galatians 3:16." *SBJT* 14.3 (2010): 36–48.

DeYoung, Kevin, and Greg Gilbert. *What Is the Mission of the Church? Making Sense of Social Justice, Shalom, and the Great Commission.* Wheaton, IL: Crossway, 2011.

Dickens, Charles. *A Christmas Carol*. Repr. ed. Cambridge, MA: Candlewick, 2006.

Dillard, Raymond B. "Joel." Pages 239–313 in *The Minor Prophets: An Exegetical and Expository Commentary*. Edited by Thomas E. McComiskey, vol. 1. 3 vols. Grand Rapids, MI: Baker Academic, 1992.

Dillon, Richard J. "Easter Revelation and Mission Program in Luke 24:46–48." Pages 240–70 in *Sin, Salvation and the Spirit*. Edited by Daniel Durken. Collegeville, MN: Liturgical, 1979.

Dumais, Marcel. *Le langage de l'évangélisation: L'annonce missionnaire en milieu juif (Actes 13,16–41)*. Montréal: Bellarmin, 1976.

Dumas, Alexander. *The Count of Monte Cristo*. Translated by David Coward. OWC. Oxford: Oxford University Press, 1990.

Dumbrell, William J. *Covenant and Creation: An Old Testament Covenantal Theology*. Exeter: Paternoster, 1984.

Dunn, James D. G. *Romans*. 2 vols. WBC 38A–B. Dallas: Word, 1988.

Dupont, Jacques. *The Salvation of the Gentiles: Essays on the Acts of the Apostles*. Translated by John R. Keating. New York: Paulist, 1979.

Edwards, James R. *The Gospel according to Luke*. PNTC. Grand Rapids, MI: Eerdmans, 2015.

Elliott, John H. *1 Peter: A New Translation with Introduction and Commentary*. AB 37B. New Haven: Yale University Press, 2000.

Evans, Craig A. "Prophet, Paul as." Pages 761–64 in *Dictionary of Paul and His Letters*. Edited by Gerald F. Hawthorne, Ralph P. Martin, and Daniel G. Reid. Downers Grove, IL: InterVarsity Press, 1993.

Evans, Craig A. "On the Quotation Formulas in the Fourth Gospel." *BZ* 26 (1982): 79–83.

Evans, Craig A. *To See and Not Perceive: Isaiah 6.9–10 in Early Jewish and Christian Interpretation*. JSOTSup 64. Sheffield: JSOT Press, 1989.

Fitzmyer, Joseph A. "David, 'Being Therefore a Prophet' (Acts 2:30)." *CBQ* 34 (1972): 332–39.

Fitzmyer, Joseph A. *The Gospel according to Luke*. 2 vols. AB 28–28A. Garden City, NY: Doubleday, 1981–1985.

France, R. T. *The Gospel of Matthew*. NICNT. Grand Rapids, MI: Eerdmans, 2007.

France, R. T. *Jesus and the Old Testament*. Repr. ed. Vancouver: Regent College, 1998.

France, R. T. "The Servant of the Lord in the Teaching of Jesus." *TynBul* 19 (1968): 26–52.

Frein, Brigid C. "Narrative Predictions, Old Testament Prophecies and Luke's Sense of Fulfilment." *NTS* 40 (1994): 22–37.

Garland, David E. *Luke*. ZECNT. Grand Rapids, MI: Zondervan, 2011.

Garrett, Duane A. *Hosea, Joel*. NAC 19A. Nashville: Broadman & Holman, 1997.

Garrett, Susan R. "Exodus from Bondage: Luke 9:31 and Acts 12:1–24." *CBQ* 52 (1990): 656–80.

Gelston, Anthony. "Some Hebrew Misreadings in the Septuagint of Amos." *VT* 52 (2002): 493–500.

Gentry, Peter J. "'Christotelic Preaching': Reflections on Daniel Block's Approach." *SBJT* 22.3 (2018): 93–101.

Gentry, Peter J. *How to Read and Understand the Biblical Prophets*. Wheaton, IL: Crossway, 2017.

Gentry, Peter J., and Stephen J. Wellum. *God's Kingdom through God's Covenants: A Concise Biblical Theology*. Wheaton, IL: Crossway, 2015.

Gladd, Benjamin L., and Matthew S. Harmon. *Making All Things New: Inaugurated Eschatology for the Life of the Church*. Grand Rapids, MI: Baker Academic, 2016.

Glenny, W. Edward. *Finding Meaning in the Text: Translation Technique and Theology in the Septuagint of Amos*. VTSup 126. Leiden: Brill, 2009.

Glenny, W. Edward. *Hosea: A Commentary Based on Hosea in Codex Vaticanus*. SCS. Boston: Brill, 2013.

Glenny, W. Edward. "The Septuagint and Apostolic Hermeneutics: Amos 9 in Acts 15." *BBR* 22 (2012): 1–26.

Goldingay, John. *The Message of Isaiah 40–55: A Literary-Theological Commentary*. London: T&T Clark, 2005.

Goldingay, John. *The Theology of the Book of Isaiah*. Downers Grove, IL: InterVarsity Press, 2014.

Goldingay, John, and David Payne. *Isaiah 40–55: A Critical and Exegetical Commentary*. 2 vols. ICC. London: T&T Clark, 2006.

Goppelt, Leonhard. *Typos: The Typological Interpretation of the Old Testament in the New*. Translated by Donald H. Madvig. Grand Rapids, MI: Eerdmans, 1982.

Goswell, Greg. "Messianic Expectation in Isaiah 11." *WTJ* 79 (2017): 123–35.

Green, Joel B. *The Gospel of Luke.* NICNT. Grand Rapids, MI: Eerdmans, 1997.

Hadjiev, Tchavdar S. *Joel and Amos: An Introduction and Commentary.* TOTC 25. Downers Grove, IL: InterVarsity Press, 2020.

Hafemann, Scott J. "Eschatology and Ethics: The Future of Israel and the Nations in Romans 15:1–13." *TynBul* 51 (2000): 161–92.

Hamilton, James M. *God's Glory in Salvation through Judgment: A Biblical Theology.* Wheaton, IL: Crossway, 2010.

Hamilton, James M. *God's Indwelling Presence: The Holy Spirit in the Old and New Testaments.* NAC Studies in Bible and Theology 1. Nashville: B&H Academic, 2006.

Harmon, Matthew S. *The Servant of the Lord and His Servant People: Tracing a Biblical Theme through the Canon.* NSBT 54. Downers Grove, IL: InterVarsity Press, 2021.

Harris, Sarah. *The Davidic Shepherd King in the Lukan Narrative.* LNTS 558. London: Bloomsbury T&T Clark, 2016.

Hays, Richard B. *Echoes of Scripture in the Gospels.* Waco, TX: Baylor University Press, 2016.

Hays, Richard B. *Reading with the Grain of Scripture.* Grand Rapids, MI: Eerdmans, 2020.

Helm, David R. *Expositional Preaching: How We Speak God's Word Today.* 9Marks. Wheaton, IL: Crossway, 2014.

Hengel, Martin. "Sit at My Right Hand!" Pages 119–225 in *Studies in Early Christology.* Edinburgh: T&T Clark, 1995.

Holladay, Carl R. *Acts: A Commentary.* NTL. Louisville: Westminister John Knox, 2016.

Homer. *The Odyssey.* Translated by Emily R. Wilson. New York: Norton, 2018.

Hooker, Morna D. *Jesus and the Servant: The Influence of the Servant Concept of Deutero-Isaiah in the New Testament.* London: SPCK, 1959.

Horrell, David G. "'Race,' 'Nation,' 'People': Ethnic Identity-Construction in 1 Peter 2.9." *NTS* 58 (2012): 123–43.

Hossfeld, Frank Lothar, and Eric Zenger. *Psalms 3: A Commentary on Psalms 101–150.* Translated by Linda Maloney. Hermeneia. Minneapolis: Fortress, 2011.

House, Paul R. *Isaiah.* 2 vols. Mentor. Ross-Shire, UK: Christian Focus, 2019.

House, Paul R. "Suffering and the Purpose of Acts." *JETS* 33 (1990): 317–30.

Iannazzone, Al. "Super Bowl LIV: Chiefs' Tyreek Hill, 49ers' Richard Sherman Express Shock over Kobe Bryant's Tragic Death." *Newsday,* January 28, 2020. http://newsday.com/.

James, LeBron. @kingjames. Instagram post. January 27, 2020. https://www. instagram.com/.

Janowski, Bernd. "He Bore Our Sins: Isaiah 53 and the Drama of Taking Another's Place." Pages 48–74 in *The Suffering Servant: Isaiah 53 in Jewish and Christian Sources.* Edited by Bernd Janowski and Peter Stuhlmacher. Translated by Daniel P. Bailey. Grand Rapids, MI: Eerdmans, 2004.

Jervell, Jacob. *Die Apostelgeschichte.* KEK 17. Göttingen: Vandenhoeck & Ruprecht, 1998.

Jipp, Joshua W. "Luke's Scriptural Suffering Messiah: A Search for Precedent, a Search for Identity." *CBQ* 72 (2010): 255–74.

Jipp, Joshua W. *The Messianic Theology of the New Testament.* Grand Rapids, MI: Eerdmans, 2020.

Jobes, Karen H. *1 Peter.* BECNT. Grand Rapids, MI: Baker Academic, 2005.

Jobes, Karen H., and Moisés Silva. *Invitation to the Septuagint.* 2nd ed. Grand Rapids, MI: Baker Academic, 2015.

Johnson, Dennis E. "Jesus against the Idols: The Use of Isaianic Servant Songs in the Missiology of Acts." *WTJ* 52 (1990): 343–53.

Johnson, Dennis E. *Walking with Jesus through His Word: Discovering Christ in All the Scriptures.* Phillipsburg, NJ: P&R, 2015.

Johnston, Joe, dir. *Captain America: The First Avenger.* Burbank, CA: Marvel Studios, 2011.

Josephus, Flavius. *Jewish Antiquities.* Translated by H. St. J. Thackeray et al. 9 vols. LCL. Cambridge, MA: Harvard University Press, 1930–1965.

Josephus, Flavius. *Jewish War.* Translated by H. St. J. Thackeray and Ralph Marcus. 3 vols. LCL. Cambridge, MA: Harvard University Press, 1927–1930.

Josephus, Flavius. *The Life, Against Apion.* Translated by H. St. J. Thackeray. LCL 186. Cambridge, MA: Harvard University Press, 1926.

Kaiser, Walter C., Jr. *The Uses of the Old Testament in the New.* Chicago: Moody, 1985.

Karris, Robert J. "Luke 23:47 and the Lucan View of Jesus' Death." *JBL* 105 (1986): 65–74.

Keener, Craig S. *Acts: An Exegetical Commentary.* 4 vols. Grand Rapids, MI: Baker Academic, 2012–2015.

Keener, Craig S. *The Gospel of John: A Commentary.* 2 vols. Peabody, MA: Hendrickson, 2003.

Keener, Craig S. *The Gospel of Matthew: A Socio-Rhetorical Commentary.* Grand Rapids, MI: Eerdmans, 2009.

Keener, Craig S. "Sent like Jesus: Johannine Missiology (John 20:21–22)." *AJPS* 12 (2009): 21–45.

Keesee, Tim. *Dispatches from the Front: Stories of Gospel Advance in the World's Difficult Places.* Wheaton, IL: Crossway, 2014.

Kilgallen, John J. "The Sadducees and Resurrection from the Dead: Luke 20:27–40." *Bib* 67 (1986): 478–95.

Koester, Craig R. *The Word of Life: A Theology of John's Gospel.* Grand Rapids, MI: Eerdmans, 2008.

Konradt, Matthias. *Israel, Church, and the Gentiles in the Gospel of Matthew.* Translated by Kathleen Ess. Waco, TX: Baylor University Press, 2014.

Köstenberger, Andreas J. "John." Pages 415–512 in *Commentary on the New Testament Use of the Old Testament.* Edited by G. K. Beale and D. A. Carson. Grand Rapids, MI: Baker Academic, 2007.

Köstenberger, Andreas J. *The Missions of Jesus and the Disciples according to the Fourth Gospel: With Implications for the Fourth Gospel's Purpose and the Mission of the Contemporary Church.* Grand Rapids, MI: Eerdmans, 1998.

Köstenberger, Andreas J. "The Seventh Johannine Sign: A Study in John's Christology." *BBR* 5 (1995): 87–103.

Köstenberger, Andreas J., and T. Desmond Alexander. *Salvation to the Ends of the Earth: A Biblical Theology of Mission.* 2nd ed. NSBT 53. Downers Grove, IL: IVP Academic, 2020.

Kraus, Hans-Joachim. *Psalms: A Commentary.* Translated by H. C. Oswald. 2 vols. Minneapolis: Augsburg, 1988–1989.

Kruger, Michael J. *Christianity at the Crossroads: How the Second Century Shaped the Future of the Church.* Downers Grove, IL: InterVarsity Press, 2018.

Larkin, William J. "Luke's Use of the Old Testament as a Key to His Soteriology." *JETS* 20 (1977): 325–35.

Leeman, Jonathan. "Soteriological Mission." Pages 17–45 in *Four Views on the Church's Mission.* Edited by Jason S. Sexton. Counterpoints. Grand Rapids, MI: Zondervan, 2017.

Lehmann, Karl. *Auferweckt am dritten Tag nach der Schrift, früheste Christologie, Bekenntnisbildung und Schriftauslegung im Lichte von 1 Kor. 15, 3–5.* Freiburg: Herder, 1969.

Leithart, Peter J. *Brightest Heaven of Invention: A Christian Guide to Six Shakespeare Plays.* Moscow, ID: Canon, 2006.

Levenson, Jon D. *Resurrection and the Restoration of Israel: The Ultimate Victory of the God of Life*. New Haven: Yale University Press, 2006.

Lewis, C. S. "Is Theology Poetry?" Pages 116–40 in *The Weight of Glory, and Other Addresses*. Rev. ed. San Francisco: HarperCollins, 1980.

Lewis, C. S. *Miracles: A Preliminary Study*. Repr. ed. New York: Simon & Schuster, 1966.

Lewis, C. S. *The Voyage of the Dawn Treader*. The Chronicles of Narnia. New York: HarperCollins, 1952.

Lewis, Charlton T., and Charles Short. *Harper's Latin Dictionary*. Rev. ed. New York: Harper & Brothers, 1891.

Liefeld, Walter L., and David W. Pao. "Luke." Pages 21–356 in *Luke-Acts*. Edited by Tremper Longman III and David E. Garland. Rev. ed. EBC 10. Grand Rapids, MI: Zondervan, 2007.

Lincoln, Andrew T. *The Gospel according to Saint John*. BNTC 4. Peabody, MA: Hendrickson, 2005.

Litwak, Kenneth Duncan. *Echoes of Scripture in Luke-Acts: Telling the History of God's People Intertextually*. JSNTSup 282. London: T&T Clark, 2005.

Longenecker, Richard N. "Acts." Pages 665–1102 in *Luke-Acts*. Edited by Tremper Longman III and David E. Garland. Rev. ed. EBC 10. Grand Rapids, MI: Zondervan, 2007.

Longman, Tremper, III. *Psalms: An Introduction and Commentary*. 2 vols. TOTC 15–16. Downers Grove, IL: InterVarsity Press, 2014.

Longman, Tremper, III. "'What Was Said in All the Scriptures concerning Himself' (Luke 24:27)." Pages 119–36 in *Evangelical Scholarship, Retrospects and Prospects: Essays in Honor of Stanley N. Gundry*. Edited by Verlyn D. Verbrugge. Grand Rapids, MI: Zondervan, 2017.

Luz, Ulrich. *Matthew 8–20: A Commentary*. Translated by James E. Crouch. Hermeneia. Minneapolis: Fortress, 2001.

Macintosh, A. A. *A Critical and Exegetical Commentary on Hosea*. ICC. Edinburgh: T&T Clark, 2014.

Mallen, Peter. *The Reading and Transformation of Isaiah in Luke-Acts*. LNTS 367. London: T&T Clark, 2008.

Marguerat, Daniel. *The First Christian Historian: Writing the 'Acts of the Apostles.'* Translated by Richard Bauckham. SNTSMS 121. Cambridge: Cambridge University Press, 2002.

Marguerat, Daniel. *Les Actes des Apôtres*. 2 vols. CNT 5A–B. Genève: Labor et Fides, 2007–2015.

Marguerat, Daniel. "Quand la résurrection se fait clef de lecture de l'histoire (Luc-Actes)." Pages 183–202 in *Resurrection of the Dead: Biblical Traditions in Dialogue*. Edited by Geert Van Oyen and Tom Shepherd. BETL 249. Leuven: Peters, 2012.

Marshall, I. Howard. "Acts." Pages 513–606 in *Commentary on the New Testament Use of the Old Testament*. Edited by G. K. Beale and D. A. Carson. Grand Rapids, MI: Baker Academic, 2007.

Marshall, I. Howard. *The Gospel of Luke: A Commentary on the Greek Text*. NIGTC. Grand Rapids, MI: Eerdmans, 1978.

Marshall, I. Howard. *Last Supper and Lord's Supper*. Grand Rapids, MI: Eerdmans, 1980.

Mathews, Joshua G. *Melchizedek's Alternative Priestly Order: A Compositional Analysis of Genesis 14:18–20 and Its Echoes throughout the Tanak*. BBRSup 8. Winona Lake, IN: Eisenbrauns, 2013.

Mays, James L. *Psalms*. Interpretation. Philadelphia: Westminster John Knox, 1994.

McCasland, S. Vernon. "The Scripture Basis of 'on the Third Day.'" *JBL* 48 (1929): 124–43.

McKelvey, Michael G. "Amos." Pages 301–70 in *Daniel–Malachi*. ESVEC 7. Wheaton, IL: Crossway, 2018.

Meacham, Jon. *The Hope of Glory: Reflections on the Last Words of Jesus from the Cross*. New York: Convergent, 2020.

Meek, James A. *The Gentile Mission in Old Testament Citations in Acts: Text, Hermeneutic, and Purpose*. LNTS 385. London: T&T Clark, 2008.

Menken, M. J. J. *Old Testament Quotations in the Fourth Gospel: Studies in Textual Form*. Kampen: Kok Pharos, 1996.

Metzger, Bruce M. *A Textual Commentary on the Greek New Testament*. 2nd ed. Stuttgart: Deutsche Bibelgesellschaft, 1994.

Michaels, J. Ramsey. *1 Peter*. WBC 49. Waco, TX: Word, 1988.

Michaels, J. Ramsey. *The Gospel of John*. NICNT. Grand Rapids, MI: Eerdmans, 2010.

Moessner, David P. "The 'Script' of the Scripture in the Acts of the Apostles: Suffering as God's 'Plan' (βουλή) for the World for the 'Release of Sins.'" Pages

218–50 in *History, Literature, and Society in the Book of Acts*. Edited by Ben Witherington III. New York: Cambridge University Press, 1996.

Moessner, David P. "Two Lords 'at the Right Hand'? The Psalms and an Intertextual Reading of Peter's Pentecost Speech (Acts 2:14–36)." Pages 215–32 in *Literary Studies in Luke-Acts: Essays in Honor of Joseph B. Tyson*. Edited by Richard P. Thompson and Thomas E. Phillips. Macon, GA: Mercer University Press, 1998.

Moo, Douglas J. *The Letter to the Romans*. 2nd ed. NICNT. Grand Rapids, MI: Eerdmans, 2018.

Moore, Thomas S. "The Lucan Great Commission and the Isaianic Servant." *BSac* 154 (1997): 47–60.

Morales, L. Michael. *Exodus Old and New: A Biblical Theology of Redemption*. ESBT Downers Grove, IL: InterVarsity Press, 2020.

Moreau, A. Scott, Gary R. Corwin, and Gary B. McGee. *Introducing World Missions: A Biblical, Historical, and Practical Survey*. 2nd ed. Grand Rapids, MI: Baker Academic, 2015.

Morgan-Wynne, John Eifion. *Paul's Pisidian Antioch Speech (Acts 13)*. Cambridge: James Clarke, 2014.

Motyer, J. Alec. *Isaiah: An Introduction and Commentary*. TOTC 20. Downers Grove, IL: InterVarsity Press, 1999.

Niehaus, Jeffrey. "Amos." Pages 315–494 in *The Minor Prophets: An Exegetical and Expository Commentary*, vol. 1. Edited by Thomas E. McComiskey. 3 vols. Grand Rapids, MI: Baker Academic, 1992.

Nolland, John. *Luke*. 3 vols. WBC 35A–C. Dallas: Word, 1989–1993.

Novakovic, Lidija. "Matthew's Atomistic Use of Scripture: Messianic Interpretation of Isaiah 53.4 in Matthew 8.17." Pages 147–62 in *Biblical Interpretation in Early Christian Gospels: The Gospel of Matthew*. Edited by Thomas R. Hatina. London: T&T Clark, 2008.

Novakovic, Lidija. *Raised from the Dead according to Scripture: The Role of Israel's Scripture in the Early Christian Interpretations of Jesus' Resurrection*. JCTCRS 12. London: Bloomsbury T&T Clark, 2012.

Obermann, Andreas. *Die christologische Erfüllung der Schrift im Johannesevangelium: eine Untersuchung zur johanneischen Hermeneutik anhand der Schriftzitate*. WUNT 2/83. Tübingen: Mohr, 1996.

Ortlund, Dane C. "'And Their Eyes Were Opened, and They Knew': An Inter-Canonical Note on Luke 24:31." *JETS* 53 (2010): 717–28.

Ortlund, Raymond C. *God's Unfaithful Wife: A Biblical Theology of Spiritual Adultery*. NSBT 2. Downers Grove, IL: InterVarsity Press, 1996.

Oswalt, John N. *The Book of Isaiah*. 2 vols. NICOT. Grand Rapids, MI: Eerdmans, 1986–1998.

O'Toole, Robert F. "Christ's Resurrection in Acts 13,13–52." *Bib* 60 (1979): 361–72.

O'Toole, Robert F. "How Does Luke Portray Jesus as Servant of YHWH." *Bib* 81 (2000): 328–46.

Ott, Craig, ed. *The Mission of the Church: Five Views in Conversation*. Grand Rapids, MI: Baker Academic, 2016.

Ott, Craig, and Stephen J. Strauss. *Encountering Theology of Mission: Biblical Foundations, Historical Developments, and Contemporary Issues*. Grand Rapids, MI: Baker Academic, 2010.

Ovey, Michael J. *The Feasts of Repentance: From Luke-Acts to Systematic and Pastoral Theology*. NSBT 49. London: Apollos, 2019.

Pao, David W. *Acts and the Isaianic New Exodus*. BSL. Grand Rapids, MI: Baker Academic, 2002.

Pao, David W., and Eckhard J. Schnabel. "Luke." Pages 251–414 in *Commentary on the New Testament Use of the Old Testament*. Edited by G. K. Beale and D. A. Carson. Grand Rapids, MI: Baker Academic, 2007.

Paul, Shalom M. *Isaiah 40–66: Translation and Commentary*. ECC. Grand Rapids, MI: Eerdmans, 2012.

Pervo, Richard I. *Acts: A Commentary*. Hermeneia. Minneapolis: Fortress, 2009.

Peterson, Andrew. *Resurrection Letters: Prologue*. Franklin, TN: Centricity Music, 2018.

Peterson, David G. *The Acts of the Apostles*. PNTC. Grand Rapids, MI: Eerdmans, 2009.

Peterson, David G. "Atonement Theology in Luke-Acts: Some Methodological Reflections." Pages 56–71 in *The New Testament in Its First Century Setting: Essays on Context and Background in Honour of B. W. Winter on His 65th Birthday*. Edited by Peter J. Williams, Andrew D. Clarke, Peter M. Head, and David Instone-Brewer. Grand Rapids, MI: Eerdmans, 2004.

Philo. *Questions and Answers on Genesis*. Translated by Ralph Marcus. LCL 380. Cambridge, MA: Harvard University Press, 1953.

Philo. *On Abraham. On Joseph. On Moses*. Translated by F. H. Colson. LCL 289. Cambridge, MA: Harvard University Press, 1935.

Philo. *On the Cherubim. The Sacrifices of Abel and Cain. The Worse Attacks the Better. On the Posterity and Exile of Cain. On the Giants.* Translated by F. H. Colson and G. H. Whitaker. LCL 227. Cambridge, MA: Harvard University Press, 1929).

Piper, John. "Let the Nations Be Glad! The Supremacy of God in Missions." Pages 433–700 in *The Collected Works of John Piper, Volume 3.* 13 vols. Edited by David Mathis and Justin Taylor. Wheaton, IL: Crossway, 2017.

Plato. *Euthyphro, Apology, Crito, Phaedo.* Translated by Christopher Emlyn-Jones and William Preddy. LCL 36. Cambridge, MA: Harvard University Press, 2017.

Porter, Stanley E. "Composite Citations in Luke-Acts." Pages 62–93 in *Composite Citations in Antiquity, Volume Two: New Testament Uses.* Edited by Sean A. Adams and Seth M. Ehorn. LNTS 593. London: Bloomsbury T&T Clark, 2018.

Potter, D. S. "Augustus (Emperor)." Pages 524–28 in *The Anchor Yale Bible Dictionary,* vol. 1. 6 vols. New Haven: Yale University Press, 1992.

Ray, Jerry L. *Narrative Irony in Luke-Acts: The Paradoxical Interaction of Prophetic Fulfillment and Jewish Rejection.* Lewiston, NY: Mellen, 1996.

Rese, Martin. "Die Funktion der altttesttamentliche Zitate und Anspielungen in den Reden der Apostelgeschickte." Pages 61–79 in *Les Actes des Apôtres: Traditions, Rédaction, Théologie.* Edited by Jacob Kremer. BETL 48. Leuven: Leuven University Press, 1979.

Ringe, Sharon H. "Luke 9:28–36: The Beginning of an Exodus." *Semeia* 28 (1983): 83–99.

Robertson, O. Palmer. *The Flow of the Psalms: Discovering Their Structure and Theology.* Phillipsburg, NJ: P&R, 2015.

Rosner, Brian. "The Progress of the Word." Pages 215–33 in *Witness to the Gospel.* Edited by I. Howard Marshall and David G. Peterson. Grand Rapids, MI: Eerdmans, 1998.

Rowe, C. Kavin. *Early Narrative Christology: The Lord in the Gospel of Luke.* BZNW 139. Berlin: de Gruyter, 2006.

Runge, Steven E. "Joel 2.28–32A in Acts 2.17–21: The Discourse and Text-Critical Implications of Variation from the LXX." Pages 103–13 in *Early Christian Literature and Intertextuality,* vol. 2, *Exegetical Studies.* Edited by Craig A. Evans and Zacharias H. Daniel. LNTS 392. London: T&T Clark, 2009.

Rusam, Dietrich. *Das Alte Testament bei Lukas*. BZNW 112. Berlin: de Gruyter, 2003.

Russell, Michael. "On the Third Day, according to the Scriptures." *RTR* 67 (2008): 1–17.

Schnabel, Eckhard J. *Acts*. ZECNT. Grand Rapids, MI: Zondervan, 2012.

Schnabel, Eckhard J. *Der Brief des Paulus an die Römer: Kapitel 6–16*. HTA. Witten: Brockhaus, 2016.

Schnabel, Eckhard J. *Early Christian Mission*. 2 vols. Downers Grove, IL: InterVarsity Press, 2004.

Schnabel, Eckhard J. *Paul the Missionary: Realities, Strategies and Methods*. Downers Grove, IL: IVP Academic, 2008.

Schnabel, Eckhard J., and David W. Chapman. *The Trial and Crucifixion of Jesus: Texts and Commentary*. Peabody, MA: Hendrickson, 2019.

Schnackenburg, Rudolf. "Joh 12,39–41: Zur christologischen Schriftauslegung des vierten Evangelisten." Pages 167–77 in *Neues Testament und Geschichte: Historisches Geschehen und Deutung im Neuen Testament: FS Oscar Cullmann*. Edited by H. Baltensweiler and B. Reicke. Zürich: Theologischer Verlag, 1972.

Schreiner, Patrick. *Matthew, Disciple and Scribe: The First Gospel and Its Portrait of Jesus*. Grand Rapids, MI: Baker Academic, 2019.

Schreiner, Thomas R. *Romans*. 2nd ed. BECNT. Grand Rapids, MI: Baker Academic, 2018.

Schweitzer, Albert. *The Quest of the Historical Jesus: A Critical Study of its Progress from Reimarus to Wrede*. New York: Macmillan, 1968.

Schwemer, Anna M. "Jesu letzte Worte am Kreuz (Mk 15,34; Lk 23,46; Joh 19,28ff)." *TBei* 29 (1998): 5–29.

Seifrid, Mark. "Romans." Pages 607–94 in *Commentary on the New Testament Use of the Old Testament*. Edited by G. K. Beale and D. A. Carson. Grand Rapids, MI: Baker Academic, 2007.

Seitz, Christopher R. "The Book of Isaiah 40–66." Pages 307–552 in *The New Interpreter's Bible*, vol. 6. Edited by Leander E. Keck. Nashville: Abingdon, 2001.

Seneca. *Dialogues and Essays*. Translated by John N. Davie and Tobias Reinhardt. OWC. Oxford: Oxford University Press, 2007.

Sexton, Jason S., ed. *Four Views on the Church's Mission*. Counterpoints. Grand Rapids, MI: Zondervan, 2017.

Shakespeare, William. *Macbeth.* Edited by Barbara A. Mowat and Paul Werstine. Folger Shakespeare Library. New York: Simon & Schuster, 2010.

Shakespeare, William. *The Tragedy of Julius Caesar.* Edited by Barbara A. Mowat and Paul Werstine. Folger Shakespeare Library. New York: Simon & Schuster, 1992.

Siker, Jeffrey S. "'First to the Gentiles': A Literary Analysis of Luke 4:16–30." *JBL* 111 (1992): 73–90.

Silva, Moisés, ed. *New International Dictionary of New Testament Theology and Exegesis.* 2nd ed. 5 vols. Grand Rapids, MI: Zondervan, 2014.

Sleeman, Matthew. *Geography and the Ascension Narrative in Acts.* SNTSMS 146. Cambridge: Cambridge University Press, 2009.

Snodgrass, Klyne. *Stories with Intent: A Comprehensive Guide to the Parables of Jesus.* 2nd ed. Grand Rapids, MI: Eerdmans, 2018.

Stanley, Andy. *Irresistible: Reclaiming the New That Jesus Unleashed for the World.* Grand Rapids, MI: Zondervan, 2018.

Stanley, Andy. "Jesus Ended the Old Covenant Once and for All." *Christianity Today*, October 18, 2018.

Starling, David I. *Not My People: Gentiles as Exiles in Pauline Hermeneutics.* BZNW 184. Berlin: de Gruyter, 2011.

Stemberger, Günter. "Sadducees." Pages 1179–81 in *The Eerdmans Dictionary of Early Judaism.* Edited by John J. Collins and Daniel C. Harlow. Grand Rapids, MI: Eerdmans, 2010.

Strauss, Mark L. *The Davidic Messiah in Luke-Acts: The Promise and Its Fulfillment in Lukan Christology.* JSNTSup 110. Sheffield: Sheffield Academic, 1995.

Stuart, Douglas K. *Hosea–Jonah.* WBC 31. Waco, TX: Word, 1987.

Stuhlmacher, Peter. "Isaiah 53 in the Gospels and Acts." Pages 147–62 in *The Suffering Servant: Isaiah 53 in Jewish and Christian Sources.* Edited by Bernd Janowski and Peter Stuhlmacher. Translated by Daniel P. Bailey. Grand Rapids, MI: Eerdmans, 2004.

Suetonius. *Lives of the Caesars*, vol. 1. Translated by John C. Rolfe. 2 vols. LCL 31. Cambridge, MA: Harvard University Press, 1914.

Tabb, Brian J. *All Things New: Revelation as Canonical Capstone.* NSBT 48. London: Apollos, 2019.

Tabb, Brian J. "God's Answer to Human Suffering: The Cross of Christ and Problem of Pain." Desiring God, May 21, 2020. http://www.desiringgod.org/.

Tabb, Brian J. "Is the Lukan Jesus a 'Martyr'? A Critical Assessment of a Scholarly Consensus." *CBQ* 77 (2015): 280–301.

Tabb, Brian J. "Jesus's Thirst at the Cross: Irony and Intertextuality in John 19:28." *EvQ* 85 (2013): 338–51.

Tabb, Brian J. "Johannine Fulfillment of Scripture: Continuity and Escalation." *BBR* 21 (2011): 495–505.

Tabb, Brian J. "Salvation, Spreading, and Suffering: God's Unfolding Plan in Luke-Acts." *JETS* 58 (2015): 43–61.

Tabb, Brian J. *Suffering in Ancient Worldview: Luke, Seneca, and 4 Maccabees in Dialogue.* LNTS 569. London: Bloomsbury T&T Clark, 2017.

Tabb, Brian J. "Theological Reflections on the Pandemic." *Themelios* 45 (2020): 1–7.

Tabb, Brian J. "The Unexpected God: How He Meets Us in Disappointment." Desiring God, May 8, 2017. http://www.desiringgod.org/.

Tabb, Brian J., and Andrew M. King, eds. *Five Views on Christ in the Old Testament: Genre, Authorial Intent, and the Nature of Scripture.* Counterpoints. Grand Rapids, MI: Zondervan, forthcoming.

Tabb, Brian J., and Steve Walton. "Exodus in Luke-Acts." In *Exodus in the New Testament.* Edited by Seth Ehorn and Sarah Whittle. LNTS. London: Bloomsbury T&T Clark, forthcoming

Talbert, Charles H. "The Place of the Resurrection in the Theology of Luke." *Interpretation* 46 (1992): 19–30.

Talbert, Charles H. *Reading Luke: A Literary and Theological Commentary on the Third Gospel.* Rev. ed. Reading the New Testament. Macon, GA: Smyth & Helwys, 2002.

Tannehill, Robert C. "Israel in Luke-Acts: A Tragic Story." *JBL* 104 (1985): 69–85.

Tannehill, Robert C. *The Narrative Unity of Luke-Acts: A Literary Interpretation.* 2 vols. Philadelphia: Fortress, 1986–1990.

Tennent, Timothy C. *Invitation to World Missions: A Trinitarian Missiology for the Twenty-First Century.* Grand Rapids, MI: Kregel, 2010.

Thompson, Alan J. *The Acts of the Risen Lord Jesus: Luke's Account of God's Unfolding Plan.* NSBT 27. Downers Grove, IL: InterVarsity Press, 2011.

Thompson, Alan J. *Luke.* EGGNT. Nashville: Broadman & Holman, 2017.

Thompson, Marianne Meye. *John: A Commentary.* NTL. Louisville: Westminister John Knox, 2015.

Timmins, Will N. "A Faith Unlike Abraham's: Matthew Bates on Salvation by Allegiance Alone." *JETS* 61 (2018): 595–616.

Timmins, Will N. "Why Paul Wrote Romans: Putting the Pieces Together." *Themelios* 43 (2018): 387–404.

Trites, Allison A. *The New Testament Concept of Witness*. SNTSMS 31. Cambridge: Cambridge University Press, 1977.

Turner, Max. *Power from on High: The Spirit in Israel's Restoration and Witness in Luke-Acts*. JPTSup 9. Sheffield: Sheffield Academic, 1996.

Turner, Max. "The 'Spirit of Prophecy' as the Power of Israel's Restoration and Witness." Pages 327–48 in *Witness to the Gospel*. Edited by I. Howard Marshall and David G. Peterson. Grand Rapids, MI: Eerdmans, 1998.

VanGemeren, Willem A. *Psalms*. Rev. ed. EBC 5. Grand Rapids, MI: Zondervan, 2008.

Vanhoozer, Kevin J. *Hearers and Doers: A Pastor's Guide to Making Disciples through Scripture and Doctrine*. Bellingham, WA: Lexham, 2019.

Velázquez, Diego. *The Supper at Emmaus*. 1622–1623. Oil on canvas. The Metropolitan Museum of Art, New York. https://www.metmuseum.org/.

Virgil. *Eclogues. Georgics. Aeneid: Books 1–6*. Translated by H. R. Fairclough and G. P. Goold. LCL 63. Cambridge, MA: Harvard University Press, 1916.

Wagner, J. Ross. *Heralds of the Good News: Isaiah and Paul 'in Concert' in the Letter to the Romans*. Leiden: Brill, 2002.

Wagner, J. Ross. "Psalm 118 in Luke-Acts: Tracing a Narrative Thread." Pages 154–78 in *Early Christian Interpretation of the Scriptures of Israel: Investigations and Proposals*. Edited by Craig A. Evans and James A. Sanders. JSNTSup 148. Sheffield: Sheffield Academic, 1997.

Waters, Guy Prentiss. *The Lord's Supper as the Sign and Meal of the New Covenant*. SSBT. Wheaton, IL: Crossway, 2019.

Watts, Rikk E. "Mark." Pages 111–249 in *Commentary on the New Testament Use of the Old Testament*. Edited by G. K. Beale and D. A. Carson. Grand Rapids, MI: Baker Academic, 2007.

White, Aaron W. "Revisiting the 'Creative' Use of Amos in Acts and What It Tells Us About Luke." *BTB* 46.2 (2016): 79–90.

Whybray, R. N. *Isaiah 40–66*. NCB. Grand Rapids, MI: Eerdmans, 1975.

Wilcox, M. "'Upon the Tree': Deut. 21:22–23 in the New Testament." *JBL* 96 (1977): 85–99.

Williamson, Paul R. *Death and the Afterlife: Biblical Perspectives on Ultimate Questions*. NSBT 44. Downers Grove, IL: InterVarsity Press, 2017.

Willson, Mary A. "'Cursed Is Everyone Who Is Hanged on a Tree': Paul's Citation of Deut 21:23 in Gal 3:13." *TrinJ* 36 (2015): 217–40.

Wilson, Benjamin R. *The Saving Cross of the Suffering Christ: The Death of Jesus in Lukan Soteriology*. BZNW 223. Berlin: de Gruyter, 2016.

Wilson, Benjamin R. "'Upon a Tree' Again and Again: Redundancy and Deuteronomy 21:23 in Acts." *Neot* 47 (2013): 47–67.

Wise, Michael O., Martin G. Abegg, and Edward M. Cook. *The Dead Sea Scrolls: A New Translation*. San Francisco: HarperSanFrancisco, 1996.

Witherington, Ben, III. *The Acts of the Apostles: A Socio-Rhetorical Commentary*. Grand Rapids, MI: Eerdmans, 1998.

Wolff, Hans Walter. *Hosea: A Commentary on the Book of the Prophet Hosea*. Edited by Paul D. Hanson. Translated by Gary Stansell. Hermeneia. Philadelphia: Fortress, 1974.

Wolff, Hans Walter. *Joel and Amos: A Commentary on the Books of the Prophets Joel and Amos*. Edited by S. Dean McBride Jr. Translated by Waldemar Janzen, S. Dean McBride, and C. A. Muenchow. Hermeneia. Philadelphia: Fortress, 1977.

Wolter, Michael. *The Gospel according to Luke*. Translated by Wayne Coppins and Christoph Heilig. 2 vols. Baylor-Mohr Siebeck Studies in Early Christianity. Waco, TX: Baylor University Press, 2016–2017.

Wright, Christopher J. H. *The Mission of God: Unlocking the Bible's Grand Narrative*. Downers Grove, IL: IVP Academic, 2006.

Wright, Christopher J. H. "Participatory Mission." Pages 63–91 in *Four Views on the Church's Mission*. Edited by Jason S. Sexton. Counterpoints. Grand Rapids, MI: Zondervan, 2017.

Wright, N. T. *Jesus and the Victory of God*. Christian Origins and the Question of God 2. Minneapolis: Fortress, 1997.

Wright, N. T. *The Resurrection of the Son of God*. Christian Origins and the Question of God 3. Minneapolis: Fortress, 2003.

Yong, Amos. *Mission after Pentecost: The Witness of the Spirit from Genesis to Revelation*. The Mission in Global Community. Grand Rapids, MI: Baker Academic, 2019.

Zwiep, Arie W. *The Ascension of the Messiah in Lukan Christology*. NovTSup 87. Leiden: Brill, 1997.

General Index

Abernethy, Andrew T., 52n50, 53n52, 96n42, 151, 152n69, 152n71, 153n75, 173n24, 174
Abraham, 62, 66, 79, 165, 176
Abrahamic covenant, 147–49
Achtemeier, Paul J., 196n115
Adam, 183
Adams, Sean A., 144n34
Adonai, 124
adversity, 42
Aeschylus, 63n8
Agrippa II, 30
Alexander, 34n45
Allen, Leslie C., 143n31
all flesh, 142–43
Allison, Dale C., 171n14, 171n18, 173n22, 174n30, 176n35
allusion, 35, 54, 70, 72, 74, 89, 104
Amos, 157
analogy, 193n103
anastasis, 69
Andersen, Francis I., 157n88
Anderson, Kevin L., 64n16, 65n21, 65n24, 66n29, 75n66, 81n97
Andrew, 134
angels, 65, 75
Anna, 73–74, 86
anoikodomeō, 160
anointed, 111–14, 122
Antioch, 140, 145, 155, 163
Antiochus IV, 85
Antipater of Thessalonike, 203n1
aphesis, 96n40, 98

apokalypsis, 88
apostellō, 96n40
apostles, 27, 108, 139
Artaxerxes, 90n24
Athens, 155
Augustine, 76, 182n59
Augustus, 84n5
authority, 22
  of Christ, 81, 113
  of prophets, 31
  of Scripture, 35–36
Azariah, 62

Babel, 146–47
Babylonian captivity, 62
Barabbas, 55
Barnabas, 32, 89, 128, 139, 149–50, 153, 154, 155, 156, 165, 207
Barrett, C. K., 140n21
Bates, Matthew, 26n26, 186, 188n82, 211
Batluck, Mark, 26n26
Bauckham, Richard, 156n84, 159n97, 159n98, 160, 181n55, 193n103
Bayer, Hans F., 73n57, 73n58, 73n60
Beale, G. K., 24n20, 35n48, 35n49, 35n52, 45n21, 47n29, 99n52, 110n9, 124n61, 132n93, 143n30, 144n36, 146, 153n73, 154n79, 156n85, 159n94, 174n31, 184n66, 184n67, 195n111, 196n117, 196n119, 198n130
Beaton, Richard, 169n4, 171n19, 175n33, 175n34

Scripture Index

Ancient Sources Index